I am inspired and grown by those around me, not only family and friends but also that great cloud of witnesses and thinkers and scholars who have gone before us all and whose legacies have both shaded and illuminated our paths.

RRJ

passeggiata

Strolling through a life

ROSEMARY ROSS JOHNSTON

Published in Australia by Rosemary Ross Johnston

First published in Australia 2025

This edition published 2025

Copyright © Rosemary Ross Johnston 2025

Edited by Peter Vaughan-Reid | EditingPlus

Cover design by Annabel Robinson

Typesetting by WorkingType (www.workingtype.com.au)

Post-editing by Robert Johnston and Sarah Johnston

The right of Rosemary Ross Johnston to be identified as the Author of the Work has been asserted in accordance with the Copyright, Designs and Patents Act 1988.

All rights reserved. No part of this publication may be reproduced, stored in a retrieval system, or transmitted, in any form or by any means without the prior written permission of the author, nor be otherwise circulated in any form of binding or cover other than that in which it is published and without a similar condition being imposed on the subsequent purchaser.

Every effort has been made to credit copyright holders for material reproduced in this book. We would be pleased to rectify any omissions in subsequent editions should they be drawn to our attention.

ISBN: 978-1-922923-27-1

Thoughts on a wisteria bloom

(On the eve of a new decade RRJ 27.01.24)

My daughter brought it to me yesterday
A perfect bloom, dew-fingered, out of season;
Comported in a glorious defiance
Of scent and colour nuzzling mauves and violets,
Full of itself, plump, robust in its roundness,
How fresh, how firm, how jubilant the bloom!
     I put it in a vase beside my bed.

Waking up this morning, one day later,
The bloom is sagging, wizened, sadly flat,
Fragrant still but not so confident,
   Losing figure, losing innocence,
     Seduced by gravity.
No longer taut and proud and other-worldly,
But of this day, invaded by the heat.

      It's evening now.
Bloom's less of glorious self, and more of core.
Its cascade droops
   and petals fall brown on the floor.
Yet deep within the crêpe I see the heart –
the genesis –
   revealing all, right from the start:

Look closely!
It's all there!
The psalmist sings!

Not depletion
But completion,
Not depleted
Just replete.

Past and present into future,
    Time's dimensions all in scope,
See the oneness, see the fullness,
    Seeds of wonder, seeds of hope!

Not depletion
But completion,
Not depleted
Just replete.

'*You make known to me the path of life; in your presence there is fullness of joy*' …
(Psalm 16:11)

depleted – run down, used up, diminished
replete – filled up, very full, abundantly supplied and provided for

Passeggiata **(particularly in Italy or Italian-speaking areas) – a leisurely walk or stroll, especially one taken in the evening for the purpose of socialising**

Muhibbah (**Malay**) – friendship, living in harmony, camaraderie, tolerance and understanding

Hiraeth (**Welsh**) – nostalgia, longing for home, yearning, bittersweet memories mixed with feelings of gratitude for times past

Merak (**Serbian**) – a sense of oneness with the universe that comes from the simplest of pleasures, contentment when the soul has settled

Habseligkeiten (**German**) – belongings (Goethe Institute winner of a competition for Germany's most beautiful word)

Resfeber (**Swedish**) – tangled feelings between fear and excitement before a journey begins

Querencia (**Spanish**) – fondness, homing instinct, homeland

Firdaus (**Arabic**) – paradise, garden, a lush garden with flowing water

Suaimhneas (**Irish**) – peace, tranquillity, contentment

Dobrodosli (**Slovenian**) – welcome, 'You came in a good way'

Namaste (**Hindi**) – Sanskrit for 'I bow to the divine in you'

Geluksalig (**Afrikaans**) – the highest form of happiness, blissful happiness and luck, the joys of paradise

Contents

Introduction and Dedication		1
1.	Garden the First – The Crag	5
2.	Garden the Second – Braeside	21
3.	Garden the Third – Oasis	31
4.	Garden the Fourth – Cameo	52
5.	Intermezzo – University Days	64
6.	Back to Cameo – Until …	84
7.	Garden the Fifth – Kerensa	100
8.	Sprouts and Seedlings	116
9.	Revelations	139
	9.1 Preamble	139
	9.2 Infant Joy	141
	9.3 Frederick George Reay-Edwards (c. 1915 to c. 1920)	144
	9.4 Royston Frederick Reay-Edwards (c. 1922 to 1956)	147
	9.5 Roy Darling's crusade	149
	9.6 In the beginning	174
10.	A Well-Watered Garden	190
	10.1 Teaching again	190
	10.2 Adventures with CREA	195
	10.3 The adventure in Finland	199
	10.4 Working against disadvantage	204
11.	Requiem	221
12.	Keeping On	228
13.	A Blessed Congruence	242
	13.1 A cosmic symphony	242
	13.2 'This world is not conclusion'	248
Benediction		257
Thank You		264

Introduction and Dedication

A *passeggiata*, in Italy, is a leisurely stroll, generally taken in the late afternoon, often with pauses and stops to admire the view or exchange pleasantries with others met along the way. The *passeggiata* might take you to the town square: the hub of activities, with wafts of chatter and busyness as shops stir again after siesta and cafes and restaurants begin preparations for long and leisurely evening meals. It might take you to a place where you can sit for a while and with a sense of quiet awe watch the whole world tilting away below you.

On a *passeggiata* years ago in the old Tuscan hill town of Cortona, I remember being almost mesmerised by the green slopes and hazes of olive that stretched every which way, down and around and up, holding fast to the scatter of sturdy stone farmhouses. It's where I first saw grapes in rows and olives planted together – the old practice of *coltura promiscua* (evocative name!), a form of polyculture that mixes crops.

In the late afternoon, everyone walked comfortably toward the market square – a real and convivial meeting place for locals, a charming embrace into village life for visitors. There was no sense of rush, just a placid participation in the present.

This book emerges out of that sense. It is a leisurely stroll through memories and reflections on life experience and on those who so intimately share and inform it, both in person, through ideas and chat and walks and meals together, as well as in thought, through books and poems and paintings and other creative expressions. It is a *coltura promiscua* that juxtaposes bits and pieces of the everyday with bits and pieces of the communal. Memory jumps around – past and present can run into one another very easily when you are strolling and remembering – so the *passeggiata* reflects a sort of polytempo, a *tempo promiscua*, if you like.

Along the visual depiction of the path of our *passeggiata* (in the introduction), I have included words from many languages (and am always on the lookout for more). These words seem to encapsulate hopes and dreams and relationships that we all share, all aspire to, despite cultural and linguistic differences. They move the personal and communal into a sense of the universal. They represent an 'us' at our deepest, at our best.

I am using the gardens of our various family houses as a way in, an entry point, to this chronicle and as pause points in the *passeggiata*. The gardens give context and focus to the houses and are what I remember most. As children, we were always playing outside in the garden; it was where my little mother, Dorothy Patricia, most loved to be and where I watched my grandmother, Elsie Emily, at the age of eighty carrying rocks and plants and buckets of manure to make a large rock garden at Dorset Cottage, her home next door to our Oasis.

These gardens were and are not grand (some of them far from it), but they held (and hold) the houses they surround with a sense of responsibility and nurture. Sometimes they were immaculate and sometimes not so much, as life pressed in with other commitments and distractions. Sometimes they might have become a bit scrappy, but they were always faithful: a flower here, a bud there, an upright sprout of a forgotten bulb confidently asserting spring.

Gardens are connections to the earth. They are earthed. They are grounded. They sponsor growing, and growing is an expression of hope. Flowers and plants grow, even in little pots of earth on a deck or balcony, and every growing is a little miracle.

So, this is not a garden book but a book about the life that came and went and comes and goes around gardens: into them, through them.

It is my family that are (yes, it has to be plural) at the core of the story, who came and went through these gardens and who have coloured and textured them with their own individual spirits. I am reminded of one of my favourite poets – indeed, my most favourite – Gerard Manley Hopkins, and his idea of 'inscape'. He used this term to describe the array of characteristics that make each thing unique and different even to other very similar things. He writes in his journal:

> There is one notable dead tree … the inscape markedly holding **its most simple and beautiful oneness** up from the ground … I saw the inscape freshly, as if my mind were still growing.

His eyes were attuned to this idea of 'simple and beautiful oneness', which he saw in the world around him. Wonder in the ordinary and everyday is also expressed in this line from his sonnet 'God's Grandeur':

There lives the dearest freshness deep down things.

It is family and extended family, in all its different shapes and configurations over the years, in all its identities, who fill and have filled my life with their 'dearest freshness', their individual and 'beautiful oneness'. They have made, and continue to make, my mind 'as if still growing'.

This book is dedicated to them all, past and present and still to come.

Post Script: Why, you may wonder, have I included in this introduction a picture of an imperfect rose? This is explained more fully in a later chapter. Suffice it to say that being not quite perfect does not destroy the beauty that remains, that was and is.

1. Garden the First – The Crag

Tread Softly ...

Had I the heavens' embroidered cloths,
Enwrought with golden and silver light,
The blue and the dim and the dark cloths
Of night and light and the half light,
I would spread the cloths under your feet:
But I, being poor, have only my dreams;
I have spread my dreams under your feet;
Tread softly because you tread on my dreams.

'Wishes for the Cloths of Heaven' by WB Yeats (1865–1939)

There is the beginning and then there is the remembered beginning. The beginning is hard to find. Where does it actually begin? What and when is past? And, indeed, present? (The present in which I wrote those words has already faded into some sort of past.) What is remembered as 'beginning' may also be elusive; even when coated with confident assurance it can later be pierced and challenged and almost certainly will undergo edits and unexpected rewrites. Some of these corrections may be incidental ('oh, so that's what *that* meant', '*that*' referring to a comment or some event we didn't really understand at the time), or so dramatic that they change our thinking, our relationships and even our own sense of identity. I have had personal experience of all of these 'corrections'.

Our sense of beingness – our concept of self, our histories, our geographies, our awareness of presence in the world – goes through many stages, doesn't it? Perspectives change and shift and sometimes shrink, hopefully to grow again, perhaps when a different lens is applied or when an original premise is altered or a new discovery made that is startlingly different to previous knowledge or convictions. So it is with my story. Up until my mid-thirties, I had a solid and unquestioned view of my immediate history and of the immediate origins of my family. It was not until then that I was told a whole different story about a whole different world that claimed part of my own.

My remembered sense of beingness begins with the Crag, the childhood home of my mother and maternal grandparents, perched in the rugged but gloriously aromatic bushland around Sydney's beautiful Middle Harbour. After they married, my parents also lived there for a time. And so, as a ten-day-old baby, I was carried home down its long rows of sandstone steps from the car (an old Chev?), which had to be left back along the rough narrow track of Tor Walk way above. It is with the Crag that the gardens of my life begin and my story starts.

* * *

The Crag sat on the very edge of Sydney's Middle Harbour. It was perched on a large slab of steep land with the lovely address of 'Tor Walk, Castlecrag'. Although officially the house was called The Pines, it was the Crag to us and always featured as such in our family annals. The Tor Walk at that time *was* only a walk, a rough and rocky lane that ran off the then unmade end of Edinburgh Road. When my grandparents first moved there in the early 1920s, the main access was by boat to and from The Spit (near Mosman). Decades later, car access was still difficult, especially in wet weather. I have childhood memories from the fifties of my father, or an aunty or uncle or family friend, coming halfway down the long winding stone steps from the lane above, calling out that they needed help back along the track because they had ventured too far and 'The car is bogged!'

My grandmother, Elsie Emily Ross, was proud to be the daughter of South Australian free settlers. Her father, William Ronald Ross, emigrated as a five-year-old child with his family from Edinburgh, Scotland, in 1859. Her mother's parents, Thomas and Mary Ann Allen, had emigrated earlier from Dorset, England, in 1853. Both families settled in Gawler, a pioneering town almost one hundred kilometres from Adelaide (now connected to the Barossa through the Barossa Valley Way). Thomas and Mary Ann Allen had a large family, including my maternal great-grandmother, Emily Jane Allen, born in Gawler in 1858.

The two families came together when Emily Jane Allen married William Ronald Ross on Christmas Day 1879. They were to have eight children; their eldest daughter, my grandmother, Elsie Emily ('Grandma'), was born in 1892.

Elsie grew up in Gawler but met and married Harry Leslie Bevege in Sydney in 1910. Their first baby, a boy they named Jack, was born a year later. Baby Jack was to become a sad family legend: he died of pneumonia as an infant. It had been a scorching hot day; Grandma took him outside in the gloaming to cool off during a southerly buster and he apparently caught a chill. Grandma, who was an everyday part of our lives growing up, was fanatical about us not catching cold, especially if we stripped off during a warm day.

More tragedy was to come for our lovely grandmother. After Baby Jack she had a daughter, Hilda Mary, named after Harry's sister Hilda, a wisp of a woman with a rich deep contralto voice, who was a well-known Sydney elocutionist. We, when we emerged, called her Big Aunty Hilda; Hilda Mary was our Little Aunty Hilda. In 1919, another son, Leslie Ross, was born. Elsie was in hospital with the new baby and kept asking why Harry wasn't coming to see her. Unbeknown to her, Harry was desperately ill with the Spanish flu, a deadly strain of the virus that swept through the new nation in 1919. (The disconnected Australian states had federated in 1901.) Out of a population of just over five million, twelve thousand Australians lost their lives during this pandemic. Harry died when Uncle Les was eight days old.

Elsie, shattered but resourceful, set about preparing their Neutral Bay house for taking in boarders, the only possible source of income for her with two small children, one of whom was a baby. Her family were all back in Gawler, South Australia. She took in two gentlemen boarders, Joe and Jimmy. Joseph Edwin Cowley was a tallish, slim, good-looking seafarer from the Isle of Man, who had been seriously injured during the Great War at Polygon Wood in West Flanders, Belgium. James Witherspoon was short and rotund and wore thick round glasses. Both men proposed marriage to Grandma Elsie, who was a wonderful cook. She accepted Joseph (he was always 'Joe' to the family) and they married and had my mother, Dorothy Patricia, in 1925.

Elsie Emily (née Ross) and Harry Leslie Bevege with Baby Jack (1912)

I am not sure exactly how the move to the Crag took place, but it happened sometime early in the marriage, before Mum was born and while Hilda and Les, Grandma's two children, were still small. Perhaps Joe, descended from a long line of sea captains, just wanted to be near the water. It was an inspired move. Castlecrag was being developed, with almost utopian vision, by Walter Burley Griffin, the American architect and landscape architect who in 1912 won (controversially) the international competition to design Australia's new federal capital, Canberra. His wife, Marion Mahony Griffin, an artist and architect, did the drawings. Griffin named the south side of Edinburgh Road 'Castlecrag' because it reminded him of Castle Rock, on which Edinburgh Castle stands. It was to become quite an artistic little community.

The Griffins very much admired the bushy, rocky area around Middle Harbour and acquired several parcels of land, on which they were designing a new estate that respected the natural beauty and contours of the land. They came to live there in 1925, just a few years after Grandma and Joe moved in. The Crag was not a Griffin house, which were mostly further up the hill. It practically sat in the water. The Griffin houses were charming and unique, but they were also, my family thought, too flat on the ground, a bit pokey and their flat roofs were notoriously prone to leaking. I remember as a small girl visiting one in particular and being fascinated by the buckets collecting drips in various parts of the sitting room.

The Crag, from the waters of Middle Harbour

Joe and Grandma extended the bottom level of the house, which was built on the side of a steep slope, to make several new rooms, and I think Jimmy continued to visit with them until we moved to our next house, Braeside. Indeed, even after the move to Braeside and the later move to Dorset Cottage, Jimmy visited Joe almost every weekend, often carrying a suspiciously clanking bag. By that time, years later, the marriage of Elsie and Joe was no longer close, and Joe now had his own quarters elsewhere in the back of the house. Grandma was a Methodist teetotaller. She told me that she had chosen Joe because of his looks and often warned me that looks could be deceiving.

During World War II (1939–45), the fear of Japanese invasion became very real, especially for Sydney Harbour dwellers. On 31 May 1942, three Japanese midget submarines (launched from a group of five larger ones waiting off Sydney Heads) entered the harbour. Two were destroyed before firing torpedoes, but one fired at the USS *Chicago*, missed it but sank HMAS *Kuttabul*, a converted ferry, killing twenty-one sailors who were sleeping on board.

I have been told that some people sold their water frontages at this time, but my family had a big rock cave further up the cliff to which they planned to go (I think just near or under Sugarloaf Point) if the worst happened. It is not clear how this would have saved them had there been an actual invasion.

The war took Les to New Guinea, where he contracted malaria. He suffered from dreadful fevers for some time after coming home; they shook him and shook up the whole house.

Sometime later he became a salesman, married Eileen and had five children (actually seven, they had twins who very sadly died at birth). He was made a state manager. Later, a promotion to national manager necessitated the family moving to Melbourne.

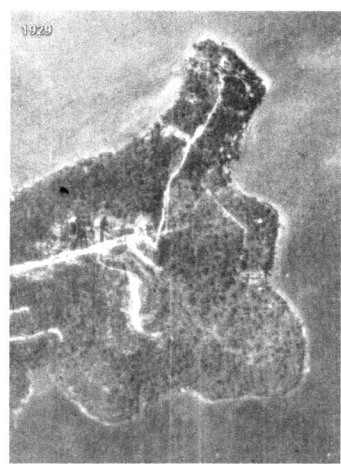

Map of Castlecrag in 1929 (NSW Spatial Services)

Hilda, always musical, had become a pianist, and as 'Miss Melody' had a half hour radio program in Adelaide, where she met and married Basil Norris, a South Australian. Basil had also served in New Guinea as an ambulance driver. He was to become a successful landscape artist. I am proud to have many of his paintings in my home (Kerensa, Garden the Fifth).

Daughter of the Crag – Dorothy Patricia (my mother) aged 11

My mother, Dorothy Patricia, six years younger than Les and twelve years younger than Hilda, trained as an actress at the Independent Theatre with the well-known Doris Fitton, giving her an abiding love for Shakespeare that she passed on to me. She always kissed us good night with Juliet's words to Romeo: 'Good night, good night! Parting is such sweet sorrow/That I shall say good night till it be morrow.'

Leslie Ross Bevege

Hilda Mary Bevege (Miss Melody)

At a very young age, Dorothy married Royston Frederick Darling, a much older film producer, who had an exciting and rather mysterious past. As a teenager during World War I, he had run away from home, put his age up by several years and enlisted in the South African Motor

Cyclist Corps. We were not to find out Roy's whole story until many years later, when we were grown up and some of us had children of our own.

Dorothy's family was not initially pleased about this union (to say the least); Roy had been married before and Dorothy was very young. But it was to prove an exceptionally happy marriage, producing four children: my three brothers and me.

The first three of us were born at the small private hospital, the Cabarisha (now Castlecrag Private Hospital) at the top of Edinburgh Road, which Dr Edward Rivett had established in a converted Walter Burley Griffin house. We were all delivered by Dr Rivett. Like the Griffins, he was a dreamer; he tried to create his hospital as a place of healing and beauty. I remember

Roy on set

Dorothy Patricia Cowley

being taken to see Mum when she had my second little brother; we walked through lovely gardens and the room seemed full of flowers and pretty pale blue tissue paper.

Roy was also at this time writing Australian country music, which seems very odd for someone with such a strong British accent and manner. I never had the opportunity of asking him about this, but he was clearly fascinated by Australia and Australian history. He was a leading early crusader for the local film industry. The National Film and Sound Archive of Australia lists some of his early productions, which are now very dated; the better ones have not survived. Sheet music for many of his songs, including the 'Overlander Trail' and 'Eureka: The Stockade Song', was published by

Cabarisha Private Hospital, formerly King O'Malley House (designed by Walter Burley Griffin)

Elsie, Dorothy and Rosemary (6 months)

Dorothy and children:
(l) Dorothy, Rosemary Ross and Royston Ross
(c) Rosemary and Royston
(r) Rosemary and Christian Ross

Boosey & Hawkes (1945–50); these are now part of the National Library of Australia's Trove collection. The 'Overlander Trail', 'Eureka: The Stockade Song' and 'Lightning Ridge' were also included in a Boosey and Hawkes collection titled *Nine Australian Folk Songs*, along with works by Henry Lawson, AB Paterson and Will Lawson. His songs have been recorded by leading artists such as, among others, Buddy Williams, Slim Dusty, Wayne Horsburgh, Lindsay Butler, Col Edmonds, Smoky Dawson and Reg Lindsay. The most recent version that I am aware of is that of the 'Overlander Trail' recorded by Lee Kernaghan, with choruses by Slim Dusty, Reg Lindsay and Smoky Dawson.

Roy's 'Overlander Trail'

> https://catalogue.nla.gov.au/Record/1785602
>
> Description   Sydney: Boosey & Hawkes (Aust.), c1964
>   1 score (27 p.); 28 cm.
>
> **Full contents**
>
> - Ballad of the drover / words by Henry Lawson; music by Hal Evans
>
> - The shearers' jamboree / arr. by Hal Evans; words and music by Eric Tutin
>
> - Overlander Trail / arr. by Hal Evans; words and music by Roy Darling
>
> - A bush Christening / words by A.B. (Banjo) Paterson; music by Hal Evans
>
> - What makes it snow / words by A.B. (Banjo) Paterson; music by Hall Evans
>
> - Over hill-top and hollow / arr. by Hal Evans; words and music by Stanley Robinson
>
> - A song of wind / words by Will Lawson; music by Hal Evans
>
> - Eureka (The Stockade song) arr. by Hal Evans; words and music by Buddy Williams [**Incorrect – by Roy Darling**]
>
> - Lightning Ridge / arr. by Hal Evans; words and music by Roy Darling.
>
> The composition of 'Eureka: The Stockade Song' is incorrectly attributed here to Buddy Williams, who recorded the song but <u>did not write it.</u>

Some of the happiest days at the Crag were the singalongs, when Aunty Hilda played the piano, my father, Roy, the banjo mandolin and/or violin, and Grandma sang with her strong contralto. Uncle Les, who was a great admirer of Fred Astaire (when I inherited his boyhood wardrobe for my first baby it had pictures of Fred pasted inside), would tap dance with real flair, and we children just danced and jumped around, often with Mum, who didn't sing and always said she was tone-deaf.

The Crag, in my memory, was a combination of rocky tracks, long rows of steep sandstone steps, aromatic bush, diamond and sapphire waters, music, flowers and water play. Less pleasant is my memory of our swimming costumes – they were knitted by Mum and quickly became heavy, clammy and sagging, especially when filled with sand. But the garden in my recollection was a fairyland, particularly in spring, when the wisteria draped the pergola along the whole front of the house (the western, Tor Walk, frontage); I can still see the magic patterns made by the sun shining through the voluminous cascades of mauvy-purple blossom, the honeyed buzzitude of busy bees and the backdrop extravaganza of blues of sky and harbour. And of course the perfume! I have loved wisteria ever since, and when we built our own home in 1969, I planted four, somewhat to my husband's consternation. He also liked it, however, because it had – rather more sedately – covered the lattice joining the garage to the back door of his childhood home at Strathfield.

Jumping in a sort of *tempo promiscua* (mixing different times), the Crag stars in a schoolgirl story I wrote at the age of eleven/twelve called *Stella of the Crag*. In a not unfamiliar narrative pattern, an orphaned cousin (Stella) comes from New Zealand to live with the family at the Crag.

The manuscript was never published – don't think it was ever sent anywhere – but below is the description written then about my memories as a small girl of the garden.

Because the Crag had a long water frontage, we had a harbour pool and a rowboat, which in the early days would take Elsie and Joe to the post office and shops. For some years the most convenient post office was not up along Edinburgh Road on the way to the city (which was only eleven kilometres away), as our address would suggest, but instead, to quote Stella again, a quick trip down the harbour to 'the low sandy spit of land which lay between the hills. Its name indicated its shape – the Spit.'

My first novel

As well as the wisteria, what I remember most about the garden of the Crag was the

> From *Stella of the Crag,* Chapter 1
>
> The Crag was situated on a promontory overlooking the Harbour … The surrounding garden was steep, but very picturesque. On the southern side the fresh green lawn, where stately gum trees stood in silence, sloped upwards until it reached a grove of young wattle trees, beyond which was a sheer cliff. The front of the home, the western side, was much steeper; it had been a cliff also, but a landslide of days gone by had reduced the precipitous drop to more gentle lines. The front lawn slanted upwards to where the massive rocks formed the remaining part of the cliff. The rocks were covered with dainty fernery which hung in a green and feathery curtain.
>
> An archway of wisteria framed the stone steps that led round and round, round and round, until they reached the top of the cliff and gave way to a stone path, bordered with pretty little pink stars of wild boronia growing in front of plump banksias and rustling, secretive she-oaks.

Elsie and little Les rowing to the Spit (above)

An older Les and Beauty on the steep path winding down from Tor Walk through the Glade to the Crag

terraced area of flattish land about halfway between the house level and the Tor Walk level high above. This was called The Glade. It was a sheltered natural bush house, and here Grandma Elsie grew her ferns – bird's nest, wild maidenhair and a fern our family called mother of thousand – and her lovely red, pink and purple fuchsias. Tom Thumb was my favourite and I took a cutting from a plant that Mum had struck from the Crag original to grow in my own garden many years later. For ages it thrived, then one long hot summer some years ago, while caught up with work, I lost it.

The waters of Sydney Harbour, day and night, provided a fascinating, ever-active backdrop to the story of our lives. They sometimes brandished the bold brilliance of precious gems – splendid, mind-stretching blues and greens of every shade – and sometimes the colours were more nuanced – gentle and fleeting greys, mauves, rose and amber.

I remember kneeling on a window seat one Christmas Eve and watching the Showboat with all its bright lights gliding past, wafting 'Jingle Bells' and dance music in its wake. I also remember my little brother and I watching the sailing boats flying across the top of the water on windy days, and I'm sorry to say we found it very exciting when they were blown over and the people sailing them bobbed about in the water struggling to get their craft upright again.

I started school while at the Crag and spent several years at a private prep school that I liked very much, mainly because of the uniform (navy blue tunic and white blouse) and the endless little books and fancy padded stickers I was given for reading them. I had been reading since at least four; I don't really remember how I learnt, but presume my mother and father read to me and so demonstrated how letter and sound worked together.

Childhood in the beautiful setting of the Crag set up an appreciation of homes and gardens for life. But there is one unhappy kindergarten memory that has stayed with me for years and made me aware from a very early age of how easily children's actions can be misinterpreted. We were lying on the floor for rest time, and a teacher (not my usual one) or perhaps assistant was standing very near and just above me. As I looked up, I saw her pretty dress and the wide froth of lace of her petticoat. There were little pink satin bows dotted with a tiny pearl sewn into the top of the lace and I reached up and shifted her skirt slightly so I could see them better. She reacted very angrily and called me a dirty little girl. I don't really remember if I said anything to explain, but I had no idea at the time what she thought I had done. There is a vague recollection that my usual teacher may have come to my defence, but that may be a wishful memory.

Apart from this experience, my first school was a very happy time. Books – both reading and writing – became a part of my every day, and I have loved them ever since. It was at the Crag that I was given my first little desk, which was placed in my room so that when the lid was down I could sit and look out over the harbour. And there was a Bambi transfer on the lid, which I loved.

My first school

Indeed, they were halcyon days – or so it seems now – and the Crag and its clasp of the harbour has remained a part of my inner geography all my life. But things were changing. The Sydney Harbour Bridge had been opened in March 1932; Joe took little six-year-old Dorothy to walk across it on the first day. For many years there had been talk of plans to build another harbour crossing at Sugarloaf Point, which was very close to us at the Crag and which would have put us under or near its approaches. The fear of this (it has never eventuated), along with the steepness, no flat play space for three growing children and the fact that the house

Women of the Crag: (l-r) Hilda, Hilda, and Elsie with Dorothy

lost winter sun so early in the afternoon, were some of the reasons that the family decided to leave the Crag and move to a house on several acres of flat land then considered in the bush (or 'in the sticks', as I heard someone say), in a small village with a one-teacher school near Camden, about eighty kilometres south-west of Sydney.

'Sydney Harbour 1894' by Arthur Streeton (Mitchell Library, State Library of New South Wales)

A legacy of love

In the 1920s, at the Crag, Grandma Elsie Emily was given a fuchsia, Tom Thumb. Delicate and dainty, it became a family favourite. Grandma took many cuttings and gave a plant to Mum who also loved it and later took cuttings and gave a plant to me. It flourished for years but while away over one hot summer I lost it. I was upset.

That I thought was the end of the story. But it wasn't. Before we lost it, my daughter Sarah was showing the garden to a friend's mother, a keen gardener, and gave her a cutting of the unusual fuchsia. Years passed, and Sarah was visiting the friend's family and mentioned this. She was shown a flourishing plant which had one solitary flower. Yes, it was Tom Thumb!

Unbeknown to me she requested a cutting which she struck. Last birthday she presented me with a beautiful Tom Thumb plant (pictured). In over a century of history and through a heritage of caring hands, it had come full circle: a legacy of love.

Sydney Harbour (*New Year's Eve, 1897*)

The jewelled city glitters through the night,
The jewelled boats glide softly through the gloom;
On either hand dark isles and headlands loom,
And overhead stars flood the heavens with light.

Our vessel trembles, as the bronze blades smite
The quiet waters, and the engines urge
Our forward way to where the sounding surge
Washes the cliff, and all the waves are white.

'Tis midnight; from the distant city spires;
The bells peal out a welcome to the year,
And ruddy glows the smoke of festal fires.

The lighthouse now, unbonneted and free,
Throws out pale spokes of light that wheel and veer,
And one great planet burns above the sea.

Mary E. Richmond. *Poems*, Elkin Mathews, London, (1903), pp. 83–88

'The Bridge in Curve' (1930) Grace Cossington-Smith (National Gallery of Victoria)

Harbour Dusk

She and I came wandering there through an empty park,
and we laid our hands on a stone parapet's
fading life. Before us, across the oily, aubergine dark
of the harbour, we could make out yachts –

beneath an overcast sky, that was mauve underlit,
against a far shore of dark, crumbling bush.
Part of the city, to our left, was fruit shop bright
After the summer day, a huge, moist hush.

The yachts were far across their empty fields of water.
One, at times, was gently rested like a quill.
They seemed to whisper, slipping amongst each other,
always hovering, as though resolve were ill.

Away off, through the strung Bridge, a sky of mulberry
and orange chiffon. Mauve-grey, each cloven sail –
like nursing sisters in a deep corridor, some melancholy;
or nuns, going to an evening confessional.

Robert Gray (1945 –)

Portrait of Sydney, 1952

The water is like silk, like pewter, like blood, like a leopard's skin, and occasionally merely like water. Its pigments run into themselves, from amber and aquamarine through cobalt to the deep and tranquil molasses of a summer midnight. Sometimes it dances with flakes of fire, sometimes it is blank and anonymous with fog, sometimes it shouts as joyously as a mirror.

Kenneth Slessor (1901–1971)

(*Portrait of Sydney: a photographic impression with an illuminating article by Kenneth Slessor* Eds. Gwen Morton Spencer and Sam Ure Smith, National Library of Australia)

Sydney Harbour beautifully captured by Ken Done (Ken Done Gallery, The Rocks Sydney)

2. Garden the Second – Braeside

'Core of my heart, my country'
From 'My Country' by Dorothea Mackellar

I can't remember much about the move to Braeside besides being very sorry to leave my protected little school. I was able to take my treasured desk with its lid that lifted, which Father Christmas had delivered a few years before, and I remember setting it up very carefully in my new room. My two dolls, Elizabeth and Margaret Ruth, were also set possessively on my newly made bed.

Braeside opened up a new world to us Crag cliff dwellers. When we arrived it was a smallish house with a nondescript garden, but it had open fields and paddocks all around and for the first time trikes and bikes entered our world. We must have moved in spring, because the paddock across the road was a dream of wildflowers; there are old photos of us all picking these very soon after arrival. In my memory it was the next day, but it probably wasn't.

Braeside also expanded our mindscape of Australia. We were surrounded here not by the rugged bushy hills and cliffs of Castlecrag, nor by the pervasive sensory sparkle of Sydney Harbour, but by rich land, with lovely tracks and miles of unmade roads behind the back paddocks. We went for long, long walks every day. We had

With my brothers picking wildflowers at Braeside

chooks, and several old round chicken coops became our favourite places to play; not inside but on the top of their curved tin roof, which got burning hot in summer. We were reading *Mandrake the Magician* comics by this time and we told our little blonde brother, who was being big strong Lothar (my older young brother was Mandrake and I was Princess Narda),

'View upon the Nepean River, at the Cow Pastures New South Wales 1824–1825', Joseph Lycett (State Library of NSW)

that there were crocodiles on the ground below. I can still see him sliding but clinging to the hot rounded sides for dear life.

Trains also entered our experience for the first time – the lovely old steam engine that puffed its way across the willow-fringed Nepean River into Camden. We could hang out of the carriage window and watch the train snaking along behind us.

The famous Cowpastures were all around: the rich and fertile soil of the Nepean floodplain to which the cattle of the First Fleet (two bulls and five cows) had escaped about five months after landing in 1788. They had a bonanza. By 1810, when Governor Macquarie (the fifth governor of the new colony) visited the area, he estimated that there were then between four and five thousand head of cattle. Fertile indeed!

John Macarthur, of Merino fame, was granted an initial two thousand hectares here to develop the colony's wool industry; he named his grant Camden. By 1837 the Macarthur Camden Estate was 11,209 hectares.

Camden and nearby Campbelltown were then both delightfully pretty rural and historical areas, and my father used to take us for drives and picnics on Sunday afternoons: another new type of adventure. And Mum and Grandma set about making a garden, which transformed Braeside (as gardens were to transform our later houses). The Crag was framed by the harbour, which was its main and obvious landscape feature, but subsequent houses needed their gardens both to frame them and to give them character and identity.

We all gardened. There was a very different climate at Braeside to the Crag, with bitingly-cold frosty winters. I'd never seen a frost and at first found the sharp crunch of glassy grass exciting. Joe dug a massive vegetable garden. I think he must have produced everything we ate as I remember a grocer delivering to Braeside but never a greengrocer. Our father was not much of a gardener – although he was later to plant the long row of *Pinus insignis* that became the well-known local signature of our next homes and that of Grandma next door – but he did grow and love radishes, which he ate, brushed, straight from the garden. We called him 'Dadda Radish' for years.

I made the acquaintance of English daisies, which thrived in the cool Braeside soil. Mum and Grandma grew beautiful and fragrant roses. Mum also grew some amazing sweet corn. We loved running through it. We also loved eating it on the cob and drizzled with butter. Dahlias, zinnias and other annuals flourished. But Grandma's treasured ferns from the Crag and the delicate fuchsias faltered. Thus, the first of many protective bush-houses and ferneries was built.

The laundry at Braeside was separate to the house, connected by a small courtyard with a trellis over which a Black-eyed Susan sprawled rather flagrantly. The little flowers dropped in squashy messes onto the paving below, and for some time I ran a flower hospital for these in the two concrete tubs in the laundry. Survivors went into water in one tub, non-survivors into the other. This did not go over very well with the adults, as I would often forget my flower ministrations and they would be faced with a brown congealed mess in the tubs to deal with as well as their baskets of dirty washing.

Myself and my brother gardening. Note the trellis, the back of which was soon to be covered by the Black-eyed Susan vine. The building on the left is the laundry/flower hospital

I had to go to school, and this was a very different experience to the school to which I had gone while living at the Crag. At first I went to the bigger school in Camden – the only school I have ever hated. I'm not sure exactly why I left after only a short time, but I was glad I did. I was teased unmercifully because I dressed differently (in the tunic and blouse I had worn previously, which got tossed as soon as I could get out of them), I spoke differently and, according to one of the teachers, I ran differently. She told Mum (remember, these were politically incorrect times) I 'ran like a spastic'.

Mum, with the haughty indignation she could produce very well in defence of one of her offspring, removed me and I went instead to the tiny one-teacher school down in the village and across from the small but pretty Anglican church. A few months later I was joined by my little brother, now of school age.

This was an experience that whilst it wasn't always happy I am very glad to have had: one teacher in one classroom with about fifteen boys and girls from kindergarten to sixth class. (It's possible kindergarten were mostly with some sort of carer or aid in another small room in the adjoining building.) The teacher was a male who, from memory, lived or roomed next door to the school. He was cranky and volatile. He swung a cane menacingly, pretty much every day (at least that's how I remember it). I was petrified but fascinated; he was almost a storybook ogre figure.

But I think I learnt. My brother certainly did. You could always tune into a more interesting lesson going on with another group, and my brother – perhaps less sociable than I – did so. His remarkable mind and our wide and sometimes out-of-order knowledges were fed and encouraged by this regime of choosing our own lesson.

We were a family of avid readers. I already had Mum's collection of the *Anne* books by L. M. Montgomery and my brother was already into *Biggles*, which we acted out endlessly (he was, of course, Biggles, I was Algy and our little brother was Bertie). After we learnt – or rather we overheard from the older class lessons – about the crossing of the Blue Mountains in 1813, we played at being Blaxland, Wentworth and Lawson, endlessly exploring the paddocks and tracks around us.

We started going to the church near the school, where I think services were on alternate Sundays, and went to Sunday School for the first time. Mum became a Sunday School teacher. Again, I enjoyed the stories and loved the stickers. These ones had Bible verses and pretty flowers. I also loved the hymns. We were used to Grandma (a staunch Methodist) continually singing rousing hymns whilst cooking and working at home. Now I found I could recognise some of them: 'Mothers of Salem', 'Onward Christian Soldiers', 'The Lord's My Shepherd'.

For a short time – and my recollection of this is foggy – our father flirted with the idea of being a builder and started construction of a small house on a piece of sloping land adjoining and just down the hill from Braeside that fronted onto the unmade road at the side. It got to lock-up stage, and Mum and the boys moved in, almost camping whilst he finished it off. It was a rather wonderful but messy adventure, and we children roamed freely, exploring the adjoining bush. I remember a spring season with a sky seemingly festooned as we looked up with huge puffs of heart-stoppingly beautiful golden wattle. We moved my desk down to the new house, but my room wasn't really ready and I stayed sleeping at Braeside; Mum wanted me to keep Grandma company at nights anyway. The building adventure didn't last long; unfortunately our father had a very bad fall through some floor joists at the steepest part of the house and broke a number of ribs. I remember a doctor coming and wrapping his whole torso, it seemed, in wide white adhesive. His chest was very hairy and I also remember hearing about the horrible and painful process of the adhesive removal.

Braeside and this little building adventure were, in a way, a stepping-stone between the Crag and the home we all grew to love: Oasis. Our father had found out about two houses for sale that sat on adjoining huge blocks: one with several acres of land and both cement-rendered, which satisfied his sense for the solid. They were a mile from the local station and just a little closer to the city, and we didn't need to change trains for the Camden Puffing Billy.

So we moved. Our family moved into the house Mum named Oasis and, just next door, with two large empty blocks between, was the house Grandma moved into, which she called Dorset Cottage after the family home of her maternal grandmother (Mary Anne Ross née Allen) in England.

With my two brothers just before leaving Braeside

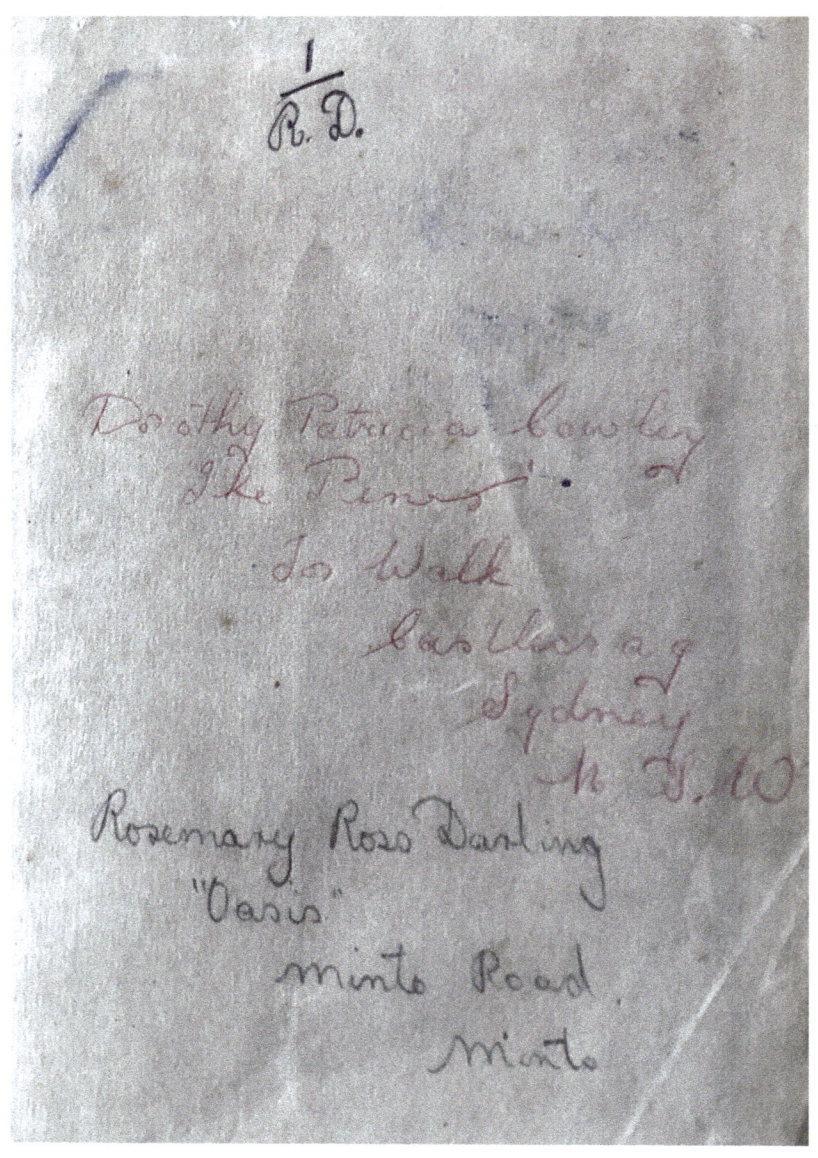

Books were our most treasured possessions. My grandmother, Elsie Emily, loved her books, as did Mum (and, as I would find out later, Malcolm's mother, Queenie). Grandma often wrote not her name but rather the name of her house on the first page. This is Mum's precious *Anne of Green Gables*, given to her by her parents when she was about nine (and then given to me at nine). You can just discern where she wrote her name in the middle – 'Dorothy Cowley, The Pines, Tor Walk, Castlercrag' (written in red pencil). A treasured palimpsest.

I created my own library referencing system for my books – this is proudly 1/R.D. (Rosemary Darling)

Grandma Elsie's Recipes
Grandma's Cornish Pasties:

Grandma's pasties looked better than this! They were fat and full and sometimes oozing deliciously tasty juices. They were an event in themselves.

Grandma was proud of her South Australian and Scottish heritages, and her cooking, which was amazing, reflected this. Cornish Pasties were a great favourite, and she often made these for family events, especially in winter. I can still remember the lovely aromatic steam that escaped, tantalisingly, when you made the first cut through the pastry into the almost-overflowing stash of vegetables and meat within.

She used her version of short crust pastry, which was very short and well-seasoned with salt and pepper and delicious in itself. She was fussy that everything for the pastry had to be cold, even the implements used, and she always made the pastry first, rolled it into a ball and stored it in the fridge (sometimes she called it the 'icebox') whilst she made the filling. I have a vague recollection that she may have used old-fashioned suet (or lard?) instead of or as well as butter. (Just as an aside, my favourite pudding from those days was Grandma's apricot suet pudding – it was scrumptious. Of course, I didn't know then what suet or lard was. I couldn't eat either now. Mum, one of my brothers, my daughter-in-law and I are all long-term vegetarians.)

The filling was completely cooked within the pastry: meat, potatoes, onions, swedes/turnips (rather old-fashioned vegetables), and sometimes carrot and pumpkin. I think she used the more economical cuts, but modern recipes say rump steak. Whatever she used, it was always succulent and tender. Everything was diced or cut into small, bite-sized cubes, not the big lazy chunks of today.

When she had the meat and vegetables all mixed, she rolled the pastry into oval shapes and piled the well-seasoned filling on top, leaving a good inch around the inside edges, which she brushed with the beaten egg (my job as a small child was to beat the egg). Then she wrapped the pastry around to completely enclose the filling and basted the top with the rest of the beaten egg (also my job – it was like painting). Grandma always crimped the pastry together along the side (the traditional way), not along the top.

Grandma's, and indeed Mum's, table was always generous, and she made the pasties to fit the size of each person, from the smallest child to well and truly man-sized. When unexpected guests came and food was a bit limited, we children all knew the code – 'FHB' (family hold back). It didn't happen often, but (mostly) we abided by this instruction.

Pastry has gone out of favour in more recent years and I haven't made these for ages. But when I did, I increasingly experimented with adding more vegetables, no meat and lots of herbs – not traditional but very warming and appetising on a cold winter's day.

Grandma's Lemon Cheese *(as copied into my recipe book, which I compiled just before I was married): The adults all loved this, but as children it wasn't our favourite. (I enjoy it now.) Mum and Grandma would have this on a biscuit (Sao?) with their regular morning cup of milk coffee. This all happened in that long-ago time before all things of the everyday were recorded (with mobiles).*

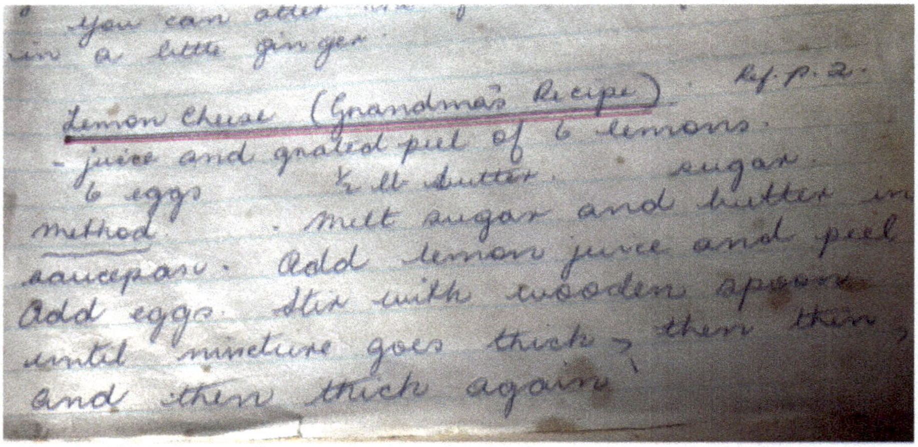

you can alter
in a little ginger.

Lemon Cheese (Grandma's Recipe) Ref. p. 2.
- juice and grated peel of 6 lemons.
6 eggs ½ lb butter. sugar.
method. Melt sugar and butter in saucepan. Add lemon juice and peel Add eggs. Stir with wooden spoon until mixture goes thick, then thin, and then thick again.

My Country

The love of field and coppice,
Of green and shaded lanes,
Of ordered woods and gardens,
Is running in your veins.
Strong love of grey-blue distance,
Brown streams and soft, dim skies …
I know, but cannot share it,
My love is otherwise.

I love a sunburnt country,
A land of sweeping plains,
Of ragged mountain ranges,
Of droughts and flooding rains.
I love her far horizons,
I love her jewel-sea,
Her beauty and her terror –
The wide brown land for me!

The stark white ring-barked forests,
All tragic to the moon,
The sapphire-misted mountains,
The hot gold hush of noon –
Green tangle of the brushes
Where lithe lianas coil,
And orchids deck the tree-tops,
And ferns the warm dark soil.

Core of my heart, my country!
Her pitiless blue sky,
When, sick at heart, around us
We see the cattle die …
But then the grey clouds gather,
And we can bless again
The drumming of an army,
The steady soaking rain.

Core of my heart, my country!
Land of the rainbow gold –
For flood and fire and famine
She pays us back threefold …
Over the thirsty paddocks,

'Beyond the Crag: Australia'

Braeside and our long walks and Sunday afternoon road trips gave me a sense of a spacious, expansive country that I did not have earlier. The *Anne* books were set in the Canadian Maritime province of Prince Edward Island, and my increasing library of schoolgirl novels, apart from *Billabong,* which I didn't love, were set in the United Kingdom. For some years I yearned for snow and white Christmases. But Braeside, and perhaps growing up a bit more, gave me eyes to see a different beauty. It was in that little one-teacher school, and possibly in a School Magazine for an older grade, that I first came across the heart-stirring poem 'My Country'.

'A Day to Remember' painting by our Uncle Basil Norris, 16 Feb 1982

Watch, after many days,
The filmy veil of greenness
That thickens as you gaze …

An opal-hearted country,
A wilful, lavish land –
All you who have not loved her,
You will not understand …
Though Earth holds many splendours,
Wherever I may die,
I know to what brown country
My homing thoughts will fly.

Dorothea Mackellar (1885–1968)

Tarrangaua (above), home of poet Dorothea Mackellar (left) at Lovett Bay on Pittwater (built 1925). Contemporary author, Susan Duncan, has written about her own life here in several books. I have lived in the Pittwater area for many years

3. Garden the Third – Oasis

Oasis
'A fertile spot in a desert, where water is found'
'A place in a desert where water comes up to the surface from deep underground'

'Love is … an ever-fixed mark … and is never shaken'

My mother, Dorothy, loved Shakespeare and she loved our father. She married him as a seventeen-year-old girl, stubbornly, even defiantly, in the face of strong family opposition. Grandma Elsie eventually relented and she and Grandpa Joe gave their reluctant consent. But Dorothy loved her family and cared for Elsie all her life.

My father, Roy, was much older, a divorced film producer and songwriter, who in an earlier life had helped to subdivide the valuable 'golden triangle' of Newport and had given names such as 'Hollywood Road' and 'The Boulevarde' to streets in the area. He had various ages because he had put his age up when he left home to enlist in the South African Motorcyclist Corps during World War I (the records of which were destroyed during World War II) and put it down when he met Mum. He was probably sixteen when he joined up and I now know he was forty-four when they married. His story, which is still being unravelled, is told more fully in Chapter 9. We weren't aware of most of this for many years. I was in my thirties and had five children before I knew any of it.

Dorothy Patricia

They married in a registry office on 1 May 1943. Mum carried a posy of yellow and orange nasturtiums, picked from the rocky garden at the Crag. Dorothy's father, Grandpa Joe, and siblings Hilda and Les, were the witnesses. There are no wedding photos.

My father was a dreamer and a crusader, perhaps an unusual mixture of idealism and pragmatism. When he arrived in Australia, and because of his experiences in South Africa and India, he was horrified at the limited space and conditions of the elephants at Taronga Park Zoo and wrote many letters of protest to the Taronga Zoological Park Trust. As a film director but non-Australian, he fought vigorously for an Australian film industry; we have letters and signed replies about this from then Prime Minister Ben Chifley, among others.

He had enormous charisma, and I remember an amazing presence and a truly beautiful voice. When I first heard Roger Moore (playing Simon 'The Saint' Templar – James Bond came later) I heard the timbre and intonation of my father's voice. I am sure he wasn't necessarily an easy person to be in love with, but I only once ever heard my parents have a serious disagreement.

My father enjoyed cooking and cooked quite often. His meals were delicious. We all enjoyed what he called bubble and squeak. Mum preferred gardening and painting the house; she painted the roof at one stage and created all sorts of artistic effects inside the house. I remember a colourful frieze of fish and coral, shells and sea creatures all around our bath, which made it very easy to imagine we were swimming in the Great Barrier Reef.

> **Sonnet 116**
>
> Let me not to the marriage of true minds
> Admit impediments. Love is not love
> Which alters when it alteration finds,
> Or bends with the remover to remove:
> O no; it is an ever-fixed mark,
> That looks on tempests, and is never shaken;
> It is the star to every wandering bark,
> Whose worth's unknown, although his height be taken.
> Love's not Time's fool, though rosy lips and cheeks
> Within his bending sickle's compass come;
> Love alters not with his brief hours and weeks,
> But bears it out even to the edge of doom.
> If this be error and upon me proved,
> I never writ, nor no man ever loved.
>
> **William Shakespeare**

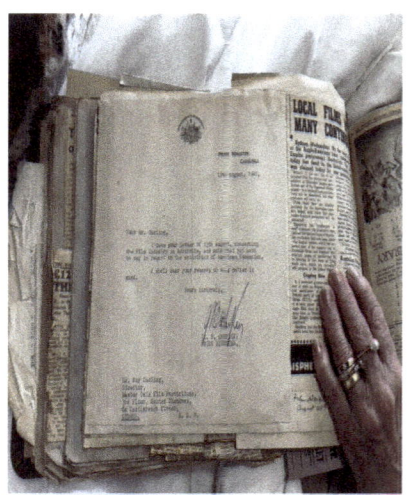

Letter from Prime Minister Ben Chifley

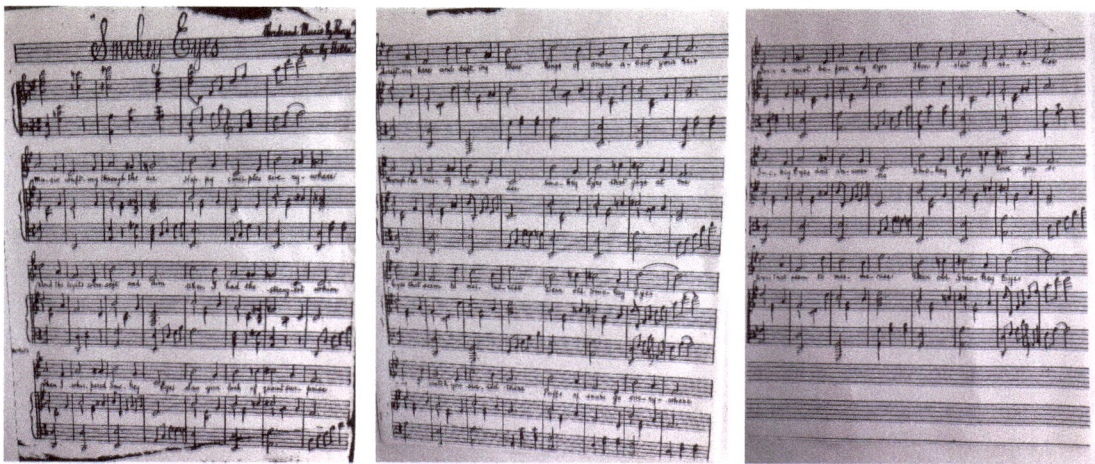

Unpublished song 'Smokey Eyes' © Roy Darling. Written for Dorothy, whom he called 'Smokey Eyes'. Arranged by Aunty Hilda Norris

I don't remember Roy as being a particularly 'hands-on' father, although we all enjoyed being tucked in by him at night – he was a great tucker-inner. He had been brought up with maids and his own father was, I was told years later, very strict. We all knew, without it ever being said, that there were certain things we couldn't do when he was home. For example, I knew I could only play dress-ups and put on Mum's high heels and make-up when he wasn't around. Mum told me years afterwards that he had a horror of 'showgirls' (and presumably of me turning out like one).

I know Oasis was an idyllic place for Mum and am so, so happy and grateful that they had this joyous and fulfilling experience together.

This chapter (Garden the Third – Oasis) is inspired by and dedicated to them both. But it is written in homage to Mum, Dorothy Patricia Darling.

* * *

I remember the excitement of the move to Oasis – Mum's name for a little world of our own (but please see Chapter 9). And it was. But while it was to be a home of much joy, it was also to be a home of much unexpected sorrow.

The small village to which we had moved consisted of a general store and tiny post office (doubling as the local telephone exchange) on our side of the railway station and, perhaps strangely, a small haberdashery shop with the proprietor's home above it on the other side. At that time it was an even sleepier village than the one at Braeside. Now it is more-or-less a suburb of Sydney and you can pick up traffic reports on the radio.

Oasis in the very early days. Note the baby Pinus insignis tube stock planted by our father just beginning its stretch to the sky. The Oasis nameplate was on the increasingly rose-covered pergola

Groceries were delivered every week by the storekeeper, and Johnny, a colourful Italian, brought weekly deliveries of fruit and vegetables from a nearby market garden. A milk and bakery delivery came each day. Oh, the warm fragrance of that fresh fluffy bread! We all loved the crusts with butter and vegemite, and often well before nightfall a proud loaf would remarkably still be standing after having lost some or all of its crusty (and delectable) sides. We vied for the top one, which was usually the crustiest. In the early days milk came in a billy left out at night, and I remember thinking how smart it was, years later, when milk came in glass bottles (just like in the grand houses on American television, which had by then come into our lives).

In those early days, the only regular traffic up our road were the cows. These came from the dairy farm across the road. Every morning the sister of the farmer moved the cows to the creek pastures a little further down, which were probably rich and alluvial because they flooded periodically, and every night she moved them back up again. It would be nice to say she was on horseback – by now we were very much into Roy Rogers, Hopalong Cassidy and Dale Evans – but in fact she was languidly astride an old rusty bike. Aunty Syl, as she was known, and her to-ings and fro-ings, was a marker of our long, lazy Oasis days.

It was very exciting to gallop on our pretend horses (mine was called Moonlight) down to Grandma's place, especially when there were tantalising smells of her baking. Sometimes we scored a basin or spoon to 'lick out'. (We often thought the cake mixture was even nicer than the cooked cake.)

Cow paddocks across the road from Oasis

The early days at Dorset Cottage, before Grandma made the garden

In the very early days at Oasis, our toilet was a small room open to the outside but attached to the back of the house. ('Toilet' was a word that wasn't ever used then, not by us anyway. It was considered very poor usage by both Grandma and our father; it was always the 'lavatory'.) The toilet had newspaper, torn rather meticulously into squares by our father and stuck on a nail, and a large can, which did not bear looking into, with a flip-top lid that we put up rather fast and closed even faster. This was emptied once a week by the night cart man, a mysterious figure I never actually saw. We did hear him, however: quick steps running down the side path in the dark. It was too unpleasant to think about what he was carrying and how. At Christmas, our father left out two bottles of beer for him. I remember worrying how he would carry them, as he needed two hands (I supposed) to fulfil his mission.

It was not long after we moved in, however, that we had a septic tank installed, and the 'lavatory' became a fancy new shiny white bowl, with clean flushes of water replacing the big, dark, ominous can.

Again we had chooks and watched twenty-four fluffy day-old chicks grow into hens. We also had a beautiful white rooster called, rather oddly, Marie Antoinette. Perhaps it was Grandpa Joe's sense of humour.

Grandpa Joe's quarters were in the two rooms of a remodelled garage at the back of Dorset Cottage. He made another spectacular vegetable garden: new potatoes (which Mum steamed deliciously with mint), cabbages, cauliflowers, lettuce, carrots, parsnips, turnips and swedes.

In 2008, I did an extensive tour of the war cemeteries and battlegrounds of France and Belgium with my younger son, who is a keen historian. We deliberately chose to go to Polygon Wood, where Grandpa Joe had been badly injured during World War I. We were very moved to see, all around the cemetery, acres and acres of lush fertile vegetable gardens growing prolific crops of cabbages and cauliflowers in neat and almost unending rows. In a flash, and with a lump in my throat, I was transported back through decades of years to a fresh and lovely morning at Oasis. I am wearing my high school uniform and about to go out to the bus when Joe comes up to the kitchen carrying a huge cauliflower and presents it to Mum. I can still smell its tangy and earthy freshness and see the droplets of dew hanging on its florets and leaves.

Mum once again grew a small plantation of sweet corn, and our father, as noted earlier, bought and planted a long row of *Pinus insignis* all along the front road border of both houses. (This was the south side. The back faced the north, which gave us beautiful sun-drenched acres in which to play.)

With the *Pinus insignis* shooting up like crazy and Mum's wonderful gardening (helped by copious supplies of poultry and cow manure), the house soon lost its bare look. Red roses grew over the pergola at the front, and the front garden shrubs and flowers were flourishing. Along the western side of the house were three plum trees and two apple trees – how I loved the blossom – that the previous owners had planted. The apples were too sour to eat uncooked (Mum stewed them and Grandma made apple pies – both with generous amounts of sugar), but the plums were messily delicious. What I loved most of all, and what was growing prolifically when we moved in, was a whole dense one-metre-wide and six-metre-long bed of violets, crammed with huge, deeply purple flowers that were oh so fragrant. The previous owners had sold them to the markets: hundreds of corsages and little posies. I called this area Violet Vale after *Anne of Green Gables*.

There were three mulberry trees growing along the eastern side fence at the back; we loved climbing these, especially when they were in fruit. They were havens of shade in the long hot summers. We children were always outside, playing our endless games inspired by our endless reading. Our father at this stage was travelling to and from the city and was a frequenter of auction sales. He brought us home boxes and boxes of second-hand books, which was always exciting. Mine were all, even then, slightly old-fashioned schoolgirl stories about the upper

The front of Oasis after about two years – Pinus insignis at the front fence, roses, may bush, plumbago, yellow banksia rose over the front porch and my specialty, English daisies, pinks and primulas, in bed against front porch (not visible here)

fourth, boarding school and snowy Christmases. But that little girl from an upside-down world devoured them eagerly and still has many of them!

The house itself was cosy and it had a very effective wood heater in the lounge room. I can still see it with the afternoon sunlight streaming in through the lounge room window. The boys slept in a blue room together, but I had what was effectively a glassed-in verandah that I absolutely loved, which opened off their room. Mum painted it a soft sunshine yellow and pasted a frieze of tawny autumn leaves along the top, where wall met sloping ceiling. Grandma made me a wonderful old-gold silk quilt and pillow sham. I kept these for years (and I still have a yellow bedroom).

It was about this time that we three children invented and started playing an exciting going-to-bed game called The Secret Tunnel. One of my brothers was for a while scared about putting his feet down the end of his bed, and perhaps we dreamed up this game, possibly inspired by Enid Blyton's *Magic Faraway Tree*, to help him.

Indicator board at Central railway station, Sydney

Every night, burrowing down in our kapok mattresses, we would take it in turns to tell each other the stories of our adventures; we would transport ourselves in magic cars, boats, aeroplanes and rocket ships down the tunnel to the Giant Indicator Board. This was modelled on the indicator board at Central railway station. (We had little experience of any other travel at this time.) The game was, of course, all imaginary, and we were each under the blankets and quilt in our own bed. But it felt amazingly real. We would decide where we would go, how we would each get there and then all take off and drive, sail or fly while calling out to each other, compounding the

The Secret Tunnel
Many years later, when I had my own children, I turned these imaginary adventures into a story. We all had special tunnel names in that long-ago game with my brothers – an alter-ego. Our first port of call was always the Giant Indicator Board, which had endless destinations, including Ancient Greece, Buckingham Palace, Deepest Africa and Outer Space!

adventure, all adding to and reacting to the story along the way, playing it endlessly (I don't quite know for how long) until one or t'other of us fell asleep.

The move to Oasis took us to a new school. Our little brother was now also accompanying us. For a few months it was quite a long walk: down to the station, across the railway line and up the hill to a very old one classroom building swamped in the magical leaves and scent of pepper trees, which were great for climbing. The headmaster and his family lived more-or-less on site, just across the play area. This was another experience of an old historical schoolroom. It had started as a tiny Catholic school, but in 1867 it was transferred to the government so that the teacher could actually receive a salary! Until 1884 it was known as Saggart Field Provisional School. But by the time we got there it was already well and truly the 'old school', and at the end of our first Oasis year a brand new – and bland – weatherboard building was opened on our side of the railway line, just up from the oval where some years later my brothers would distinguish themselves at cricket.

Pepper trees, Schinus molle, were frequently planted in NSW schools in the early days

exploration. For example, a ragged old creek just wide enough for a big jump, or sometimes a little too wide (the shoes had to be cleaned for the next day anyway), was always a welcome diversion from the mere process of getting to and from school.

The school was a small and shabby two-room building which was very old. Actually, it was one of the oldest schools in NSW (and therefore in Australia) but in those days that fact generated neither interest nor historical enthusiasm. This was a time when old was just old, and run-down, and out-of-date, and, simply, a Disgrace. For all that, it was not without its charm, especially in retrospect. It was built of weatherboard, and both rooms opened on to a verandah, with a splintery railing around it and a short row of steps leading down to the playground (which was just a patch of often yellow grass - no fancy equipment then). The whole building was all but covered by the spicy and keenly-green branches of a huge, drooping pepper tree. There was a tumbledown weather shed at one end of the playground, and over at the other side was the Headmaster's residence, to which place the teacher beat many retreats, especially on hot and dry afternoons.

Description of the old schoolhouse from Oasis days, as later written in The Secret Tunnel

This new school was big. It had two or perhaps three classrooms, a staff room, a headmaster's office, from which the swish of the cane could be heard now and then (we all flinched in sympathy), a cloak room, which doubled as a canteen on Mondays, and a verandah along the front, where the three teachers stood when we had an assembly and where we recited the pledge every week: 'I honour my God, I serve my Queen, I salute my flag.'

The 'canteen' consisted of volunteer mothers using a teacher's table to make sandwiches – exotic luxuries such as baked beans (which I always had on Mondays, the one day we bought our lunches), vegemite, corned beef and Spam. Notwithstanding hygiene issues, those Monday sandwiches, on morning-fresh white bread that was aromatically delivered in a basket by the baker, were scrumptious!

Not so scrumptious – in fact, terrible – was the half pint bottle of milk delivered to all students at all schools every morning. This was no doubt a worthwhile government initiative, but at our school, anyway, the milk was delivered early (we heard the clank of the bottles in their trays) and was drunk at playtime (11.00-ish). This was fine in winter, which was frosty and freezing, but in summer, with the trays parked under the building because the school did not have adequate refrigeration, the milk was warm and revolting by the time we drank it. Also, because it was basically straight from the cow, about three centimetres of cream sat on the top. I enjoy cream now but didn't eat it for years because of the school milk experience.

But I liked school very much. I gobbled up the stories and the neat sensible sums and the fascinating grammar and the spelling and the projects: the wool industry, the explorers. I think we must have had longer lunch times, because some days we would 'go home' for lunch. We didn't actually go home; Mum met us with a basket about halfway and we had a picnic sitting on a log under huge gum trees and playing near a trickle of a stream. I wrote just recently in another book a few lines about that memory:

And here's our mother, at one with the gentle haze of the day,
Coming to meet us on the way home.

I think we all loved Oasis. The boys had a scrappy, uneven, idiosyncratic cricket pitch down in the back paddock and played cricket endlessly. There was also a dam down there that was mostly dry and which, I'm sad to say, we used as a sort of rubbish disposal. There was at that time and in that place no garbage collection and no recycling, but because we had the chooks there was no food

And just remembering that weatherboard schoolroom,
I feel the searing heat of creamy paddocks,
the squish and squash of shoes in melting asphalt.
and smell the steamy whiff of hay and cow dung.
 A hundred memories tumble in, unguarded …
            playlunch and lunch in crinkly greaseproof paper,
green apple stirred by warm leather of satchel,
        and eucalyptus air,
    the smooth-rough coat of our cow, Honey,
    the sound of a tractor down the road,
and here's our mother,
at one with the gentle haze of the day,
        coming to meet us
on the way home ….
From Growing Young Minds (in press) **RRJ**

wastage. And Mum and Grandma diligently composted way before their time. (Mum and Grandma also inveigled us into many collecting-manure-for-the-garden excursions along the back roads.) The dam and whatever was in it caused a problem for fielders but added to the general excitement of the game. Could the ball actually be retrieved or even seen?

We always looked forward to when Uncle Les and his growing family came to visit because he was a wonderful sportsman and a star tennis player (an ex-NSW doubles champion). He always found time to play with us and was a great encourager.

Play seemed so full in those days. I had my books, my dolls (Margaret Ruth was turning a bit rubbery and smelt a bit if I left her in the sun, and Elizabeth had a leg that fell out if I wasn't careful, but they were survivors). I also had my box of magazine cut-outs: people and backgrounds that were endlessly arranged and rearranged to create different stories. And I had Grandma's button jar. The buttons all had personalities of their own and I had many adventures with them.

We built a tree house, which was actually just two thick pieces of Masonite (?) resting on a few bricks and was virtually flat on the ground. This was covered with a faded and frayed rug. It was under a large tree clump and had an old wind-up gramophone on which we played – and endlessly sang along to – our small supply of records. Davy Crockett was a favourite:

Born on a mountain top in Tennessee
Greenest state in the land of the free
Raised in the woods so he knew ev'ry tree
Kilt him a be 'are when he was only three ...

We sang it out lustily across the paddocks and listened over and over to Bing Crosby's 'The Small One'. At this time, and certainly after television came to Australia in September 1956, we knew much more about that 'land of the free' than we did about our own beautiful country. Most of our knowledge was of the Hollywood variety, however – illusory.

Even at Braeside, and certainly at Oasis and later Cameo, we were regular attendees at the Saturday afternoon matinee at the local 'pictures'. This referred to buildings that were not grand enough to be called 'theatres' and would today probably be called 'cinemas'. In those days regional towns had a 'picture show', but the smaller places, near us, showed films in what was then the local 'School of Arts'.

From the earliest days we loved musicals. Bing Crosby was a favourite, as were Ginger Rogers and Fred Astaire. My parents had taken me to see *The Wizard of Oz* as a very small girl, but I found it frightening and apparently spent most of the time under the seat. Later we liked cowboys, and a bit later still Crosby and Hope's 'Road' films. I liked the glamorous women and remember seeing a Loretta Young drama, *Paula*, and thinking how lovely she looked. (She reminded me of Mum.) I also saw the Danny Kaye film about the life of Hans Christian Andersen and sang 'Wonderful, Wonderful Copenhagen' for years. As we grew older we enjoyed the Doris Day and Rock Hudson films, but we completely missed the innuendo and subtexts of these. I really liked Doris's clothes. (I still do: such pert, immaculate smartness.) And what a smooth and easy listening voice!

This fascination with movies (my recollection is that we followed the British tradition and called them 'films' in those days) continued, perhaps unsurprisingly. The film (or movie) world was intoxicating. A few years afterwards, by then on our own small television set (more on this later), we watched and admired (and yes, perhaps sometimes envied) the very tidy houses and front yards with no fences, and the mothers in pretty dresses and high heels (and perfectly coiffed hair) smiling and carrying baskets of clean folded washing, and the children who didn't have to wear school uniform, and the teenagers driving long shiny cars, and the camaraderie of the milk-bars, and all the 'Alices' in the kitchen who helped Mom with the dirty work (which actually didn't look all that dirty). It was a very different world.

A year or so after moving into Oasis, like half the school at the time, we all caught the measles. In those pre-vaccination days this was quite common. But for us it created a terrible problem, as Mum had never had them and caught them also, and she was pregnant. It was not German measles, which is so dangerous, but Mum became very ill and was hospitalised for a short period. My father was beside himself with worry, and Grandma came up from her place next door to look after us (actually, we ate down at her place). When Mum came home she seemed very weak, but my father

The growing garden – back and side

made what he called 'bone soup' (not sure what was in it, but he had a bubbling cauldron of it on the fuel stove) and she recovered.

One day, at the beginning of the following year, our father took Mum off to the local private hospital. This was no Cabarisha, just a rather shabby extended house, but the matron was very kind. I can remember Mum getting ready, putting on the blue crepe maternity dress Grandma had made her and doing her hair in front of their bedroom mirror. In those days fathers were kept out of labour wards, but he told me he sat outside in the car, waiting. When he came back home late that afternoon, we were watching for him on the front porch. I have always remembered his words: 'Mummy said for me to tell you that you have a little baby brother.'

At the time I was very disappointed; I wanted a sister. And when we all trooped in the next afternoon to see our new little brother, we were not very impressed. He was 'rashy' and unsettled. But the rash soon went and a beautiful and gentle nature emerged; and I forgot any disappointment about the pink and pale green baby rug I had rather tediously knitted and I fell in love with him.

That first year of our little brother's life feels like, in my memory, another one of those halcyon times. The family were all so happy and were all enjoying Oasis so much. Trees were growing and plants and flowers were thriving. Grandma built a bush house for her ferns and Joe kept us in a never-ending supply of vegetables.

Mum with her third little son

School for me was now no longer the sleepy little primary school up the road but a brand-new high school (with two science rooms, a music room and a library) in the local town. I had qualified for Fort Street, then the major selective girls' school in the city, but my parents decided it was too far to travel each day (round about a two hour trip each way, plus an almost two kilometre walk to and from the local station). So I caught the school bus, which stopped right outside our door, to the new school. Suddenly there were new friends from different places. There were also some knowing boys – very popular with everyone else – who made deliberate fun of this very naive, very

With our beautiful baby brother

fair girl: I burnt terribly and could never get a tan, which in those years was the order of the day. Again, I was teased.

But that school and its teachers were very good to me. It was, for all intents and purposes, a country school, and I remember the librarian used to disappear with some senior staff up the street at lunch time for refreshments. But when he got to know me, he would allow me to go into the locked library to browse and read. Thus the library became, as libraries have been many times, not a hiding place, exactly, but a place of refuge and solace. It had 'modern' books that I had never come across, like the *Cherry Ames Nurse* series, as well as some of the classics that I grew to love, such as George Eliot's *Silas Marner* and Charles Dickens' *Great Expectations*. As a prelude to later reading of writers such as Toni Morrison, I started to read and was moved by other places and problems, such as in Alan Paton's *Cry, the Beloved Country*. I was increasingly beguiled by the magic of words and story and devoured them all. Each one made me feel as if my mind was developing new shaky tentacles of thinking and thought.

But one terrible winter's night our life changed.

I am going to tell it briefly. We said good night and went to bed as usual, but I was woken just after ten by Mum, who said: 'Dadda is very sick, darling. I am going around to Mrs Gorn's to ring the doctor. I need you to be with him.'

We had a telephone, but it was, at this stage, on the local exchange operated in the little post office down near the station and switched off at ten. Our neighbour, Mrs Gorn, who lived almost a kilometre away across the paddocks, was on the main continuous exchange of the next village.

Mum left. Our father walked out on the back verandah to the laundry, where he was sick into the tub. I stood helplessly by and held his hand as he went back into the lounge room and lay down on the divan.

Mum returned, the doctor came, and it all became a nightmare of unreality. Our father seemed to be breathing very loudly. And louder still. Then I heard the breathing stop and the doctor's soft words. Mum gave one short sharp cry. I heard the winter wood fire crackling. That particular sound, along with a certain awareness of deep cold, always reminds me, dreadfully, of this night. Mrs Gorn arrived with Mrs Stroud, another neighbour she had picked up on the way. They came in with sympathetic eyes to where I was standing in the little hallway leading from the lounge to the bedrooms, but I did not react in any way: if I didn't cry or look upset it couldn't be really happening. Mum told them not to disturb Grandma next door. When they left, Mum came and sat on the chair in the main bedroom (where I had got into their bed) and wrapped herself in my father's dressing gown. She stayed there, quite silent, all night. In the morning she went into the boys' room and told my brothers. 'Dadda was very sick last night. He was so sick he died.' She then went down and told Grandma.

The nightmare continued. Mum had four young children, one a baby of eighteen months. Grandma was amazing. She made us breakfast, lunch and dinner; she kept the everyday going. Looking back, things are a blur. I can't recall much about the following weeks and months, even some parts of years, but somehow life went on. For ages I slept with Mum in her bed, our baby brother in the big cot alongside. It was a messy, messed-up time. There were also some financial problems to do with the estate; our dynamic father had not expected to die and had died intestate.

The family were all thoughtful and kind. Uncle Les, with a demanding job and five children of his own, still managed to visit quite often to play cricket with the boys and talk cricket with Grandma. Aunty Hilda and Uncle Basil invited us frequently for holidays to their waterfront home in Octavia Street, Narrabeen, where Uncle Basil took us all out fishing (we never caught anything). During this period, they gave us a particularly kind and thoughtful gift (one of many): our

'Big Aunty Hilda', a well-known elocutionist, still performing late in life, here with the Governor of NSW (1966–1981) Sir Roden Cutler, VC, who lost a leg during WWII

very own television set. Television had only just arrived in Australia (in 1956), and this was a real luxury. It was a little seventeen-inch black and white set, and while it couldn't take away the pain of our loss, it did provide a distraction, probably not for Mum so much but certainly for us children. It seemed miraculous to have moving pictures in our own lounge room.

We spent the first Christmas after our father's death with Aunty Hilda and Uncle Basil at Narrabeen, and my only real memory of that time is of a sort of false jollity and Mum sitting very still and composed looking but with streams of tears running down her cheeks. 'Big Aunty', a well-known figure in Sydney artistic circles and a real character, who was used to being the star of the show, was there as well. She tried to cheer us all up. Unfortunately, we children found her very embarrassing. I remember walking with her along the beach one day as she scooped up her skirt to collect seashells. This revealed her long pink bloomers underneath, which seemed to reach her knees. Without saying anything to each other, we all walked as far away from the adult group as we could, lest anyone connect us.

It was a difficult, terrible time for all of us. I felt deeply guilty that I could do nothing to help our father whilst we were waiting together for Mum to return and for the doctor to arrive. I felt like I should have said something meaningful to him. But I didn't know that it would be my last chance. There was also now a growing and insidious fear deep inside me that someone else I loved would suddenly die. If my little brother was asleep and too still, I would poke him to make him stir, to check if he were still alive. If Grandma nodded off in her chair watching the television, I would cough or make a sudden noise to make her start. I would even panic that our dog, a dear little Scottish terrier, had stopped breathing and give it a little jab to check. Worst of all, over and over again and wherever we went, and even at school, I would think I saw the figure of my father in the distance or walking towards me, only to find that it wasn't. Once I was sure I saw him and that he was coming to pick me up; then the awful reality of his death re-hit and I saw it was someone else. This was complicated no doubt by the fact that around about this time, and without anyone realising it, I had developed short-sightedness, so all distant figures were blurry.

But Oasis was kept safe as he had it registered in Mum's name, and the garden was thriving; it was beautiful. Every day as I got off the school bus, which stopped right at our door, it felt like a haven. It truly was an oasis. The long row of *Pinus insignis*, now tall and adolescent with gangling limbs, was like a dense dark green beacon 'signalling' to us as the bus brought us home from school or as we walked up from the station.

And Oasis had another gift for us. Mum had tried going to work in various ways but hated it. She had sold the car because she was always very nervous in cars and didn't drive. (We all had to travel by train or bus, and our new little brother was still a baby.) So, that daughter of the Crag bought a cow, Honey, a pretty little Jersey. It kept us in milk and cream (I still didn't like it!) and Mum took to making butter. The chooks were supplemented and kept us and others in eggs and allowed us the occasional roast chicken, which in those days was a real treat. Although I haven't eaten meat for over twenty-five years and we children did feel sad about the chooks (Joe did the deed), we all loved and looked forward to that succulent treat. Joe continued to grow our vegetables and Grandma made many of our clothes. She was a wonderful designer and made the entire smart outfits and hats worn by Hilda and Dorothy in various photographs of those bygone years. That flair for design and creative sewing has been inherited by all three of our daughters in different ways but by one in particular. And it came from both sides; my husband's mother, Queenie, was also a clever dressmaker.

The biggest gift (legacy) was to do with our Oasis land: the big spare garden block with its long front road frontage that adjoined Grandma's spare block. It was mixed with the gift of Mum's vision and initiative and Grandma's never-ending creativity and care. Somehow, she (or they) decided to subdivide our land, separating the one Oasis block from the rest of our land: our other front block adjoining Grandma's spare and the back blocks that ran along the back of the whole property and fronted an unmade road. We helped Mum measure where the dividing fence should go, and I remember holding the string and trying desperately to get the three precious plum trees onto our new side. I couldn't quite manage it, but we did get the May bush, and though it spilled on both sides, we, through some subtle manoeuvring on my part, had the clumpy root.

Our new little brother growing up with the garden

So, Mum sold Oasis. It should have felt sad, and I'm sure Mum must have been heavy about it, but it was actually quite exciting. We were not moving away; we were going to build a new house, designed especially for us by Mum. In the interim, we all (five of us, four getting bigger), moved into Grandma's small Dorset Cottage next door, and Mum set about organising the building of our new home. Money was a concern, so it was to be a simple rectangle across the large front block next to Oasis. There was to be a row of five small bedrooms all along the back and simple living areas along the front. And, of course, there now also had to be a redesign of the whole garden.

The front garden

Dreamscape (song)

I dreamt last night of days gone by
Of overflowing days, and summer sky
Of rainbow colours bright, like tinted cellophane,
I dreamt last night I was a child again.

Why can't the world be like my memories, when roads were long, and mountains high?
When just the branches of a pepper tree became a fortress, reaching to the sky?
And I could keep my tryst with destiny, with laughing eyes as dreams fulfil.

Yet as I dreamed I heard you say
Tomorrow's yesterday will be today
So let it come to me, I'll take it on the chin!
I'll make the best of all that life may bring.

The world can be like memories, its roads are long, its mountains high!
And just the branches of a pepper tree can be a fortress, reaching to the sky!
And I will keep my tryst with destiny, with laughing eyes as dreams fulfil.

RRJ

Safe in the house

Before our father died, I think Oasis was an idyllic place for Mum – for us all. This poem, 'Song of the Rain', by Hugh McCrae (1876–1958) sums up that sense of quiet and ordinary and precious contentment. It expresses, powerfully, how Malcolm and I were to feel later in Kerensa. McCrae lived in Camden for several years in the early 1930s. 'Song of the Rain', one of my favourites, first appeared in a limited collection entitled *Colombine*.

> *Night,*
> *and the yellow pleasure of candle-light …*
> *old brown books and the kind, fine face of the clock*
> *fogged in the veils of the fire - its cuddling tock.*
> *The cat,*
> *greening her eyes on the flame-litten mat;*
> *wickedly, wakeful she yawns at the rain*
> *bending the roses over the pane,*
> *and a bird in my heart begins to sing*
> *over and over the same sweet thing –*
> > Safe in the house with my boyhood's love
> > And our children asleep in the attic above.

A legacy of love

I treasure a geranium which we call 'Grandma Darling'. It's a plant my mum gave me years ago to help start our Kerensa garden – a 'garden-warming' gift – and its flowers are a variegated bright red and white. Mum loved colour and the red expresses the passion of that love while the white symbolises her peace-making and 'essential essence' of purity.

Cuttings of this special geranium now thrive at the homes of my children – the one seen here on Robert's balcony.

Poets are environmentalists: Gerard Manley Hopkins (1844–1889) saw beauty and a unique 'oneness' in the world of nature. He called it 'inscape'. I understand the beauty of this 'sweet especial rural scene' and mourn with Hopkins the 'unselving' of trees, and the loss of 'beauty been'. Poplars first entered our orbit at Oasis. We had so much ground that Mum planted one on the side of the front garden. As far as I know, they didn't do anything terrible to the water pipes – whilst we were there anyway.

Binsey Poplars *felled 1879*

My aspens dear, whose airy cages quelled,
Quelled or quenched in leaves the leaping sun,
All felled, felled, are all felled;
    Of a fresh and following folded rank
        Not spared, not one
        That dandled a sandalled
        Shadow that swam or sank
On meadow and river and wind-wandering weed-winding bank.

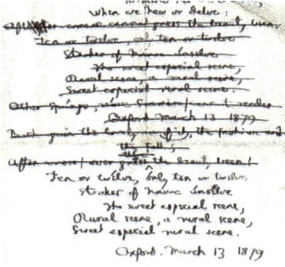

In the Bodleian Library, Oxford

O if we but knew what we do
    When we delve or hew—
     Hack and rack the growing green!
      Since country is so tender
To touch, her being so slender,
That, like this sleek and seeing ball
But a prick will make no eye at all,
    Where we, even where we mean
    To mend her we end her,
    When we hew or delve:
After-comers cannot guess the beauty been.
    Ten or twelve, only ten or twelve
      Strokes of havoc unselve
       The sweet especial scene,
       Rural scene, a rural scene,
       Sweet especial rural scene.

Claude Monet (1840–1926) Poplars at Giverny

'Danny Boy' – my father's favourite song – a ballad written in 1910 by English songwriter Frederic Weatherly and set to the traditional Irish melody of 'Londonderry Air'. It has both Irish and Scottish connections.

Oh, Danny boy, the pipes, the pipes are calling
From glen to glen, and down the mountain side.
The summer's gone, and all the roses falling,
It's you, it's you must go and I must bide.

But come ye back when summer's in the meadow,
Or when the valley's hushed and white with snow,
I'll be here in sunshine or in shadow,
Oh, Danny boy, oh Danny boy, I love you so!

But when ye come, and all the flowers are dying,
If I am dead, as dead I well may be,
You'll come and find the place where I am lying,
And kneel and say an Ave there for me.
And I shall hear, though soft you tread above me,
And all my grave will warmer, sweeter be,
For you will bend and tell me that you love me,
And I shall sleep in peace until you come to me!

'Skye Boat Song' – my mother's favourite song – lyrics by Harold Boulton to an air collected by Anne Campbell MacLeod. Mum only ever sang the first verse, but I do remember an occasional dramatic declamation of the last verse.

Speed bonnie boat like a bird on the wing
Onward the sailors cry
Carry the lad that's born to be king
Over the sea to Skye

Loud the wind howls, loud the waves roar,
Thunderclaps rend the air
Baffled our foes, stand by the shore
Follow they will not dare
Speed bonnie boat like a bird on the wing
Onward the sailors cry
Carry the lad that's born to be king
Over the sea to Skye …

> *Burned are our homes, exile and death*
> *Scatter the loyal men*
> *Yet e'er the sword cool in the sheath*
> *Charlie will come again.*

'The Holy City' – my grandmother's favourite song – 1892, music by Michael Maybrick (Stephen Adams) and lyrics (I just discovered this!) also by Frederic Weatherly. Elsie Emily had a lovely contralto voice, and she often belted this out in the kitchen and elsewhere.

Last night whilst I was sleeping
There came a dream so fair,
I stood in old Jerusalem
Beside the temple there.
I heard the children singing,
And ever as they sang,
I thought the voice of angels
From heaven in answer rang
I thought the voice of angels
From heaven in answer rang!   *Jerusalem! Jerusalem! Lift up your gates and sing,*
                                       Hosanna in the highest! Hosanna to your King!

And then I thought my dream was changed,
The streets no longer rang,
Hushed were the glad Hosannas
The little children sang.
The sun grew dark with mystery,
The morn was cold and chill,
As the shadow of a cross arose
Upon a lonely hill.   *Jerusalem! Jerusalem! Hark! How the angels sing,*
                              Hosanna in the highest! Hosanna to your King!

And once again the scene was changed;
New earth there seemed to be;
I saw the Holy City
Beside the crystal sea.
The light of God was on its streets,
The gates were open wide,
And all who might enter,
And no one was denied.
No need of moon or stars by night,
Or sun to shine by day;
It was the new Jerusalem
That would not pass away.   *Jerusalem! Jerusalem! Sing for the night is o'er!*
                                    Hosanna in the highest! Hosanna for evermore!

4. Garden the Fourth – Cameo

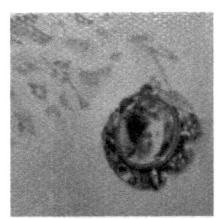

'Where's morning gone?' – From 'The Violets' by Gwen Harwood

The new house was called Cameo from the start. Both Mum and Grandma had pretty cameo brooches, and I think it was the idea of a private enclosure guarding something precious, a small safe protected world, that Mum loved. I wore Grandma's cameo brooch, which had belonged to her mother, Emily Jane Ross, as the 'something old' on my wedding dress. It opened at the back, and when Grandma had it, it contained a very faded picture of Baby Jack (the infant son who died), but I think she took that out when she gave it to Mum, who then gave it to me. I had Grandma's photo in it on my wedding day but now have a photo of Mum.

Cameo was a modest house, but we thought it wonderful because we each were to have our own bedroom with a big window and a built-in wardrobe. Four bedrooms and a sunroom

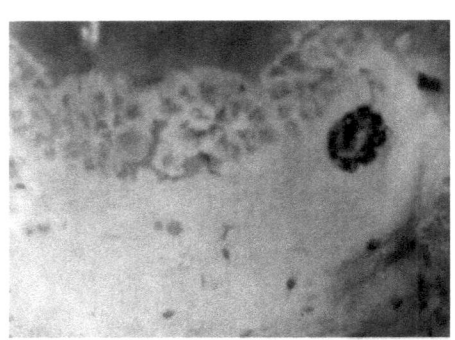

'Something old' on my wedding day

(this became Mum's bedroom when our little brother needed his own) ran along the back northern side, looking down over the paddocks and the creek. How lovely was the winter sun pouring in: the apricity! The living areas were all along the front, facing the road. The house was set much further back on the land than Oasis, so we had an expansive front garden that spilled into Grandma's large spare block and her garden next door. The plum trees were along the side border. They were on the other side of the fence, but we could still see them. Soon after moving in, however, Mum added a garage (not for a car but for bikes and gardening tools) and a breezeway, where, as the boys got older, a beautiful ancient mahogany table, too big for the dining room, was used for table tennis.

Some years later, when Grandma needed more help, we added a large new room behind the garage. Today it would be called a studio apartment. It wasn't fancy, but Grandma brought her favourite dark green leather bucket armchair, her large old-fashioned high bed, her books, her sewing machine, her favourite bits and pieces and her television. This meant there were now two active televisions in the house, which was often handy. Grandma had astonishingly youthful tastes. A lovely classical singer and a walking hymnal, she enjoyed the pop shows *Bandstand* and *Six O'Clock Rock*. She did not like Johnny O'Keefe ('he yells') but enjoyed Col Joye, the Bee Gees, the Allen Brothers, Sandy Scott, Olivia Newton-John, Jimmy Little, Helen Reddy, Johnny Farnham and, most of all, the Delltones. Later she also enjoyed the Seekers. And she was a huge cricket fan; to this day, the sound of night-time cricket broadcasts coming from England (Old Trafford, Lord's) reminds me of Grandma. When test matches were on, it was a steady hum punctuated by muted, excited barracking from the silver-haired lady sitting in a shabby green leather chair late at night on the other side of the world.

The house itself was not big, but it felt spacious. It was built of fibro, which my father would have hated, with a very pretty and quite unusual yellow tiled roof. It had some wonderful design features and was an incredibly comfortable house. All the bedrooms were filled with winter sun but shaded and breezy in summer. The kitchen was separated from dining and living rooms by an L-shaped counter, which had another higher narrow counter on the dining room side. This maintained the feeling of openness but gave the cook some privacy and hid any cooking mess. We thought the laminex countertops exceptionally modern.

Mum, who was on a very tight budget so I don't know how, splurged on a wonderful slow combustion stove. It was large, had two ovens, one a warming oven, and a firebox. I haven't got a photo and can't remember the brand, but it was a magnificent asset. It heated our hot water, heated the house in winter and heated the bricks that were wrapped in old towels and put into our beds at night. Was it an AGA? I don't know. It may have been a Rayburn; that name seems familiar. Whatever it was, it was excellent. When my husband and I came to build our house years later, I really wanted one. But they were $10,000, which was almost as much as we were spending on the whole house. I don't know how we did it for Cameo.

That stove was indeed the heart of the house: the sound, smell and flavours of home and family. It gave us hot baths, plates were warmed, dinners were cooked, clothes (and sometimes shoes and boots) were dried and arriving-home bodies were welcomed and cheered. Every day a small saucepan slowly brewed the milk coffee with grains at the bottom that Grandma would come up to share with Mum after breakfast. I wish I had noted how they actually made it. I have never been able quite to recapture that flavour. Perhaps it is the gloss of memory.

I loved Cameo. It was the house I grew up in and the house I got married from. Its garden was truly pretty, not with flowers so much but with lovely trees and shrubs. An old-fashioned Dorothy Perkins rose sprawled thornily and adventurously over the front fence just behind the grove of willows that we children loved to climb. Indeed, we started climbing those willows when they were still too spindly to hold us, and one bad day we broke off a big branch. Knowing we had been told not to climb the young trees, we all desperately tried to camouflage the long, jagged tear by wrapping fat streamers of willow leaves around it. It didn't work, but the willow recovered in no time.

A *Lasiandra* – now called *Tibouchina* – made a huge clump of regal purple just under the front kitchen window. And Grandma's rose bed was glorious. This was where one morning, walking around with Mum and Grandma on their daily inspection, I first saw and smelt 'Peace', a soft gold rose with delicate blushes of pink: 'dew-pearled' (Browning's lovely image) on that particular

'Peace'

occasion. And truly, despite the desperate unhappiness and the necessity that had provoked this move, for me certainly, and I think in different ways for us all, Cameo days had many moments of gentle peace.

High school now played a very important part in my life. I was doing languages – French and Latin – which I very much enjoyed. I was making new friends, several of whom remained close to me in later years; indeed, two friends from these long-ago days attended my UTS retirement function in 2019. We were a very protected, innocent little group.

I did a lot of things – all now a bit of a blur – but also had a very active inner life. I was drawn more and more to Christianity. (Mum wasn't a conventional churchgoer but always said 'Keep your eyes on Jesus' and always had a Bible near her bed.) Like Grandma, I loved the hymns, and I became very involved with the church and a member of various choirs. I found my father's Bible, claimed it, made a yellow silk cover for it and embroidered a cross on the front.

I was writing more and more. *Stella of the Crag* was finished as was a long Shakespearean type play set in the Australian bush. I also wrote endless songs (including an unfinished opera) and poetry, and usually had several poems published in the annual school magazine, the *Cygnet*. I did honours in my senior years (English with some help from a dedicated teacher, History without any actual teaching or allocated time) and loved the new worlds of thought and possibility that this all opened up to me. Already – as the daughter of *that* daughter of the Crag – I knew and had read most of Shakespeare's plays and, fancying myself as a leading lady, endlessly played Lady Macbeth, Ophelia (wished it was a bigger part), Titania (ditto), the witches (all of them as one) and Puck. I knew huge slabs of the plays by heart. My favourite stage was in front of an uncurtained window at night when the light was on in the room. I could close my bedroom door, watch my reflection and declaim with drama, despite occasional thumps of complaint on the wall from my brother next door.

'Maid of the Willows'

The year's at the spring,
And day's at the morn;
Morning's at seven;
The hill-side's dew-pearl'd;
The lark's on the wing;
The snail's on the thorn;
God's in His heaven—
All's right with the world.

Song (short lyric poem) from 'Pippa Passes', a verse play by English Victorian poet Robert Browning (pub.1841). Pippa is a factory girl who winds silk, and this day is her one holiday in the whole year.

In 1846 Elizabeth Barrett eloped with Browning. She wrote:
How do I love thee? Let me count the ways.
I love thee to the depth and breadth and height
My soul can reach ... (Sonnet 43)

I had very long hair until my last year of school when, after much agonising, I had it cut. Mum took this snap on my old Brownie; she called it 'Maid of the Willows'. It felt very liberating to have hair shoulder-length after so many years of plaits.

One speech night I was asked to do a recitation and for some reason chose Lady Anne's lament from Richard III:

> Set down, set down your honourable load,
> If honour may be shrouded in a hearse,
> Whilst I awhile obsequiously lament
> Th' untimely fall of virtuous Lancaster.

Not sure how that went down with a country crowd on a summer's night just before Christmas, but I enjoyed it.

Words and their expression of thought, of idea and of emotion, had, from an early age, worked their magic on me. I was beguiled by their use in poems, speeches, stories and plays. One word, and its tumble of meanings in a particular context, could be captivating, enchanting, exhilarating.

Many years later and in another world, I wrote in a book about literacy and literature (Oxford University Press, six editions 2001–2020):

> Consider the first and subsequent *Harry Potter* books (1997 onwards). When the phenomenally popular first book became a film, much was made about the author's insistence on artistic veracity and fidelity: the film would be true to the book. The film features rich and opulent landscapes, an aristocratic cast, and brilliant special effects (some by Jim Henson's Creative Shop), while the amazing quidditch game, with Harry winning by catching the Golden Snitch in his mouth, cost a fortune to reproduce.

Literacy: Reading, Writing and Children's Literature OUP six editions (2001–2020). The book is divided into three parts. I wrote the Children's Literature section (Part 3, Chs 24–35, pp.421–619)

It is indeed interesting that so many resources were needed in order to create as a *film* a highly successful *book* that *consisted of no more than black marks on a white page.*

The book was made up of the 26 letters of the English alphabet; it was conceived and written by one person, Rowling. The settings of place, characters, events, adventures, railway station, Hogwarts were all brought into imaginative being by the words thus created in the minds of readers.

Now I also became interested in how art conveys emotion and meaning. My mother very much liked the paintings of Aboriginal artist Albert Namatjira, and I revelled in the intensity of some of his unexpected colours – purples and deep blues and olivey greens – that spoke of space and distance and seemed at once to reflect both rugged mystery and wistfulness.

Namatjira was born in Hermannsburg, near Alice Springs in the Northern Territory, and his pioneering work as a contemporary Indigenous Australian artist made him the most famous Indigenous Australian of his generation. In 1957 he and his wife became the first Aboriginals to be granted Australian citizenship.

Albert Namatjira (1902–1959)

This interest and indeed worry (why weren't they already Australian citizens?) nagged and inspired me from the beginning. At that time, Indigenous people were not treated well, not only in Australia but in many countries. I knew little of the history – it was never covered at school – but a relative of my Uncle Basil (married to Mum's sister, Hilda), Charles P Mountford, was a well-known anthropologist and ethnographer, who had led the American-Australian Scientific Expedition into Arnhem Land in 1956. I met Uncle Monty two or three times as a child and was fascinated by the books.

Paintings by Albert Namatjira
National Gallery of Australia, Albert Namatjira, Western Arrarnta people, not titled (Hermannsburg)
Art Gallery of NSW, 'Catherine Creek'

In my third year at high school (at the age of fourteen) I published in the school magazine a long poem about an Aboriginal artist who wanted to go to university but could not because of his race. It was called 'Heritage Without Hope'. He looks yearningly at 'the stately university where wealths of knowledge lie' where he would love to go and 'learn the mysteries of art'. It ends with the sad line: 'A great potential artist went his way.'

Many years later, as a professor, I supervised the work of a number of postgraduate Indigenous students. I will never forget one telling me, when I mentioned this, that my hero wasn't 'a potential artist', he *was* an artist. And of course, my student was right. He was.

I had been deeply affected by our father's sudden death and, as mentioned earlier, this created among other things a very real fear that someone else I loved would die. This was to stimulate an awareness of a spiritual sense of being and beingness, an other-worldliness that was no doubt encouraged by my keen reading of the Bible and which became alive and vibrant in the language and artistry of literature, and was increasingly heard in music and glimpsed in art. I became particularly invested in Aboriginal legends and Aboriginal artistic expressions.

'Uncle Monty' was related to our Uncle Basil. His books with Ainslie Roberts influenced my later deep interest in Aboriginal culture. Mum was also an influence; she always called a new moon a 'piccaninny moon'. (Such a melodious word, but I believe now not considered appropriate. It was to us then such a pretty, respectful image.)

At this stage it was not a very well-informed interest, but I was eager to learn. At the beginning of my final year I wrote 'A Native in my Heart', which won that year's Senior Poetry Prize and was reprinted in several local newspapers. Remember, its terminology is of its time – early sixties – but the sentiment was true and was increasingly deeply felt.

This strength of feeling is interesting in the light of later revelations. (This will be described in Chapter 9.)

School for me as I grew up comprised both moments of acute presentness and moments of deep awayness. I wrote much, thought much and dreamed much. My love affair with Shakespeare continued, and I wrote more than one Shakespearean iambic pentameter play set in various versions of the Australian bush. Probably it's good I can't find them. I was also writing poems and songs. In my first year at high school I sent a bundle of poems to Dame Mary Gilmore. She wrote a lovely letter back, saying 'Keep on!', which she underlined three times. I chose her because of her little poem 'Nationality'. I was learning to respect and understand nuance: that things aren't always clear cut and that you may act differently at different times and with different, equally compelling motivations.

I was learning to understand both the leavening power of love and its responsibilities: its capacity to influence and what you could and/or should do about it.

This powerful poem was written on 12 May 1942 in the middle of World War II. That it has been read into the Hansard record in both the Commonwealth Parliament and the New South Wales Parliament is an indicator of the power of poetry – and of simple and succinct language – to express deep complexities of thought.

Learning about – and teaching – the power, scope and influence of words, their beauty and melody, their endless capacities to trigger emotions both positive and negative, both for good and ill, has been a theme and driving passion all my life.

School finished for me on a high. I was both School Captain and Dux and won the Senior Poetry Prize as well as several other prizes and scholarships to university. I wanted to study arts and literature, but my history of public speaking and debating (I had won several prizes) also led me to briefly consider law. I was, however, advised against it because of my gender. I am glad such attitudes about

Dame Mary Gilmore (1865–1962)

Nationality

I have grown past hate and bitterness,
I see the world as one;
But though I can no longer hate,
My son is still my son.

All men at God's round table sit,
And all men must be fed;
But this loaf in my hand,
This loaf is my son's bread.

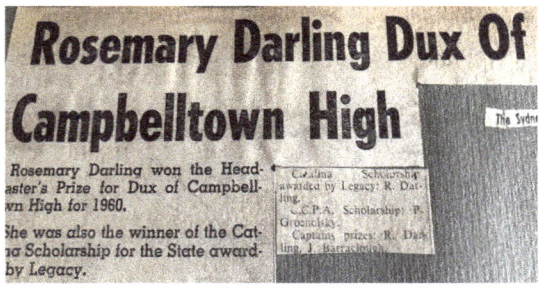

Last year of school

David Edwards, our cousin from Kenya via the UK

gender have changed but have never regretted my decision to focus on language and literature.

Around this period we met for the first time a member of my father's family, David Edwards, a young man in his early twenties. (The 'Reay-Edwards' had been dropped by now.) Dave was the son of my Uncle Ron, who owned a coffee plantation in Kitale, Kenya.

He was an excellent cricketer and had been headhunted by English selectors to go to England and play county cricket. Unfortunately, he injured his leg and this precluded any prospect of continuing a serious cricket career. He did not want to go back to Kenya but, disliking the cold, wanted to get out of England. So, he applied to come to Australia as a 'Ten Pound Pom'. (Ten English pounds bought a passage to Australia for British citizens approved as part of the Assisted Passage Migration Scheme.) To do this he had to be sponsored by an Australian family, and he wrote and asked Mum if she would sponsor him, which she was very happy to do. Part of sponsoring was to provide accommodation, and Dave lived with us at Cameo for several years. He was great fun. He played cricket with my brothers and loved the beach. He joined us for several golden

Family holidays

With my brothers and extended family: (back row l-r) self, Uncle Les, Chris, Grandma Elsie, Big Aunty Hilda (middle row l-r) Anne, Aunty Eileen, Mum (Dorothy), Danny, Uncle Basil, Aunty Hilda, and Tammy our little dog (front row l-r) Lindsay, Ross, and Hugh (Uncle Les' sons)

Literary

A NATIVE IN MY HEART

Rosemary Darling 5th yr.

For I love the scent of raindrops as they fall upon the trees;
And the music of the gum leaves as they thrill to songs of breeze;
And the light of morning breaking o'er the far and distant hill,
And the flush of dawn awaking o'er the bushland, sweet and still.
And the symphony of springtime when the earth again is born;
And the subtlety of winter when the boughs are left forlorn;
And the wonder of an echo — elusive, dim, yet sure;
And the tricks of little animals who tell me of their lore.
And the whisper of the willow weeping o'er the wavering stream;
And the wonder of the wattle like a golden wisp o' dream;
And the waratah, flamboyant, with her burning heart aflame;
And the buds of wondrous potency that spring forth with the rain.
And the beaches which like strips of gold lie shimmering in the sun;
And the foreshores which are cloaked in mist when day has just begun;
And the Southern Cross enstudded in a velvet width of sky;
And the stars like breaths o' Paradise a-floating way on high.
And the billabong indented in an endless stretch of plain;
And the hollow roar of distant surf against the rocks again . . . .
To me these mighty wonders are in life a vital part,
And I know that though a white man, I'm a native in my heart.

summer family holidays at Narrabeen and Wamberal on the Central Coast whilst he was with us.

So, school had finished with a bang, and all my hopes and dreams about doing well had come true. But the next year, my first at the University of Sydney, for which I had accepted a Commonwealth Scholarship, was not to be quite such a success, nor quite so happy.

We were to live at Cameo for another six or seven years, but I would be away in different places over the next four years, at least during university terms. So I am now going to leave the story of Cameo for a short *intermezzo* (a musical term for interspersing different bits between the main acts of a longer artistic piece).

The story continues in a following chapter.

Dorothy Patricia's Luncheon Buns

The recipe for Mum's Luncheon Buns was a family favourite and a more tender sister of Grandma's rock buns, which were a Scottish recipe crammed full of fruit and bits and pieces and which the adults liked but we children found a bit – well, rocky.

The luncheon buns can be made very quickly and with numerous short cuts, all of which at some time or other I have probably taken. The recipe underwent many edits and changes over the years, and indeed still does. I now cut the sugar more-

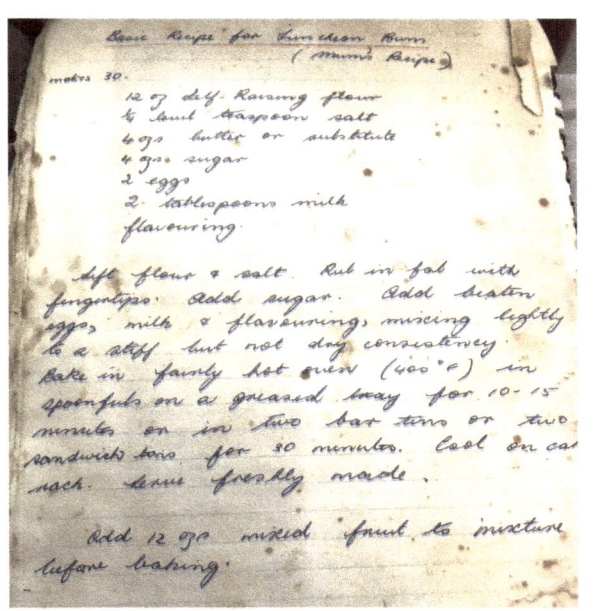

Mum's recipe for luncheon buns – as copied into one of my pre-wedding recipe books

or-less in half and add any dried fruit that takes my fancy or that is in the pantry cupboard at the time. I've also used fresh blueberries – messy, but nice.

And of course, as time went on, and we were fortunate enough to have five children, I always had to at least double the recipe!

The Violets

It is dusk, and cold. I kneel to pick
Frail melancholy flowers among
Ashes and loam. The melting west
Is stripped like ice-cream. While I try
Whistling a trill, close by his nest
Our blackbird frets and strops his beak
Indifferent to Scarlatti's song.
Ambiguous light, Ambiguous sky.

Towards nightfall, waking from the fearful
Half sleep of a hot afternoon
At our first house, in Mitchelton
I ran to find my mother, calling
For breakfast, Laughing, 'It will soon
Be night, you goose', her long hair falling
Down to her waist, she dried my tearful
Face as I sobbed, 'Where's morning gone?'

And carried me downstairs to see
Spring violets in the loamy bed.
Hungry and cross, I would not hold
The sweetness or be comforted,
Even when my father, whistling, came
From work, but used my tears to scold
The thing I could not grasp or name
That while I slept, had stolen from me.
These hours of returning light
Into my father's house we went
Young parents and their restless child

Kerensa violets

Gwendoline Harwood (1920–1995) was a celebrated Australian poet, born in Brisbane, qualified as a music teacher, married in 1945 and moved to Tasmania with her academic husband, a linguist. Her poetry is both philosophical and lyrical; I love the idea here of time present and time past overlapping – layers of time past popping up and showing through in time present.

I also love how scents – whiffs of a particular smell – can whisk you back, as it does for the poet here, into vibrant memories of other, earlier times.

Harwood was influenced by the philosophy of Ludwig Wittgenstein and his ideas of 'meaning as use' – the way we use words gives them their meaning. (Think about the usages and meanings of 'It's cool', 'He's hot'.)

We have to watch not just the word itself, but how and when it is used (world, thought, language) to understand 'meaning'.

To light the lamp and the wooden stove
While dusk surrendered pink and white
To blurring darkness. Reconciled
I took my supper and was sent
To innocent sleep.

Years cannot move
Nor death's disorienting scale
distort those lamplit presences …
'child with milk and story book'
My father, bending to inhale
the gathered flowers, with tenderness
stroking my mother's gold-brown hair.
Stone-curlews call from Kedrum Brook
Faint scent of Violets drift in air.

Gwen Harwood

> *Smell is the strongest human sense. And of all the senses, the sense of smell is the most important trigger of memory. The part of the brain that processes smell interacts with other parts of the brain that store emotional memories.*

5. Intermezzo – University Days

'Oh, they slide and they vanish
as he shuffles the years like a pack of conjuror's cards.'

From 'South of My Days' by Judith Wright

The University of Sydney Great Hall, which I could see about a kilometre away from my last office at the University of Technology Sydney

Humid the air! leafless, yet soft as spring,
The tender purple spray on copse and briers!
And that sweet city with her dreaming spires,
She needs not June for beauty's heightening.

From 'Thyrsis' by Matthew Arnold

Towery city and branchy between towers;
Cuckoo-echoing, bell-swarmèd, lark charmèd, rook-racked, river-rounded …

From 'Duns Scotus's Oxford' by Gerard Manley Hopkins

I see the coloured lilacs flame
In many an ancient Oxford lane,
And bright laburnum holds its bloom
Suspended golden in the noon.

From 'Oxford' by Tom Lovatt-Williams

Jacaranda Dreaming

A promise – (planted years ago –
transplanted twice – horizons grow) –
full bosomed now, and stretching high,
regal colours scrape the sky,
velvet purples – bold as brass –
mossy petals drift to grass …
Eyes melt at the magnificence
of beauty steeped in transience.

RRJ

University of Sydney main quadrangle, with its beautiful jacaranda tree (now gone)

Adlestrop

Yes, I remember Adlestrop
The name, because one afternoon
Of heat the express-train drew up there
Unwontedly. It was late June.

The steam hissed. Someone cleared his throat.
No one left and no one came
On the bare platform. What I saw
Was Adlestrop—only the name

And willows, willow-herb, and grass,
And meadowsweet, and haycocks dry,
No whit less still and lonely fair
Than the high cloudlets in the sky.

And for that minute a blackbird sang
Close by, and round him, mistier,
Farther and farther, all the birds
Of Oxfordshire and Gloucestershire.

Edward Thomas

Steam train at Adlestrop station

> *Inscape –*
>
> > ***Haecceitas***
> >
> > > ***This-ness …***
>
> In the Introduction, I spoke of poet Gerard Manley Hopkins and his concept of *inscape* – perception and appreciation of the unique characteristics of a particular place, at a particular moment in time. This idea has coloured and permeated and indeed imprinted my life.
>
> *Inscape* relates to what medieval scholar Johannes Duns Scotus called *haecceitas* or '*this-ness*' – capturing the unique and particular of this one among many similar others: this one place, this one object, at this time, even this second, right now.
>
> The poem above ('Adlestrop') is a simple description of a particular place (Adlestrop Railway Station in the UK) at a particular time ('one afternoon'). The little poem 'Song of the Rain' by Hugh McCrae (quoted in Chapter 3) is another example.
>
> Nothing special happened in these poems – it was ordinary, part of the everyday – but it became memorable in the way that very 'ordinariness' is observed and described. The descriptions of a particular 'this-ness', have, for an intense moment, made it so.
>
> This is how I feel about the memories in this *Passeggiata*.

The dreaming spires

I carried images of the 'dreaming spires' and all the associated literary allusions of Oxford (and Cambridge for that matter) with me on the train and bus as I set forth as a newly-enrolled student on a hot summer's day for the University of Sydney. I went to university with many dreams and high hopes. This was a time when only seven per cent of high school students (three per cent of whom were girls) went on to university. As a result, I didn't know anyone. But the university, Australia's first (it was established in 1850), was beautiful and everything I thought a university should be: Gothic buildings à la Oxbridge, tradition steeped, cloistered quadrangles, sandstone walls and a lovely old library that would grow into the smarter (but less evocative) New Fisher whilst I was there.

I liked Manning House (in those days for women only), where girls with long lacquered fingernails smoked their cigarettes artistically and were impressively cool. I, meanwhile, had the sophisticated treat of a scoop of ice cream with strawberry topping (bright pink and in retrospect probably synthetic) and crushed nuts. The Union Refectory was full of noisy men and therefore a bit daunting. But soon – too soon – my new friends and I, who were all at that stage from the country and all as equally dazzled as I, discovered the Union Theatre and its lunchtime film screenings. What excitement! We dared not skip tutorials (where absence would be noticed and noted) but bravely and excitedly skipped lectures if there was a film that sounded interesting. As that first year progressed, all too often there was.

The Union Theatre, Parramatta Road entrance to the University of Sydney, pre the pedestrian footbridge

Just to intersperse here a somewhat perplexing note about the fleeting tastes of youth. We were all smart, but we, somewhat unbelievably, really liked Peter Sellers films and even attended some twice. Just a few years on, I could not understand or justify this aberration.

Those lunchtime screenings in the old Union Theatre (renamed the Footbridge Theatre after a footbridge was built across Parramatta Road) were great fun and quite often noisy and rowdy. The screenings were occasionally frequented by the lordly postgrads and editors of the university newspaper, *Honi Soit*. They were a clever crowd, already making a name for themselves beyond the university. Germaine Greer, for example, was a towering presence, read about and talked about but soon to leave to pursue a doctorate at Cambridge.

I think I had been expecting lectures after the style of Oxford and Cambridge, or as much as I knew about them from books: small groups in a professor's room, with personal attention and deep discussion of big ideas. This began to happen in some tutorials, but these were led not by the awe-inspiring and interesting professors but by postgrad students, some of whom were more interested in the sound of their own voice than in anything the lowly students might want to say. Our lectures in first year were large, often held in the Wallace Theatre, and the lecturers tended to walk in, deliver their lecture, sometimes reading it, and walk out. There was little interaction with their audience.

Unfortunately the Psych 1 Statistics lecture frequently missed the cut. Film or lecture? No question! Why, I have always wondered, should such an interesting subject be saddled with such an unenticing introduction? But English and Modern History (which were to be my majors) I loved.

I turned seventeen at the beginning of the first year. For that year I more-or-less travelled from home, walking the mile to the station, spending about an hour and forty-five minutes on trains (two hours at least if I missed the Liverpool connection) to Central, then the walk or sometimes bus to the university. This necessary travel regime precluded much social interaction, especially as the days became shorter. I did not want to get back too late as there was still the long dark walk from the station. Often by the time we got to my station I had had to swap carriages several times. This was because, as they emptied out there were occasional scares with men who, in an otherwise empty carriage, would come and sit in the seat beside me. I learnt to stretch my coats and briefcase over the spare seat and to keep an eye on spaces and people in other carriages. When I arrived at the station, I would try to find another woman to walk near, and sometimes I would give three rings home from the telephone box near the post office and Mum or one of my brothers would come to meet me. When winter came, it was very dark and very cold for this last part of the journey.

I became sick, very sick, for one of the few times in my life. I remember feeling absolutely dreadful one particular night whilst waiting in an icy wind on the platform at Central for the train home, feeling chilled to the bone. My throat hurt as if it were being sliced with a knife every time I swallowed. The sore throat became tonsillitis and then a very severe case of quinsy, a disease we had never heard of before. I came close to needing a breathing tube inserted. After eventually having an operation to remove my tonsils, I gradually recovered in the sun at Cameo. That operation, by the way, was an horrific experience. The anaesthetic was somehow applied with a heavy dark cloth over my face, and I fought against going under. I remember counting – could it be to ninety-six? The medical staff said afterwards that I felt so unwell because they had to give more and more anaesthetic. Did they somehow blow it on? Press it on the cloth? It felt like I was in the Dark Ages, and I don't like recalling that horrible experience even now. It meant, of course, that I missed weeks and weeks of lectures and lost a lot of interest.

At the end of that first year, I re-explored my options. University was not the magical place of 'dreaming spires' I had anticipated. I discovered there was the possibility, perhaps, to ditch my four years of the prized Commonwealth Scholarship and transfer to another scholarship that would cover teachers' college training for one year and give me a qualification to teach junior secondary classes. I had little sense of vocation at this point; my dreams of being a scholar were completely disrupted. All I really wanted was to obtain the funds that would allow me to travel as soon as possible. This seemed like a good escape option, so I went to see the appropriate dean at the University of Sydney and requested to swap over. But, even though I had not done particularly well in the first year, I had not failed, and that, so I was told, prohibited me from taking this escape route.

Amazing! But there is a good ending to this unhappy hiatus, and maybe some credit for perspicacity should be attributed to the rather dry and seemingly unsympathetic dean who met with me in his dark office off the main quadrangle. He simply said that I needed to go on.

It was a difficult time, and I was ploughing through it pretty much on my own; no one could really understand how despairing I felt. My family were worried it was the travelling that was getting me down. We discovered that if I transferred to a Teacher's University Scholarship, which I had also been awarded at the end of school, I could get a good living-away-from-home allowance. So I swapped over. (Who cares about a long-time-in-the-future five-year bond!) Mum was wonderful. She looked for accommodation with me and we found an inexpensive girls' hostel in Stanmore, into which I was duly accepted.

St Margaret's was fun – a bit like my plethora of English boarding school stories about the upper sixth. In this old but pretty inner-city house with its multiple bedroom extensions tacked on at the back, there was an assortment of girls studying different courses: arts, medicine, teaching, nursing, law. The food was nothing like home, but it was fine. It was lucky, however, that I wasn't a vegetarian in those days, because mince, disguised in one form or another, was a staple feature of the menu. I usually went home at weekends.

It was at St Margaret's that I became a non-smoker for life. My girlfriend came in one night, very excited, with a packet of Alpines. 'We can smoke these,' she said, 'they aren't bad for you at all. Everyone says they're really good!'

She proceeded to take a cigarette out of the packet and lit it. She was smiling for a moment and then must have inhaled. She coughed increasingly violently and went red. Then her face turned a terrible bruised purple colour and she vomited copiously all over the floor. Luckily it was vinyl and washable.

She did, I think, later offer me a cigarette, but strangely enough I had no desire to take one. And I have never ever had even one puff. I've never wanted to. The association with the smell of vomit has remained too real.

So, although I returned to second year reluctantly, I really began to enjoy the next years of study and the friends that went with it. At the end of that year at St Margaret's, a group of us decided to move into accommodation in a terrace house on Glebe Point Road, less than a block down from its intersection with Parramatta Road and just across from Victoria Park and the university: eleven girls sharing a bathroom and kitchen. The building was owned by the Anglican Church, and we were all involved in various ways with helping at St Barnabas, Broadway. The rector was the Reverend Bernard Gook. In his honour, we called this three-storey establishment the G'Nook. My dear girlfriend Suzanne and I were on the very top (third) floor in the two single attic bedrooms, each with a dormer window. Her room was quite large; mine was small but my favourite. The bathroom was down on the next level on a sort of mezzanine. All the other rooms were doubles.

It was a happy and fun time. The church had another similar place for boys (men!) further along Glebe Point Road and we became friends with some of them. Most of these were not lowly undergrads, as we all were, but rather dashing and glamorous American postgraduates doing PhDs. Several were undertaking their postgraduate studies in radio or optical astronomy and travelling between the university and the radio telescope at Parkes. Two of the G'Nook girls ended up marrying two of these fellows, who were endlessly entertaining when we shared meals together crowded around the kitchen table. (The dining room had been turned into a double bedroom.)

One of the astronomy students was a very nice person and I secretly liked him a lot, but he had a girlfriend back home in Denver, Colorado. We did go out a few times, but not in a romantic way. We did, however, keep in contact for a while, and he sent me a lovely twenty-first birthday present a few years later. Not long ago, I was invited to Denver for an event; it was snowy and magical, and I thought of that boy for the first time in many years.

Early edition of Anne of Green Gables, presented to me on retirement by my university

One of the other students, his friend, was very different: he was also extremely erudite but annoyingly condescending towards Australians. Night after night he told us that we were completely lacking in cultural knowledge, uneducated, colonial and backward. We knew nothing, he said, about the rest of the world. One night when he had been going on about this again and again, I very rashly contradicted him and more-or-less said 'Ask me something and I'll show you!' Now, had he asked anything about American history or indeed ancient history or a million other things I probably would have been well and truly stumped. I think the other girls were all waiting with bated breath, scared of his crowing when I showed my ignorance. Very smugly, he asked what he obviously thought was a question I had no chance of knowing: 'What is the capital of Prince Edward Island?'

Now, this was, absolutely coincidentally, a gift question for me. As a kid I researched and drew maps for all my favourite stories and was an avid reader of the *Anne* and *Emily* books by L. M. Montgomery, which were set on Prince Edward Island. Quick as a flash, and much to his obvious astonishment, I replied 'Charlottetown'. The whole table was quiet for a moment and he was flabbergasted. He treated us all with a little more respect afterwards. Years later, I wrote my Master's thesis, 'Reaching Beyond the Word', on the five original *Anne* books. And years later still, I went to Prince Edward Island to present the keynote address at the annual L. M. Montgomery conference, where I was invited to become a member of L. M. Montgomery International, now located in the Robertson Library at the University of Prince Edward Island, joining people whose work I had so much admired from afar: Elizabeth Epperly, Mary Rubio, Elizabeth Waterston. The patrons of the L. M. Montgomery Institute at that time were long-time Montgomery fans: the Rt. Hon. Adrienne Clarkson, then Governor General of Canada, and Her Imperial Highness, Princess Takamado of Japan, International Patron since 2004.

On one occasion we were all invited to a formal function at Government House in Charlottetown and I was delighted to meet Adrienne Clarkson's husband, the author and philosopher John Ralston Saul, with whom I had a long conversation about his book *The Unconscious Civilisation* and about the vital significance of a broadly humanistic, rather than a narrowly specialised, education. It was one of those small but memorable epochs in academic life.

Montgomery Institute International Board, with international patron Her Imperial Highness, Princess Takamado of Japan

Back to student days. Our little group still ditched lectures if there was a good film on, and now our adventures extended to the array of cinemas in the city. One of the favourite activities of our group (there were perhaps five or six of us) was to walk along Broadway (girls looking in all the Anthony Hordern windows on the way, which are long since gone), get a cheap Chinese meal for lunch, go to the pictures and then wander along George Street and past Central Station to the G'Nook. Sometimes, to make us feel more virtuous, we might include an afternoon in the Mitchell Library, that lovely part of the State Library of New South Wales. I spent hours there, not so much studying for my actual courses, but just beguiled by the old books on so many interesting subjects.

When New Fisher Library opened it became another place I liked to go, usually on my own and usually looking for a cubicle facing out towards the city (and, coincidentally, towards where UTS Tower now stands). Many years later, as a professor at UTS, I was fortunate enough to have a wonderful corner office looking on one side straight towards the University of Sydney in the direction of the new library. A revision of T. S. Eliot's words in 'East Coker' frequently ran through my mind: 'In my beginning is my end'.

With Adrienne Clarkson, Governor General of Canada, and John Ralston Saul, Charlottetown, Prince Edward Island

My last office at UTS

Shuffling the years

However, we were all actually very insular in many ways. I had always been interested in English history. My father, whose mother, Rose Isabella Reay-Edwards, was English, had bought me a number of books about the British Royal family, including Marion Crawford's *The Little Princesses*, which as a child I read over and over

> *Time present and time past*
> *Are both perhaps present in time future,*
> *And time future contained in time past.*
> From 'Burnt Norton' No. 1 of
> *Four Quartets* by T. S. Eliot

again. I already loved Shakespeare and the English poets and was fascinated by the twists and turns of English history. Mum also kept me aware of Scottish and Irish perspectives

'In my beginning is my end.' And in my end I look out on my beginning – my last office at UTS, looking up the road towards Sydney University Great Hall, which is in the distance (on the left)

Grandchildren in my UTS office on the day of my retirement: (l-r) Caleb, Samuel, Isabella, Evelyn, Anna, Luke, Toby

and would sometimes warn me against taking too much notice of the 'Sassenachs', a rather derogatory Scottish term for the English. In retrospect, this is surprising, and I am not at all sure what informed her sentiments. Could it have been the influence of Grandfather Joe (Mum's father)? He was from the Isle of Man. Or from her mother, whose father was Scottish?

Just another little note here that may be of relevance. Only very recently I explored my ancestry – a gift from my sons. I'll write more about this in Chapter 9, but as well as other things it showed an ethnicity estimate of thirty per cent for England and north-western Europe, twenty-nine per cent for Ireland, and sixteen per cent for Scotland. I am not completely sure why the Irish is so high (perhaps the proximity to the Isle of Man), but I have two sons now very interested in family history, so there may be more to discover.

Anyway, back to those early years at university. In my third year I studied American history and became extremely interested in presidential history. This is an interest that has grown even more vigorous over the years. It was the Kennedy era, and for the first time in our experience a young and charismatic leader with a striking and intelligent wife (but with a strangely wispy, little-girl voice) had become the leader of the free world. The Kennedys were fascinating, and many of us started following American politics. Dwight and Mamie Eisenhower had not seemed particularly interesting, but the Kennedys were endlessly interesting. It was not until years afterwards that all the less pleasant facts emerged.

The momentous event that stands out in memory from those days was the terrible assassination of President Kennedy on 22 November 1963. It was a Friday in the United States, but we woke up to the news on Saturday morning. It was a weekend when we were all still at the G'Nook, packing it up for the Christmas holidays.

Presidential Motorcade in Dallas, Texas, 22 November 1963 – just moments before JFK was shot and killed

I was awoken by my girlfriend Sue banging on the bedroom door and yelling: 'President Kennedy has been shot. He's dead!' Shocked, we raced across the road to the little general store opposite and bought a paper with big black headlines that seemed hard to believe.

A little later the American boys came over, absolutely shaken. They said it felt like a death in the family. Some of us eventually set off for a walk down into the city, where we went to find either a newsreel or a television in a shopfront (perhaps both, I can't really remember) so we could watch the terrible events unfolding. When I got home the following weekend, I watched the television footage endlessly.

John-John Kennedy (1960–1999)

There is a sad subsequent memory. We had all been terribly moved by the images of little John-John saluting his father's horse-drawn caisson on the day of the funeral. Years later, in July 1999, one of my daughters and I were in London, staying near Sussex Gardens. We walked up Oxford Street and past the little paper shop on the corner, just across from Oxford Circus. We both stopped in horror at the news posters on the footpath, all repeating the same message: 'John Kennedy and wife lost in plane crash.' He was thirty-eight.

The Kennedy tragedies were to continue, and there are many sad images that are so much part of that era and of our collective conscious. Edward, the youngest son, was a long serving member of the United States Senate, and I remember being very moved after seeing a newsclip of the then president, Barack Obama, expressing concern when Ted was suddenly taken ill at the Capitol. In his 2020 memoir, *A Promised Land*, Obama, now former president, describes Ted as 'a man driven by great appetites and ambitions but also by great loss and doubt, a man making up for things'. Teddy Junior, speaking at his father's funeral, said:

> My father believed in redemption. And he never stopped trying to right wrongs, be they the results of his own failings or of ours.

Nuance, particularity and 'this-ness'

If I try to think of one word that sums up what I learnt during those undergraduate years – the texts studied, the people encountered and the events lived through, the thought-worlds of others that were revealed and explored, my own thought-world that was enlarged and provoked, not by the need to rationalise or excuse but rather by a true, deeply-felt, even compassionate desire to perceive more clearly the implicit and explicit contexts of both creation and response – if I try to describe all this in one word, that word would be 'nuance'.

Nuance expresses a recognition of subtlety: shades of difference, shades of meaning, shades of expression that complicate easy judgements and facile description. It derives from the French *nuer*, 'to shade', from the Latin *nubes*, meaning 'cloud'. But its focus is not on the cloudiness or shadiness of the subject, rather it is on the exquisite distinctions, the oh-so-subtle differences, that are subsequently enabled and perceived.

This is why, as I note several times during this *passeggiata*, I so much love the poetry of Gerard Manley Hopkins and his concept of 'inscape'. He saw everything as specially and uniquely beautiful just for what it is: a wildflower, a cloud, a tree. It is the unique complexity, the *oneness*, of the individual thing. This idea relates to what the medieval philosopher and theologian Duns Scotus, the 'Subtle Doctor', who attended Oxford University beginning around 1280, called *haecceitas* or 'this-ness'. It also overlaps with what the Irish novelist James Joyce thought of as *quidditas*, 'whatness', and the 'epiphany'.

This photo, taken by one of my daughters last spring, is a lovely example of this profoundly philosophical concept. It is a pretty rose, with beautiful colour and perfume, a little bit eaten by a caterpillar that also thought it was lovely! It is a type of rose called 'Just Joey', and of course there are many other roses of this same type. But this picture is absolutely uniquely *this* particular rose, on *this* particular day, in *this* particular light, against *this* particular wall. It has been munched and so is not perfect. But it is exquisitely distinctive.

That's *this-ness*!

A few years ago, I wrote this to my children and grandchildren:

> You and all our little people are beautiful and unique. I love the oneness, specialness, of each of you so much that it feels, like Hopkins felt when he saw the 'beautiful oneness' of the tree, 'as if my mind were still growing'.

Nuance, exquisite particularity and oneness. Human nature, human motives, human actions and interactions are all profoundly complex. Moral questions can also be profoundly complex. Novels, drama, poetry – the great ones – are case studies in nuance. Recently I gave one of my grand-daughters a copy of *The Greengage Summer* by Rumer Godden. This is a beautifully written story about a family spending a summer in France near the battlefields of the Marne. It is a subtle coming-of-age story that is sensitive and reflective, intellectually, physically and emotionally. In a way it is about displacement: of childish acceptance, of childish trust. People are baffling mixtures of both good and not-so-good. In an enchanted place, there have been horrific events. Too many delicious plums (in this case, greengages) can make you sick: 'On and off, all that hot French August, we made ourselves ill from eating the greengages.'

Good people can be sometimes bad, and bad people can be sometimes good. What is right may not always be easy to determine.

The time that I had begun with so many dreams and that had been very disappointing at first in the end finished quite happily. In retrospect, perhaps I should have taken a gap year as I was very young all the way through and had completed undergraduate studies at age nineteen. Many years later I was to go back with a deep hunger for more as a mature age student and, thanks to a supportive and caring husband, loved it.

I graduated with an arts degree and commenced my professional year for a Diploma of Education with several stints of practice teaching, which I quite enjoyed. Dip Ed lectures and tutorials were held at Sydney Teachers' College, at the other end of the university campus. A couple of things stand out in a not otherwise particularly memorable year. Graduation was one of course, which happened early in that fourth year. Another was a short drama production some friends and I did for an assessment, adapting and condensing George Bernard Shaw's rather melodramatic *St Joan*. I was Joan. This performance received very approving comments from some of the staff, including lecturer Bill Collins, an affable and kindly bear of a man who seemed always to wear a big red jumper and who was soon to become very well-known as a television and film critic. He also made kind remarks about my writing (I had some poetry published, one a poem

With my oldest brother (Royston) and youngest (Danny) and Aunty Hilda and Uncle Les, graduating as BA, University of Sydney Great Hall

in the college annual magazine, *Drylight*), albeit I now find my compositions of that period rather melancholy.

I had chosen to study a music elective, which I enjoyed greatly. It was the first time I had ever been able to study music; at school if you 'did' French and Latin it automatically precluded Art and Music. Mind you, the music elective was not exactly 'taught'; it was more of an exposure. The lecturer came in, put on a record and then stood as she listened, looking out of the window across to the university playing fields. At the end of class she nodded, retrieved her record and departed. But there was a quiet contentment and peace in this unhurried approach, and there was something quite meaningful in the way in which she just let the music speak for itself. I have no memory of how we were examined or indeed if we were examined at all. But in that large old-fashioned classroom, with a minimum of fuss, she introduced me to Tchaikovsky's Symphony No 5 and Symphony No 6 (the *Pathétique*), to Dvorak and to the idea of symphonic poems.

Thinking about Tchaikovsky has prompted another memory. Jump (or shuffle) forward with me to the year 2000, when I was on leave from the University of Technology Sydney and for just under a year was invited to assist with the introduction of new doctoral programs in Finland. Malcolm was able to come with me; it was a wonderful experience. Whilst there we took the opportunity to travel as much as possible. Everything was so close! One of my students was at the University of St Petersburg and I had to go there to see him. Catching the train to St Petersburg in Russia was an experience in itself. Crossing the Finnish/Russian border was terrifying. The guards that checked our carriage were led by a tall blonde woman who could have stepped straight out of a James Bond film – as the villain. Her face was completely impassive as she barked out orders, and I was acutely conscious of a wad of undeclared notes in my shoe. (My colleagues at Åbo Akademi University had warned us that credit cards at this time could not be used safely.) Her eyes were cold, pale blue, unblinking and penetrating, and I saw myself being tossed into a Russian prison. Fortunately, I was not asked to remove my shoes.

We spent several days at The Hermitage. (Not enough time, very addictive, almost overpowering in its riches.) But the other highlight was our one night at the famous Mariinsky Theatre. This was where, just before Christmas 1892, Tchaikovsky's *The Nutcracker* was first introduced to the world, with Tchaikovsky conducting. And after much badgering, Malcolm and I were able to get tickets to a performance by the Bolshoi Ballet of *Swan Lake*. It was booked out, but I begged and begged, telling them that we only had a few days and this would be an experience of our lifetime. And it was!

They told us to wait in an anteroom, left us for a while and then came back and beckoned us to follow. Two young men came in, each carrying a very grand velvety and almost regal chair into the crowded theatre. They placed them in the aisle just near the first row. As the lights started to dim, we were led to these. They were for us!

It was magical. The misty and translucent greys of trees and lake, the shimmer of water, and the feathery and snowy whiteness of the swans, created an almost mystical scenescape; and the deeply thrilling and melodious music pulsed with emotions of love and loss, joy and despair.

Interior of the Mariinsky Theatre, St Petersburg. Tchaikovsky's The Nutcracker was first performed here in November/ December 1892. Malcolm and I saw a magical performance of Swan Lake in this historic venue in 2000. We had to talk our way in as they were full, but they ended up carrying in two regal chairs for us, placing them on the right-hand side in the space between the front row. A treasured memory

> *South of my days' circle, part of my blood's country,*
> *rises that tableland, high delicate outline*
> *of bony slopes wincing under the winter,*
> *low trees, blue-leaved and olive, outcropping granite-*
> *clean, lean, hungry country.*
>
> ...
>
> *Oh, they slide and they vanish*
> *as he shuffles the years like a pack of conjuror's cards.*
>
> ...
>
> *South of my days' circle*
> *I know it dark against the stars, the high lean country*
> *full of old stories that still go walking in my sleep.*
> From 'South of My Days' by Judith Wright

SS 'Northern Star' – Sydney-Wellington-Auckland-Rarotonga-Tahiti-Acapulco-Panama-Curaçao-Trinidad-Barbados-Lisbon-Southampton

And do you know what? Those rather dour Russians who arranged all this refused to take any payment; they were apologetic that they couldn't give us actual tickets!

The college year flew by, and I graduated again, this time with the postgraduate Diploma of Education. Unfortunately I never really became part of the college crowd as I was usually away on weekends and busy elsewhere.

After four years of university my next plan was to save up enough money to travel. I also wanted to go home for a while to be with Mum and Grandma so had applied to be an English and History teacher at one of the regional high schools. I also booked my ticket to sail for England on the *SS Northern Star*, going via Panama. (Very few people flew in those days as fares were prohibitive.) This was now planned for towards the end of my second year of teaching. I wanted to be on the move for several years and would need that long to secure enough funds. I had begun organising for a teaching job in the upper wilds of Scotland, an area that fascinated me. The plan was to brush up on my French and go from there to France as an English teacher for another year or so. I was very happy when notification came that my application for the local high school was successful. So, with quiet satisfaction, big plans and a landscape of the mind that had expanded to embrace the British Isles, I left the big smoke of Sydney behind and came home to the gentle garden at Cameo.

The woods are lovely, dark and deep,

But I have promises to keep,

And miles to go before I sleep,

And miles to go before I sleep.

From 'Stopping by Woods on a Snowy Evening'
by Robert Frost

In my beginning is my end. In succession

Houses rise and fall, crumble, are extended,

Are removed, destroyed, restored, or in their place

Is an open field, or a factory, or a by-pass.

...

Houses live and die: there is a time for building

And a time for living and for generation

And a time for the wind to break the loosened pane

And to shake the wainscot where the field-mouse trots

And to shake the tattered arras woven with a silent motto.

In my beginning is my end ...

From 'East Coker' No. 2 of *Four Quartets* by T. S. Eliot

Convolution

A wilderness of wonderings in the night;
the tearing of the tentacles of time;
and streaking of apocalypse sublime,
a watching of the moon wane out of sight
as bidden nurture of the creeping light
makes superficial, half-effective mime.
A scrutiny of barriers, to climb
to wild surrender, ecstasy, delight:

What the answer, what the question, knows not He the task begun?
Spring to summer, autumn, winter, day to night, and moon to sun.

Hope, blinding as a flush of victory
in peaceful adulation of the way,
leads helpless night into sufficient day.
Yet he the hoper does not victor be,
and he the seer does not have to see
the lapping of the languished as they lay,
not one, but half, not whole. Yet as they pray,
they bow in fostered order to the Tree.

What the answer, what the question, knows not He the task begun?
Spring to summer, autumn, winter, day to night, and moon to sun.

Elusive shadows etch against the sky
the loneliness of loveliness forlorn,
the death that is the afterbirth of born,
the innate laws of nature that comply;
complexities of smitten earth that cry
as striving in the sunset, love is torn
by passion of the moon and of the morn—
now fleeting echoes whisper, Love, Goodbye.

What the answer, what the question, knows not He the task begun?
Spring to summer, autumn, winter, day to night, and moon to sun.

Rosemary Darling

What's past is prologue;

what to come,

In yours and my discharge.

The Tempest Act 2, Sc 1

From Drylight, Annual Magazine of Sydney Teachers' College

Copy of email sent to family on my mother's birthday, 1 Aug 2024

It's Mum's – Dorothy Patricia's – birthday today, 1 August.

These lines came to me on Sunday – I wasn't going to send the whole thing but have done so. It's real and tells a true story. A few mornings ago it was freezing and I put on an old cardigan over my nighty. In a vivid flashback, I was seeing – and being – Mum and Grandma on the cold winter mornings of long ago.

This is a poem about love and the power of words. Mum lived a life of love, and she loved words. She loved us all so deeply. Jodi, Mum loved you as well. Lindsay, we share grandmothers.

This is for her. For them. For us.

With love.

Ode to my mother and grandmother
   (Written for Mum's birthday 1 August 2024)

I put my Mum and Grandma on today.

 Waking early, wintry night.
  Dark retreats as rosy light
  flushes pink across the sky.
  It's cold.
 Still in nightgown, I grab a cardigan
 It's old.
 I pull it on – it's shabby, multi-worn,
  seams unravelling, and slightly torn.
  But warm. It's fawn.

I climb back into bed.
 My thoughts cascade and tumble through the decades …
  I'm working Uni holidays, just been paid,
  Admire it in the window for a week,
  Shop lady says 'It goes with everything!'
  The label calls it 'Oatmeal'.

I bring it home and Grandma says 'It's fawn.'

Fawn! A nothing colour favoured by old ladies,
I show its label 'Oatmeal', smart and trendy.
She nods, agrees, and says 'Oh yes, it's fawn.'

In that small house wrapped up in tawny paddocks,
The air is crisp. Birds celebrate the morn.
Frost icicles on grass, and each step crunchy,
The hens are gossips cackling in the dawn.

There's Mum in snow boots on her way to milking
our pretty Jersey.
    There are no theatre lights, but she's a star!
    She dreamed it so when at the Independent
    training with Doris Fitton.
    She made it so when kissing us good night –
    'Good night, good night, parting is such sweet sorrow.
    That we shall say good night, 'til it be morrow.'
It's love, and death, and love, that brings her here.

I pull the olden cardigan around me.

It's so warm. It's fawn.
    Embraced in fawn-ness, clasped and warmed by past,
    dimensions fired in kilns of love compress,
    transposing time, and space, and generations.
    So blest.

I put my Mum and Grandma on today.

6. Back to Cameo – Until ...

Because the birthday of my life
Is come, my love is come to me.

Christina Rossetti

Mum and my brothers in Cameo garden

It was nice coming back. I enjoyed the clean-up of my room, the sorting out of clothes and books and generally getting ready for beginning teaching. Earlier, I had bought an old car, which I thought looked a bit like a Rolls-Royce. (It was a Triumph Mayflower.) I really liked it because it was English and therefore classy and solid. England was well and truly in my sights. It was also good having a car (and driver) in the family again.

My first car, ABD 796

Those weeks between finishing my fourth year at university and starting teaching were a perfect summer holiday, despite the fact that the world beyond Australia was increasingly being fractured by the war in Vietnam, Cambodia and Laos. In 1965, Prime Minister Robert Menzies, in support of the United States' desire to maintain security in South-East Asia, committed an Australian battalion to the war. Further commitments followed. In 1964, the National Service Act introduced a scheme of selective conscription. Between 1965 and 1972 most twenty-year-old males had to register for national service, and 'birthday ballots' were drawn that could send conscripts off to serve in Vietnam. This frightened Mum, who had three young boys, two of whom were teenagers. This terrible war was to drag on until 1975.

'Big' Aunty Hilda, Mum and Grandma with 'Little' Aunty Hilda in Cameo garden

Despite this, Cameo that summer seemed drenched in quiet

peace. Grandma was now ensconced in her large, sunny bed-sitting room that had been built on the side at Cameo and we all had lots of cups of tea together, either in her room or, quite often, out in the garden. It was the era of the midday movies on television, and sometimes Mum and I would sit down with a salad sandwich (Mum made delicious sandwiches on fresh and crusty brown bread) and watch an old movie together. English ones were our favourites. Mum and Grandma still went for long walks every morning with the dogs. I sometimes went with them accompanied by our littlest brother on his bike.

It was fun arriving at school and driving into the teachers' car park. Although these days that whole area has almost become part of Greater Sydney, in those days it remained essentially a country town. The road past our place was perhaps a little busier, but the cows still went up and down each day on their way to the greener pastures across the creek. Aunty Syl was still around and in good voice, and still riding what looked like the same old rusty bicycle.

In our regional town there were a few more shops as well as the enlarged 'department store' in which, from the legal age of fourteen years and nine months, I had worked every Christmas holidays and on Saturday mornings 8.00 am to 12.00 pm. (All shops in those days closed at 12.00 pm on Saturdays.) Working there involved walking to the station, catching the train, working in the shop and then retracing my steps with another walk back home. For this I received a little pay envelope containing the princely wage of ten shillings and a penny! The envelope contained exactly the one ten-shilling note and the one penny. (In the old imperial system, prior to the introduction of decimal currency in 1966, there were twenty shillings in one pound.)

By comparison, teaching now seemed to bring a huge salary. What's more, teachers – male and female – received equal pay. My dreams of travelling were suddenly becoming a real possibility, and so I revived my Commonwealth Bank account, precisely to save for that purpose. Banks then, at least to my limited knowledge, had a good reputation – and paid interest.

Teaching was an adventure, to say the least. These days there are all sorts of protective restrictions and assistance in place for beginning teachers; I don't think there were any in those days. There were four of us first year outers, all girls, in a small town, co-educational high school. One taught Music (Kay and I became good friends over many years), one taught

Art, one Mathematics, and I taught English and History. There was a kindly principal and a deputy of whom we were more frightened than most of the naughty students were. I was to learn however, that his ferocious bark was mostly an act.

With one of my first English classes

I have written about some of my adventures as a new young teacher in *Growing Young Minds*. It was a very different time: no relief for first year outers, classes with thirty-five to forty students. We had heavy teaching loads, playground duty, sport, bus duty, lesson preparation and notes. I was also debating coach and organiser of play day. And many students were not very interested in school. But on the whole I loved it. Loved seeing dawning apprehension come into a child's face. Loved challenging myself to lead them better into a love of language, words, expression: to coax them into learning. I didn't love marking. Didn't always love some of my more challenging classes. I very much liked the winter athletics carnival, when the four of us 'girls' daringly wore pants (we called them 'slacks' then) to school. (We hadn't been allowed to prior to this historical day.) Those days seem now to belong to another world, and my world even then was about to change.

As part of my liberation from study, and because I now had a car and had always had thespian dreams, I enrolled in a drama course part-time at the Independent Theatre in North Sydney for two nights a week. This, of course, was because of Mum's experience. However, it only lasted a few months because it was a long and sometimes frightening drive, over two hours there and two hours back, in an old car that had a temperamental hand brake and blinkers that consisted of a dim little finger that spun out from the side pillar between the back and front seats. It was alright until the nights grew shorter and darker, as I often had to park some distance from the class and faced a long, lonely walk to and from the car, which was sometimes scary.

As Gretel in 'Whitehorse Inn'

Instead, I rejoined the local Theatre Group, which a girlfriend, Carole, and I had briefly joined whilst at school. I had been part of its early production of *The Pirates of Penzance*. Now I was in the chorus for various productions, including Sigmund Romberg's *The Desert Song* (harem girl) and Gilbert and Sullivan's *Iolanthe*. I then landed the ingenue role of Gretel in *White Horse Inn*, which was a really fun part, had several songs and some nice dialogue.

'Because the birthday of my life ...'

Although this was a musical, we did not practise with the orchestra until a month or so before the show. The first night the orchestra came, I was aware of being quite closely watched by the handsome young man playing trumpet.

Here I have to make a confession I would never have made publicly even a few years ago. I am very short-sighted. (I rarely wore glasses in public, and this was long before soft contact lenses.)

I *felt* his gaze rather than saw it.

I saw the *shape* of handsomeness rather than the features of it.

I saw the *glint* of a brass instrument and the *mass* of a broad chest.

He was below the stage in what would have been an orchestra pit, if our hall had had such a thing, and I could scarcely make out his face, let alone where his eyes were. But everyone, including the musical director and the producer, told me about him.

The local doctor's wife introduced us during a break later that night: he told me afterwards that he had asked her to do so. I heard her say three names and assumed my future husband's last surname was the last name I heard, which was in fact his third Christian name. When he asked me out a few days later, I told Mum his name was Malcolm Ferguson. It was some weeks before I discovered that was not actually correct.

He took me with a Theatre Group party to see the Phillip Street Revue in the city. I wore the white lace suit I had bought for my graduation. (In those days, University of Sydney undergrads

Malcolm Charles Ferguson Johnston

always had to wear white under their robes, which looks so much nicer than the hotchpotch graduands wear today.) I was not a person who wore blue much, but I had already fallen for Malcolm Ferguson's clear blue eyes so splurged on new blue accessories – shoes and matching handbag and gloves – and added a pretty crystal brooch that glinted very satisfactorily under the city and theatre lights. In those days I loved good crystals.

Malcolm's home garden was in Strathfield. It was suburban and very pretty, with a beautiful wisteria at the back and a native frangipanni at the front gate. He was the elder of two sons. His brother, Alistair, was six years younger and worked for one of the big banks and his father, Charles, had worked for many years as an engineer at AWA. His parents were very involved with the Presbyterian church.

Malcolm was an Industrial Arts teacher. He had been dux of his four-year course at Sydney Teachers' College and had been teaching for about eight years when we met. His first posting had been to Casino High School. He had then been seconded to the Correspondence School for a year to help with the creation of resource materials (because of his artistic talent and eye for detail) and was now teaching at Camden High.

Malcolm's mother, Queenie Evelyn Mary, on her wedding day

He played the trumpet and clarinet and was a member of Burwood Brass Band. Most important of all, he was such an interesting character: very quiet on the outside but a non-stop talker and teller of stories when we were together. He was thoughtful and kind. He had a beautiful voice and was very knowledgeable about music. He was extremely creative but also extremely good at the practical. It seemed as if he could fix anything.

Malcolm and his brother Alistair

I have to pause here in our *passeggiata* to tell a quick story. When our first daughter was about two, an elastic band around her small book broke. She just held it out to Malcolm and said 'Don't worry, Mummy. Daddy fix.' 'Daddy fix' was to become quite a catchphrase over the years!

Malcolm was able to grasp the big picture but was meticulous and fastidious about the tiniest detail (which is why he was asked to be one of the many illustrators of Harry Messel's famous science textbook). He was a lover of music, from Dvorak's 'New World Symphony' and Bach's whole corpus to the big bands of Benny Goodman and Glenn Miller.

Malcolm in 1958 in his first car, a c1936 Morris 8/40 Tourer, before my time. He drove it to and from Casino

His love and knowledge of music and especially of church music made him an instant hit with Grandma Elsie Emily, and his gentle spirit made him a winner with Mum.

Malcolm had just purchased a brand-new EH Holden (DOM 832) and we started going on long drives and picnics. (The old Morris in the photograph above had long since gone.) He took me to the beach, which necessitated a new swimming costume, beach bag and towel, to concerts and to movies. I remember he took me to the Sydney premiere of *Dr Zhivago*, and I made myself a short black wool crepe dress and sewed fur around the bell sleeves to make it appropriate for the ice and snow of the Russian steppes. We went to the country picnic races. It was my first and only time at the races, as I feel too sorry for the horses. Malcolm wanted to see a band performing. For that event I made a bright red fitted dress with a matching pillbox hat, thanks to a mesh shape from June Millinery (a great shop!).

First day at the beach with MCFJ

I, who had rarely sewn, suddenly loved making things and sewed for the next twenty years or more, making all our curtains and almost all the clothes for the children when they were small (except their pyjamas and swimming gear). Grandma, of course, was my inspiration. She had sewn for everyone. Later, when the babies started to come and inspired by Mum, who was a wonderful knitter, I took up knitting as well.

Sadly, my hardy and strong cricket-loving grandmother, not only a designer and maker of clothes, but also a maker of ambitious garden rockeries and delicious roasts and Cornish pasties and a singer of songs both secular and sacred, was, at eighty-four, becoming frail. She now spent more and more time in her room and we all would go in and sit with her 'to watch telly'. Mum cared for her, lovingly and gently. Grandma loved books and possessed and had read all the works of Dickens, even the lesser-known ones. Her favourite was *Little Dorrit*. When her eyes failed, we would take it in turns to read to her. I remember taking turns with Mum to read her a Georgette Heyer Regency romance. We also almost always had an Agatha Christie on the go. Grandma had been a voracious reader all her life. We found out decades later, through very old newspaper cuttings, that her mother, Emily Jane Ross (née Allen), had been a very smart student, topping her class in multiple subjects; but like so many girls then, she had left school early to help at home.

Elsie Emily Ross Bevege Cowley died quietly at Cameo just before dawn on 25 April (Anzac Day). I remember Uncle Les, a Kokoda Track veteran of World War II, coming in our back door very early that morning and hugging me with tears in his eyes, saying: 'What a special morning to go: when all the prayers are going up.'

And so it was.

> *In a sad irony, Grandma died on Anzac Day, a day that commemorates a disaster, the landing of Australian and New Zealander troops at Gallipoli (Turkey) just before dawn on 25 April 1915. This was their first major military action of World War I. It is now a national day of remembrance for all who have served Australia in wars. Dawn services are held across the country.*
>
> *Grandma died on Anzac Day, just before dawn, at home in 'Cameo'*

Mum with Malcolm on our land at Newport. Malcolm is wearing the mohair jumper I knitted for him; I had a matching one

Grandma was a dynamic and powerful influence on us all, and a huge support for Mum, most especially since the sudden death of our father. She was resourceful, creative and resilient. Widowed whilst in hospital having her baby son and with a six-year-old daughter waiting at home, and with no family in the same state, she opened her home to boarders and married one of them, a Manx ex seafarer. Despite this eventually becoming a loveless union, it produced my little mother: so loving, gentle and kind, with her own brand of resilience. Grandma died in the April and Malcolm and I married in the December of that same year. Looking back, I know it was a hard year for Mum, but she and my brothers would embark on their own new adventures (and new gardens) not long after.

Grandma knew Malcolm and I were planning to marry. Malcolm had said on our third date: 'You know we are going to get married, don't you.' I said something about going overseas, but he was not dissuaded. At that time he had no desire to travel: eight years older than me, he was ready to settle down. This was to become a bit of a problem. As our relationship grew, I suggested we use the money I had already saved to travel together, even just for a short time, perhaps getting married at Christmas, as we were planning, and flying (it was now becoming cheaper and more accessible) to the UK for a month's extravagant honeymoon.

As the wedding came closer, however, we started thinking about a house, and it seemed more important to save up for that. The idea of travel seemed to fade. We were fortunate to be able to make up for it later. Malcolm already owned a block of land near Bungan Beach, a very secluded beach (no real road access) on Sydney's beautiful Northern Beaches – a slim peninsular, with Pittwater on one side and the ocean indented with delectable bites of golden sand on the other. The land had a lovely valley view and was on one of the narrowest parts of the whole peninsula. His dream was to be able to walk to the surf each day, which he more-or-less did every day for over forty years. So we decided to save our funds towards building a house on this pretty block that was within walking distance of the ocean, with its expansive views and a northern boundary edged by a little creek and beautiful ancient cabbage tree palms, with leaves that glisten and gleam in the breeze and sun. The main road above on the beach side was, unfortunately, just being widened, which brought it a little closer to us, but we are surrounded by bush and most of the time we can't hear it. Our land is now zoned to reflect its environmental locality.

> *During the war, concerned about enemy invasion, the army had built a defensive anti-tank line across this very narrow spit of land, with Bungan Beach and the ocean on one side and Pittwater on the other.*
>
> *Years later, when our children were very small, we found an unexploded practice bomb down near our creek. The army bomb squad came to disable and remove it.*

A summer wedding

My heart is like a singing bird
Whose nest is in a water'd shoot;
My heart is like an apple-tree
Whose boughs are bent with thickset fruit;
My heart is like a rainbow shell
That paddles in a halcyon sea;
My heart is gladder than all these
Because my love is come to me.

From 'A Birthday' by Christina Rossetti

In the garden at Cameo, off to our wedding

With my three brothers: (l-r) Danny, Royston, and Christian

On 17 December, a sticky hot day, we were married in an old Macquarie church built in 1824 (only thirty-six years after Governor Phillip arrived with the first European settlers). Uncle Basil, Hilda's husband, gave me away, and my girlfriend Sue, from the G'Nook days, and cousin Anne, Uncle Les's older daughter, were my bridesmaids. Malcolm's best man was his brother, Alistair, and his groomsman was his dear friend from university days, Kevin Skelsey. Rev. Bernard Gook from St Barnabas, Broadway, also from the old G'Nook days, and Rev. James Mullan from the Presbyterian church Malcolm's family attended, St David's at West Strathfield, officiated.

We didn't like the commercial venues, so we had the reception at the historic Denham Court, which was a little shabby – old-fashioned charm, not shiny plush – but which we both liked very much. At that time it was surrounded by paddocks and acres of farmland, but all that area, now named after the old house, has become a suburb of large homes. Denham Court was designed by colonial architect John Verge around 1820–32 and is now heritage listed. It was a perfect setting for our reception.

We honeymooned at Magnetic Island, off the coast of Queensland, in perfect Queensland

Our wedding, Mum with my brother Royston at her side front left, Rev. Bernard Gook in white robes at front, Rev. James Mullan on far right, Malcolm's parents on right

summer weather. How beautiful is the Australian coastline: blues and greens and golds in every possible shade. The hues coloured and textured our days with magic.

I have carried that magnificent, heart-rending blue – blue – blue of the awe-inspiring Pacific in my heart ever since.

Denham Court

A faded snap of our table

(l-r) Father, Mum, Malcolm, self, Uncle Basil, Mother

(l-r) Kevin, Alistair, Malcolm, self, Anne, Suzanne

Love's Coming

Quietly as rosebuds
Talk to thin air,
Love came so lightly
I knew not he was there.

Quietly as lovers
Creep at the middle noon,
Softly as players tremble
In the tears of a tune;

Quietly as lilies
Their faint vows declare,
Came the shy pilgrim:
I knew not he was there.

Quietly as tears fall
On a wild sin,
Softly as griefs call
In a violin;

Without hail or tempest,
Blue sword or flame,
Love came so lightly
I knew not that he came.

John Shaw Neilson (1872–1942)

Many years later, roses at Kerensa

O my Luve is like a red, red rose
That's newly sprung in June;
O my Luve is like the melody
That's sweetly played in tune.

From 'A Red, Red Rose' by Robert Burns
(1759–1796)

'Dear Heart', recorded by Frank Sinatra and written by Henry N. Mancini, Jay Livingston and Ray Evans was, for a time, 'our song'. It is hopelessly sentimental, but that was how we were. Malcolm was a big Frank Sinatra fan and had a large collection of his records.

Dear heart, wish you were here to warm this night
My dear heart, it seems like a year since you've been out of my sight
A single room, a table for one
It's a lonesome town all right
But soon I'll kiss you hello at our front door
And dear heart, I want you to know
I'll leave your arms never more
…

> **A story inspired by my first year of teaching, described in *Growing Young Minds: Reading, Thinking and Aspiration* (RRJ)**
>
> What is the essence of play? Surely it is something to do with the freedom to imagine, to create, to roam, to re-create. As children get older, and especially for those in greatest need, we may need to consider ways that this sense of freedom (bounded) can become part of how we treat young people, both as teachers and as families.
>
> This is a true story of my own experience, not so much imaginative as desperate. As a freshly graduated high school teacher I was sent to a school in the southwest of Sydney, then very rural. In my first year I found myself working with, among other classes, a combined group comprised mainly of young people doing their time (and that is a very apt description) until they reached the magic age of fourteen years nine months when they could then, in those days, legally leave school.
>
> On my first day I met Ken (not his real name), one of the extremely unlikely students who would end up teaching me some principles I have never forgotten. In that class of burly boys

Ken was not physically large but what he lacked in size he made up for in bravado. He swore at me when I walked into the room on my first day, commenting to his mates in a loud voice, 'She's just a bloody sheila.'

The whole class was egging him on and he became progressively outrageous; the girls were all sniggering (in between criticizing my clothes). I tried all the tactics I knew, but after a while of trying to calm him to little avail I asked him to go outside the door and wait for me. I was horrified and mortified when one of the Masters walked past, and without consulting me took him away for 'six of the best'. (Common practice in those days, as I was to discover). A bit later Ken came back into class, hands in his armpits and tears in his eyes but defiantly muttering, 'Didn't hurt anyway'.

The class and I struggled on together as the weeks went by (very slowly, it seemed). The novel they were prescribed was *Kidnapped* (1886) by Robert Louis Stevenson, a great story but even in this abridged school version its language was difficult for these kids who didn't read and had no interest in trying.

Intuitively, I tried to introduce a sense of play. In the end I did a mixture of telling them the story and reading it to them with a Scottish(?) accent and freely omitting and changing words (which nobody noticed). Things started to get better and we began acting out some bits (very loosely) and I asked them to create sound effects, which they did with gusto, especially the storm and shipwreck (and we had extra storms and shipwrecks).

But this only briefly interested Ken. However, I'd been watching him, and a little later I found an opportunity to say that I had noticed how much he liked writing (a little exaggerated, perhaps, but he did tend to be quieter then). So I said I would prefer him not to do all the classwork (he wasn't anyway) but to write me a diary of what he did, liked, thought about. This was a special project, just for him.

This was about mid-year, and there was only about a term and a half left by that time (this was the era of the three-term year), but every morning almost without fail, Ken would be waiting for me in the carpark, diary (an increasingly tattered exercise book) in hand to show me what he had written the previous day – and night; he was also of his own volition doing it quite frequently at home.

He didn't suddenly become perfect by any means, but he became manageable. He knew I expected him to behave fairly, and treat me – and others – with respect.

And he became a very unusual teacher ally in the classroom, exhorting any rowdy others to 'stop mucking up!' (This was often laced with some descriptive adjectives.)

What Ken taught me about dealing with young people:
- the absolute significance of caring observation
- how such observation can kindle relationship
- the importance of teacher/parent initiative informed by that observation
- the importance of developing mutual respect
- the enabling power of being made to feel special and being guided to be so
- the enabling power of being able to enable someone to feel special
- the healing gift of positive attention and caring

Excerpts from *The Tiger Within* (RRJ), mystery/thriller set in the country landscapes surrounding *Oasis* and *Cameo*

What the anvil? what dread grasp
Dare its deadly terrors clasp?

1. **'Deadly Terrors'**

Not far away, but a world away, Jade Jardine was gardening. And Jade Jardine was very happy. The wind had now dropped (it was quite strong earlier) and it had been a good day. The sun, slowly slipping towards the western hills across the valley at the back of the house, still warmed her, but she was also warmed by the pleasurable sensation of the friable soil moving easily beneath her trowel, and the springtime bustle of blossom and bud that surrounded her.

…

She looked around her with satisfaction and not a little complacency. In the year that she had lived here the garden had grown from a few acres of scrubby wilderness to this expansive area of lawn and shrubbery reaching down the hill. Golden plants of rosa banksiae were already flourishing and lit up the fences that separated the home paddock from the other, untouched acres – about twenty of them, left to eucalypts, large clumps of bush and rock, wild grasses and, further down, the occasional triffid shapes of prickly pear.

…

20

… The bush was tipped with pink and red and terracotta shoots which glowed against the greens and soft greys of the foliage. The smell of the sun bounced off the compressed dirt of the road and the tang of the bush was herbal, fragrant, aromatic. This was the Eagleview that she loved – her Eagleview …

35

Thomas Pargetter was enjoying the early drive out into the country, despite the weather which was gradually worsening.

…

Coming into Eagleview, little more than a general store and a railway station, he consulted his map again and then took the long straight road up the hill. It was raining more heavily now, but he found the road he was looking for easily. It was an unmade track, very rough; he was glad it had not been raining for long: already its deep rutted furrows were streaming with water. But the scenery was beautiful. The valley that dipped all along on his right, and which he had just traversed, was swathed in tendrils of mist; the different hill tops on its other side were sometimes delineated clearly, sometimes completely obscured; the mist seemed to add a third dimension. He had the window just slightly open, and the smell of the rain, clear and clean, filled his nostrils.

…

As he came down the red gravel drive leading to the house, he noticed rose bushes along the side. All the same type, by the look of them; how effective it was. There weren't many flowers, just a few quite large buds here and there; it was probably too early. He didn't know many of the names, not like Anne who was an expert, but there was no missing the incipient colours of these, yellows smudging into pinks. It was 'Peace', he was sure. What a nice welcome to a home, he thought.

7. Garden the Fifth – Kerensa

The Props assist the House

The Props assist the House
Until the House is built
And then the Props withdraw
And adequate, erect,
The House support itself
And cease to recollect
The Auger and the Carpenter –
Just such a retrospect
Hath the perfected Life –
A Past of Plank and Nail
And slowness – then the Scaffolds drop
Affirming it a Soul –

Emily Dickinson

Malcolm built this large retaining wall and engraved the name of the house and date of construction in the sandstone

When we returned from our 'honey-money' (our name for that precious three weeks), we moved into the house of a teacher we knew who was going on leave for six months. This was our first home together – Lindesay Street. It was tiny and plain but very comfortable to live in. We had no furniture but now bought a bed and a Formica dining table with four chairs. A bit later, we bought two recliner chairs. The one piece of furniture I possessed, my radiogram, had pride of place. It was

Malcolm's fledgling vegetable patch at our first home, Lindesay St 1967. He is holding Bib, the little cat that seemed to come with the house

a good accompaniment to Malcolm's impressive stack of records.

The little house was on a block about a kilometre out of town but right next to a small rather haphazard group of shops: grocery, greengrocery, butcher and newsagency. I never had to 'go shopping' for our food but could shop every day as the spirit took me. It was very liberating!

Our second house – The Manse, St David's Presbyterian Church

Our third home – the caravan

In the very bare backyard, Malcolm, with much careful preparing and tilling, grew his first vegetables (from memory, carrots and lettuces), but unfortunately we had to leave before harvesting because the owners were returning.

We were fortunate enough to be invited to move into the empty manse of the local Presbyterian church, St David's, as they were between ministers and the new minister was not arriving for several months. For a nominal rent ('donation') and Malcolm mowing the lawn, we were able to make this our second home. It was a beautiful old house but very shabby and rundown, so I hope it has survived the building purge of the later twentieth century. Our bedroom was at the front right and opened out onto the top verandah: this gave us a great love of bedrooms with a door opening onto a deck or balcony and no doubt influenced the house we chose to build later.

The Manse got us through to about November, when we borrowed a small (very small) caravan and parked it in the side garden at Mum's. She and the boys were also on the move; they were selling Cameo and had bought a lovely old stone house in Terrigal on the Central Coast.

Malcolm and I had both applied for teaching transfers for the following year. Our plan was to move to the Northern Beaches area and rent the cheapest place we could find whilst we saved furiously to build a house on the Newport land.

Mum and Grandma had always spoken appreciatively about this Northern Beaches area, and my father had, years before, bought the historic old Rock Lily Hotel at Mona Vale (the suburb adjoining Newport on the city side) and lived in it for a short time as a home. It needed a lot of work, however, and was then a long way out of town, so they sold it after a relatively short time and moved back to Castlecrag.

Malcolm and I found the cheapest place, alright. Rents were high on the Beaches: much higher than we wanted to pay. We looked at dozens of places and, I am not quite sure now how and why (well, it was very cheap), we settled on the back of a garage in Surfview Road, Mona Vale. I think Malcolm just looked at the beautiful beach opposite, only steps from our front (and only) door, and I looked out the bedroom and living room windows across the wide empty expanse of sand alongside and saw the northerly sun and felt a tangy and fresh sea-flavoured breeze. It was such a contrast to all the basement flats and so-called garden flats we had been shown that felt dark and dank.

This was also called, very euphemistically, a garden flat. There was no garden, just a very unkempt small back yard with a wonky Hills Hoist (or copy) stuck in the middle and a few broken toys around the side. The house was made of

The Rock Lily Hotel at Mona Vale was built by Frenchman Leon Houreux in 1885, originally of timber. In 1886 it was rebuilt of local bricks made at the Bayview Brickworks of T. Austin. In the early 20th century, it was popular with Sydney's artistic community, including Norman and Lionel Lindsay. In 1945 it was bought by my father, who sold it in 1947

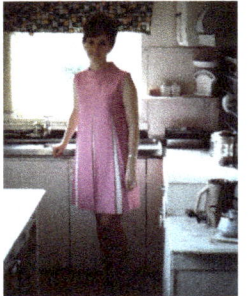

Our fourth home was almost un-photographable; it was the back of a garage in a derelict old beach house that was soon to be demolished (along with what became the council tip next door) for a park. We lived here for about eighteen months

very shabby weatherboard and fibro and was divided into two flats – three young men in the front and a family with two small children at the back. (It was to be demolished, we found out later.) Our flat was tacked on the end of the separate garage. There was a bedroom adjoining the garage, a lounge and dining alcove, and a strange little shower room inserted, very casually, at the back of the lounge, consisting of a shower that was lined with a sort of imitation Laminex and a handbasin. There was no lavatory in the flat. It was across the yard, leaning haphazardly against the back of the main house (see pic). But, as the agent said impressively, as if granting us a huge favour: 'It's just for you! No one else has a key.' There was also no kitchen per se, just a door that led into a long, sloping, narrow enclosed porch, not much more than a metre wide, which ran alongside the living room and had a counter on one wall and a sink at the end. And, there was no stove or oven. So Malcolm laid a piece of Formica on the counter to at least give us a working surface.

How the flat ever got passed by any council or rent authority I don't know. Perhaps it never did. But, for whatever reason, we weren't daunted. It was just across from the beach and virtually had a sea frontage, was wonderfully sunny and northerly facing (well, its two windows were) and we could clean and doctor it up a bit – plus, it was very cheap!

We spent two weekends at the end of the year coming down from the caravan to clean. Malcolm added a few shelves in the 'kitchen' and I scrubbed down the laminated 'bathroom' (shower cubicle, more like). Our washing machine and small second-hand fridge were placed proudly but unconventionally next to each other in the immediate entrance, which was the only possible place they could fit and at the only external door, and Malcolm brought a funny old two-burner stove from Strathfield to stand on the counter in the 'kitchen'. In reality, I did almost all the cooking in a large electric frypan (a wedding present), even a Christmas dinner for both families!

A few weekends after we moved in, we noticed some cars dumping rubbish on the large open adjoining sandy area to our north, between us and Seabeach Avenue. Then the next day some more cars came and did the same thing. We were very indignant, but then we found out the agent had neglected to inform us that this area was to be a council tip for the next year. The council was then going to fill the tip in, demolish our place, grass everything and turn it into a picnic area. I didn't like this (not at all), but Malcolm was not so worried. He liked keeping an eye out on Saturday mornings for what was being dumped and then going browsing (he called it 'checking'). He retrieved a perfectly good shovel, spade and rake one morning, and they are still here in our garage over fifty years later.

Surfview Road was a very happy time. It was a bit like another honeymoon, at least until we started building. The beach across the road gave us endless walks and swims and the sunrises were magnificent. Malcolm swam almost every day, summer and winter. On hot summer afternoons, we swam together. I would swim at the beach pool, which I liked very much; there was enough movement to feel fresh without the often hectic swirl of the surf.

We seemed to have many adventures. Living on an extreme ocean front creates its own microclimate; I would often go to work and mention the strong wind or rain in the night to be met with blank looks from my colleagues, who had not noticed anything. We had king tides and several horrific storms during this period. The waves were huge and washed all the sand away from the yards backing onto the beach further along at The Basin. The little general store at the ocean end of Seabeach Avenue was almost sitting over space. The ferocity of one overnight storm in 1968 or 69 sandblasted my car. In another, our garbage bin was washed out to sea, way past the beach swimming pool (which itself was at the end of a long sandy spit). I couldn't believe it when Malcolm swam out through the huge sea and retrieved it.

We went for a walk along the beach one afternoon after one of the worst nights to look at the grossly eroded sandbanks at the backs of the houses. One house was left with its back porch cantilevered over the sand. As we walked, a huge wave suddenly came out of nowhere and we had to scramble up and cling against the sandbank (which was above our heads). I wouldn't have been able to hold on, but Malcolm pinned his arm around me and somehow the wave retreated. It had come up to my waist and its pull was frighteningly strong. We retreated home very fast. It was scary, and we were freezing in our now sopping wet clothes.

There were so many happy days, but there was one very unpleasant experience at Surfview Road that left a nasty taste in my mouth. I used to get home before Malcolm in the afternoon and would go into the bedroom to get changed into casual clothes as later, after he got home, we almost always went for a walk or swim. I would often hear rustling noises in the adjoining garage but assumed someone was working in there. One day, when cleaning, I noticed some marks on the common wall above our bed. Investigation revealed several little pinholes. Malcolm somehow got into the garage and found that they were spyholes, all set up for watching our bedroom, with a convenient stool placed on a bit of old carpet to ensure the comfort of the voyeur. We didn't know how long they had been there. I was very upset and Malcolm went straight to the landlord and brought him back to show him the evidence. They found that the holes had been made on the garage side. I don't know precisely what happened, but it seemed like the men in the front of the house were given immediate notice. The wall was spackled up, the landlord had new locks put on the garage and the new tenants weren't allowed to use it.

I don't know now how we put up with the lavatory across the yard. (I was learning to call it a 'toilet'.) Because it adjoined the back flat, we often heard more whilst in the lavatory than we should have. Malcolm, who spent longer within than I ever did, would often come back chuckling at something funny he had overheard from the little family that lived there.

And good things were happening as well. After months of looking, we had chosen a house design that blended our diverse architectural tastes (Malcolm a 'beachcomber' on stilts, me a Cape Cod) and suited our sloping block.

The Civic 'Elmtree' was designed for Civic Constructions by Oser Fombertaux and Associates, now well-known as mid-century modernists. Researching, I find that this was 'an era that spanned the 1960s and '70s' (ours was completed in April 1969) when 'houses of the highest calibre' were being built. The 'Elmtree' was 'a split-level four-bedroom house with high ceilings, spacious rooms, timber finishes, and wrought-iron staircases'.

The Civic 'Elmtree' display home

We had walked into the display home at St Ives, pictured above, and just loved it. The house was much more expensive than we had planned – I immediately said I would work an extra year – but was so pretty and unusual.

Before we started building, however, we had made an important decision. The block in front of our battleaxe had been sold and the owners had started building their house right on our boundary and in front of our proposed building. We had not expected this. They were also now worried that the houses would be so close. We talked to the neighbour on the upper side of our block, a well-known newspaper editor, and he offered to sell us a strip of his land adjoining our rear boundary. He paced it out to about five metres and we gratefully accepted.

After bulldozing – Chris, Mum, Danny, RRJ, MCFJ

Our original view

This of course amounted to a subdivision and brought unforeseen extra costs. When it was done he said we could have had more; he had not known exactly where the boundary was. I really wish we had taken him up on this offer. But we were so pushed for funds, we let it go. As Frankie, Malcolm's favourite singer, said: 'Regrets, I've had a few.'

Some years later, and with a little more money in hand, we approached the new owner, but he wasn't interested in selling.

Jumping ahead a few more years, we did do another subdivision: we wanted to buy the actual creek on our northern boundary and the strip on the other side. This was not to use it or to subdivide but to ensure the safekeeping of the beautiful heritage of the natural water creek and cabbage tree palms. It was quite an expense. Our land, however, is now labelled Environmental Living (C4), which we love.

The 'drive', prior to the concrete being laid. Note the right-of-way on the right leading up to the beach and bus. Many years later, and at our urging, Malcolm's mother, now widowed, bought this home (in foreground) and lived here for many happy years

Back to building. We used my travel savings for the house deposit and were good at economising. We occasionally still went to shows; but we very rarely, if ever, went out for dinner. (We didn't really want to.) I made most of my clothes and knitted Malcolm's jumpers. We did a lot of walking and went to free exhibitions and events. But we were basically involved with the building – planning and amending.

We were still working and away all day, but we had to watch the builders carefully as so many things had to be decided along the way. We'd come back to find a decision already made and then it was either too late or too expensive to change. For one, the house in front of us had been radically excavated, leaving our narrow drive (our block was a battleaxe) very precarious, with a two-metre drop along one side and in front of the main area where we were planning to build.

Second, our builders excavated differently to what we had intended, telling us that if we went only a few feet higher (or deeper) we could put a garage underneath, which we had not ever planned or even considered. It was, in the end, a practical solution, but completely

The 'front steps'

changed the look of the front of the house, and necessitated more steps to get to the front door. We couldn't afford these steps at the time, so the conventional flight of six steps provided with the house just stopped in mid-air and all our early guests had to scramble up (and down) a messy slope as best they could. To make matters worse, the back door was now also way above the ground and we couldn't afford steps there either. I'll never forget an acquaintance coming; she looked unencouragingly at our dubious access and asked: 'Are you ever going to add steps?'

We could not afford a garage floor either for several years, and when we did Malcolm had the rotten job of getting rid of the messy mound of concrete the builders had left where the bricklayers had mixed their mortar.

The kitchen 'back door' (at top left). Malcolm added the steps as funds and time gradually permitted

Silly things happened. When the electrician came, we found he had placed the outside lights ridiculously high, as if the house was sitting flat on the ground. We complained, but it was, as they said, 'done'; changes would cost us. I'd argue now, but we felt helpless then. Consequently, replacing a bulb in the outside lights is fraught with difficulty (and danger). Our outside light fittings – our one splurge – were then stolen.

We cut out sanding and polishing the cypress wood floors and anything else we could. We used sandpaper whilst kneeling on our hands and knees to smooth the floors as much as possible, and Mum gave us some old rugs that we sandpapered around. In the design, there was a little toilet and restroom off the study on the lounge room level, which we also cut out. But we did have extra windows put in on the northern side, and these made easier points of connection and access many years later when, as the parents of four (soon to be five), we extended the lounge room/study level by adding a sunroom all along that northern side.

The weather wasn't helpful: it rained and rained and rained. We had to buy extra soil when they were installing the septic tank as the existing soil washed away. We then had to do it again. The drive, difficult enough anyway, was a muddy quagmire. We got some cheap gravel to make it more manoeuvrable. It also washed away. The people who had by now built the house in front of us, and who were to become dear friends, constructed a very solid retaining wall that made our access feel safer; but it was still different to what we had thought it would be when the two blocks were empty.

The house took about seventeen months to build, and when we moved in, in April 1969, it felt like a dream. We had to clamber up a messy bank to reach the front door, and the back door opened into space and onto about a three-metre drop, but *comme ci, comme ça* and *que será será*.

These casual and somewhat fatalistic attitudes were linguistically extended when, working at the university some years later, we started travelling in Thailand and Laos. Here we learnt the wonderful phrases *mai pen rai* (Thai) and *baw pen nyang* (Lao). These useful expressions have become part of our family language. If there's water flooding the floor, just stand on a chair. If it's getting higher, just stand on the table. If it's higher still, climb on the roof. You get the idea.

When we moved in, the garage had no floor (only the almost metre high mound of mortar), we had no finished and polished floors or floor coverings, we had no light fittings, blinds or curtains and we had no money! But we were in the house. And it was early autumn, with sunny days and crisper nights. The air was so clean, washed and seasoned by the acres and acres of ocean just up the path and across the road, stretching and heaving into an infinity of distance beyond the precise line of horizon, and by the bush all along the creek side, with its borders of lovely old cabbage tree palms that I was told were four hundred years old. The palm trees seemed to shine and shimmer alive in the light.

Our neighbours

We and the builders had seen a koala in a tree at the back. And there were kookaburras and rosellas and rainbow lorikeets galore, as well as possums.

The house was full of sun and air and it felt so fresh and clean and open. It *was* of course very open, indeed almost empty; we had the bed, two recliners and a small kitchen table with four chairs.

We also had a second mortgage, which worried our families considerably. However, we poured my salary into that and lived on Malcolm's. We didn't go anywhere except to visit our families. We didn't need to, as there was so much to do at home. And we were happy doing it. Malcolm made endless retaining walls and paths and I started making the garden. The excavation had removed all the lovely topsoil and left a clayey mess. We had no funds for purchasing good soil, so we had to set about trying to improve it. And it rained almost continually, turning the whole place into mud. We both ended up investing in gumboots.

Kerensa, from our creek

After much thought, we decided to call the house 'Kerensa', a Cornish word meaning 'love' and 'peace'. My father, Roy, had been born, we thought at the time (keep watching!), in Cornwall, and we liked the soft sound (reminiscent of Cameo), the romantic feel and that it was unusual. In those days there wasn't an internet to do quick searches. Doing one now, I find that Kerensa is also an unusual girl's name. So, Kerensa it was and is. Malcolm carefully engraved the name into the sandstone of the front retaining wall. That wall, part of the construction of the front steps, is still standing today.

This was a magical time. We were both teaching but put every spare minute into doing things for the house. And of course it wasn't only for 'the house'. This house was much more than just a building to us. It was a symbol; it was to be the place – the cradle, the nurturing place, the sanctuary – in which we hoped to have a family. The two bedrooms next to ours upstairs would one day, we hoped and prayed, be the places where small people would sleep and grow and dream and become strong. Similarly, the garden, we hoped, would be a place where children could play. I was almost marking off the months (still about twenty of them! Still too many!) to when I hoped this dream (which I'd had since the days of my dolls, Anne Elizabeth and Margaret Ruth) could at least begin to come true. Such a dream was already becoming quite unfashionable with my peers, but my ambition at this stage was, strongly, to be a homemaker and a mother.

Lennie, the blue-tongue lizard, came visiting one night and lived in the drive rockery for years, sometimes with a girlfriend. His offspring are still around but are more shy

The frilled neck lizard who came visiting was skittish and fierce. We encouraged the possums for years, but they were garden marauders. Brushtails are common, ringtails (at bottom) less so

In the meantime, ever practical Malcolm worked out how to construct the front and back steps – both complicated jobs, one using concrete and one wood – and built them. I made curtains and blinds and worked on the garden, grabbing cuttings from wherever I could. I always brought something back from our long walks. Perhaps a flower or a leaf or a colour of stem attracted my eye. I had no idea what some were and sometimes they weren't good choices. The things that survived were often rampant and unruly bullies of plants, but at least they were green and growing. To improve the soil, I started saving all our vegetable and fruit peelings, wrapping them in newspaper and burying them (firmly, to guard against marauders) in whatever garden I was making.

We knew we had to put in a drive as soon as possible, as access was tricky, especially when it rained – and it seemed to rain a lot. Our little creek gurgled away contentedly most of the time but occasionally became a mini torrent; it never roared, but it did become noisy enough for us to hear the swirl of water from the house.

Gradually, we started to get things done: back steps, front steps, drive and paths; the purchase of a lounge suite (economically priced) and a second-hand dining suite (also economically priced).

Making the garden filled my everyday thoughts. I borrowed gardening books and devoured them, and in any spare time at school, I drew up plans – in my head, if not on paper. Perversely, I loved English plants, some of which were not so well suited to our warm coastal environment. I really wanted autumn trees, but they needed cold to colour. I remember that Mum and Grandma, when they shifted from the Crag to the quite rugged (very hot, very cold) climate of the Camden–Campbelltown area, tried over and over again to grow the semi-tropical plants they could grow so easily by the harbour. Mum, at Oasis, had planted a jacaranda, which died back every winter in the frost but which she persevered with for years. It was only much later, on coming to the Northern Beaches, that I found out that jacarandas were more than a scrawny plant of about two-metres tall that withered and went brown every winter!

Retaining, retaining, retaining!

While Malcolm was doing all the retaining and structural work, I started clearing some of the lower slope going down to the creek, where the original soil had not been touched. It was overgrown with lantana, and although I couldn't get the big roots out, I could remove all the foliage, as multiple scratches up my arms demonstrated. Malcolm helped me make a sloping terraced bed, and I planted tomatoes, which grew prolifically. They were, in fact, the best I've ever grown, probably because I checked them and carefully watered them every day. I always remember Uncle Les and Aunty Eileen calling in one day unexpectedly, and I gave them several kilos of homegrown beautifully organic tomatoes, as well as a little box of passionfruit from the vines that had sprung up near our back door.

Kerensa, front steps in process, drive laid

We also got our first cat during these early years. I had grown up with dogs, lots of them, and loved our little Scottish terriers, but living in such a tick-prone area as the Northern Beaches (and both being away at work all day) made us hesitant to get a puppy. One day a little girl made her way up the steps to the front door with a fluffy little grey kitten in her pocket. I forget the details of what happened next, but suffice to say that when she left she wasn't carrying the kitten. He was half Persian (she said) and taking this at face value we named him Shah. Shah used to follow Malcolm around outside, just like a dog. We had him for eighteen years.

Shah was the first of many animals to share Kerensa with us. At one stage we had three tiny ducklings (Fluffus, Quacker and Dabbles). They grew into rather imperious grown-up ducks, which we eventually needed to resettle as they became so messy. The local golf club had dozens of ducks near a pond on its outskirts, and we were able to take them there. Fluffus, Quacker and Dabbles used to follow Malcolm when he drove to work in the morning, waddling in a straight line down the road after the car, looking just like a comic strip. As babies they lived in our third daughter's bedroom for a time (a very short time!).

Our first daughter brought home a baby lamb for us to look after for one of the Christmas holidays; at night we made a bed for it in our downstairs bathroom. It also grew rather dramatically during the six weeks.

We had a succession of cats: Shah of course, then Bisky (short for Biscuit), a beautiful tawny ball of fur, and Velvet, who had a smudge of blue at the tips of her dark grey fur. We had two budgerigars and a dear little canary. Our older son brought home from primary school two mice that he swore were two males. In a biological miracle those two mice doubled in numbers seemingly overnight, and before we knew it there was a whole community of mice. I rang every pet shop, but no one wanted any mice. One day, when everyone was away, my uncle and I (Uncle Basil, the artist, who was staying with us at the time) packed up the box and drove way out into the bush and let them loose. They all looked very happy, but I am not sure what their fate was. At least I felt we had given them a chance.

As you will have gathered, with the house came babies. I was going to include them in this chapter, but, except for these few heretofore quite random mentions, I find that I can't. They need their own chapter.

So the next chapter tells the story – well, the beginning of the story – of the Kerensa sprouts and seedlings.

Malcolm relaxing in our lounge room in the new chair. Note the paucity of furniture and furnishings! Mum gave me the little set of occasional tables for my birthday. We sandpapered the floorboards by hand and lacquered around the old rug. We had very little money. I eventually made the curtains. They were bright orange. It was the seventies

Malcolm in the kitchen

Family summer in the very early days at Kerensa: (back row l-r) Charles, Hugh, Ross, Lindsay, Anne, Chris, Danny, Alistair (front row l-r) Queenie, Jane, Eileen, Dorothy, Emily-Jane, Les. Photo taken by Malcolm

Our back jungle, running down to the creek, Jan 1972
Cabbage Tree palms (Livistona australis) – beautiful stately native palms, tall and slender, crowned with dark, glossy green leaves, which grow in the rich soils of the eastern Australia seaboard. Although it rarely became as immaculate as I dreamed, I am so thankful to have this little wilderness as part of our home. It attracts regular enquiries from eager estate agents, but our whole aim in extending the land was to protect this ancient coastal rainforest – our tiny piece of nature

I don't love you as if you were a rose of salt, topaz,
or arrow of carnations that propagate fire:
I love you as one loves certain obscure things,
secretly, between the shadow and the soul.

I love you as the plant that doesn't bloom but carries
the light of those flowers, hidden, within itself,
and thanks to your love the tight aroma that arose
from the earth lives dimly in my body.

I love you without knowing how, or when, or from where,
I love you directly without problems or pride:
I love you like this because I don't know any other way to love,
except in this form in which I am not nor are you,
so close that your hand upon my chest is mine,
so close that your eyes close with my dreams.

Pablo Neruda

Pablo Neruda (1904–1973) was a Chilean poet and politician who won the Nobel prize for Literature in 1971

Looking out on the jacaranda from our sunroom in late spring

The jacaranda a few years ago. Notice our chooks

The sunroom full of shade in summer and full of sun in winter

All Nature has a Feeling

All nature has a feeling: woods, fields, brooks
Are life eternal; and in silence they
Speak happiness beyond the reach of books;
There's nothing mortal in them; their decay
Is the green life of change; to pass away
And come again in blooms revivified.
Its birth was heaven, eternal is its stay,
And with the sun and moon shall still abide
Beneath their day and night and heaven wide.

John Clare (1793–1864)

Kerensa

8. Sprouts and Seedlings

here is the deepest secret nobody knows
(here is the root of the root and the bud of the bud
and the sky of the sky of a tree called life; which grows
higher than soul can hope or mind can hide)
and this is the wonder that's keeping the stars apart
i carry your heart (i carry it in my heart)
From 'I carry your heart with me' by e e cummings

Although I had enjoyed university and teaching, I had no particular ambition at this stage except to write, which I did all the time but didn't do anything really proactive about. What I looked forward to most of all was having a baby and having children. I had loved babies since Mum had my littlest brother. Mum had an old Dr Truby King baby book, which I devoured, and now we were in the house, the upstairs smaller bedroom was already in my head a nursery.

So I was delighted when we found out that first Kerensa Christmas that I was pregnant. There was, however, still the second mortgage. All my salary had been going towards it, but there was still an amount owing (which we didn't have) after I worked as long as I was then allowed. (The baby was due 19 September, so I could only work up until 31 July.)

The night of 26 August was very cold. It felt freezing. I had just finished knitting the layette and had sewn and laid it out on the table in the nursery. The room was now ready. Malcolm had restored and painted the old nappy basket and bassinette that Mum had had for my brothers and me. A girlfriend had given us her old cot. We bought new mattresses and I sewed a new lining, flounce, covers and net, all threaded with yellow satin ribbon. The net I edged with wide lace. I hunted all over the Northern Beaches for doctor flannel

e e cummings (1894–1962) was one of the most significant American poets of the twentieth century. He idiosyncratically preferred using lower case. 'I carry your heart with me' is obviously a love poem but is also sometimes seen as a love poem to country, to nation. These lines for me perfectly express the love of a mother for her babies and young children.

(recommended, if I remember correctly, by Dr Truby King) to make an enveloping blanket, which I then carefully trimmed with wide white satin ribbon. We turned an old kitchen table retrieved from the garage at Strathfield (Malcolm's parents' home) into a change table; Malcolm shaved and painted the legs with estapol antique and I made a padded elasticised and washable quilted cover. Malcolm's mother, Queenie, made a beautiful pram cover and Mum made five pretty sets of matinee jackets, booties and bonnets in different colours. Malcolm also restored the little oak wardrobe that we rescued from Mum's garage and that had belonged to a teenage Uncle Les. I painted the inside white and pasted animal transfers on the drawers.

Ready and waiting! And if you look closely, you'll see the nursery's new generation inhabitant – first day home. The bassinet was the one that my brothers and I had slept in; Malcolm repaired, painted and added the roller wheels. I made the linings and flounce and net. The nappy basket was also the one Mum had for us, similarly repaired and trimmed. The change table, not shown here, was Malcolm's parents' old kitchen table; I made a new padded and quilted cover

Imagine our surprise when in the early hours of the next morning (27 August) it became apparent that something was happening. As we got ready for bed, Malcolm said he would fill the car up with petrol the next day, just in case. Fortunately, the hospital was only a few kilometres down the road, as at 3.00 am that very morning we were on our way.

It was an anticlimax when we got there; nothing more appeared to be happening. But because my waters had broken I could not go home. The doctor came about 7.00 am and simply told me to stay put. Not long afterwards, however, it all began. They summoned Malcolm (who had been sent home), and at 12.14 pm our first child entered the world.

I was delirious with delight. I had secretly thought we'd probably have all sons, because there were so many boys in both our families. When Malcolm walked in with a big bunch of flowers trailing rose-pink satiny ribbon, I couldn't believe it. We had a little girl!

That was such a joyous time. Mum and my brothers arrived the next day from the ACT with huge bunches of fresh white chrysanthemums from a flower nursery along the road. (They had shifted from the Central Coast to Canberra because of my brothers' jobs.) The

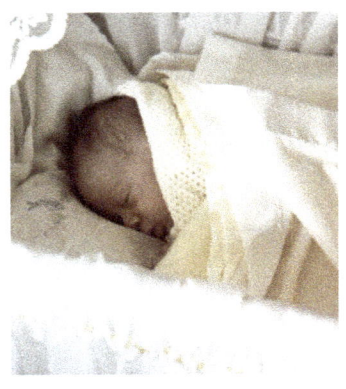

Our first daughter, first day home

smell of dewy, just-picked chrysanthemums always reminds me of that wonderful day. Malcolm's parents also came, so excited that there was now a little girl in the family. Everyone was happy.

It wasn't a time without problems. I was sore, very; it had been a high forceps delivery. And our little girl was, they thought, just slightly premature and was a very sleepy eater, and feeding times were very long. This kept me in hospital for several extra days.

Christening day

Mum and Aunty Hilda came and stayed with us during the first week home. Malcolm had had to go straight back to work the day after. (No father's leave in those days.) It was such a joy to have them. Then Malcolm's parents came for a few days and it was another happy time of celebrating this precious little baby girl. We named the baby Emily-Jane Melinda. 'Emily' and 'Jane' were names I had always loved. (My grandmother was Elsie Emily and her mother was Emily Jane.) Malcolm very much liked 'Melinda', which he thought more modern if she didn't like the then fairly rare and old-fashioned 'Emily'.

In a small serendipity, we later discovered that our little girl, bearing the name of her great-grandmother, shared her actual birthdate with that first Emily Jane's mother, the intrepid South Australian pioneer Mary Ann Allen, her great-great-grandmother, who was born on 27 August 1827.

I resigned from teaching and a little miracle happened: something that to us was unexpected but that we perhaps should have known. Because I had resigned, we were worrying about money and were planning to go to the bank to see if we could add to our

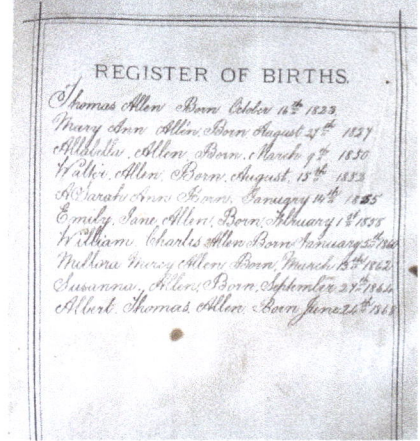

The old Allen family Bible, registering the birth of my great-grandmother; the same date as the birthdate of her great-great-granddaughter

loan. But some weeks after I handed in my resignation, we were going down the drive in the car and the postman delivered two almost identical official looking letters addressed to me. I opened up one and a cheque fell out for a sum almost exactly the same as the amount owing on the second mortgage. Then I opened the second letter, and it explained that, because I had resigned, a cheque for my superannuation payout would be sent. That was obviously what was already in my hand.

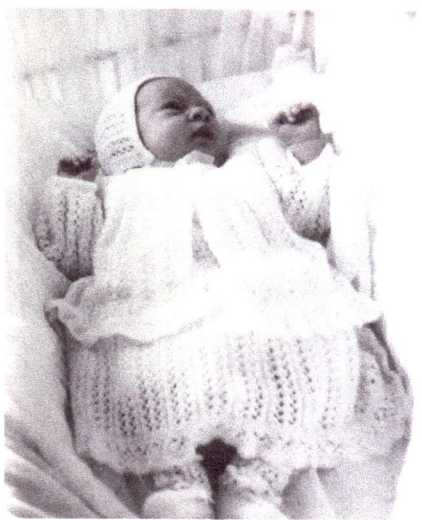

Emily-Jane at about five months (and now actually moved into her cot). The carefully knitted layette finally fits. It was way too big for bringing her home

Dorothy Patricia (Mum) with her first grandchild. Malcolm set this photo up to reference the studio portrait of Grandma, Mum and me, taken twenty-six years earlier (see Ch 1)

Of course – and again I should have known this – this original super fund was an amazingly good one, and perhaps we should have thought more about ways of keeping it going. But we didn't. And it was a wonderful and much-needed bonus for us at that time.

The next few months and years were years of energy and bounty. It was a joy watching Emily-Jane start moving: pulling herself along on her tummy and never doing an orthodox crawl, then just one day getting up and walking.

Mother and Father Johnston, now also grandparents for the first time

This all gave Malcolm another rather urgent job. I had Emily-Jane on the floor in the nursery while I was collecting the washing to take downstairs when she suddenly and unexpectedly took off towards the hallway. And I saw with horror that she could easily fit through the railings.

I suggested we rig up some fishing net, a solution I had seen at some friends' houses, but Malcolm had another idea. He started to make a decorative wrought iron filling to go between each upright. He also made a detachable gate for the bedroom level. It was very pretty and made the stair area very safe. Eventually he did the whole stair railing, and we still enjoy it today.

The whole family came to Kerensa for Emily-Jane's second Christmas. (A Kerensa

Emily-Jane and family

My brothers playing Christmas table tennis

Walking, walking, walking – Annabel on board, Emily-Jane in stroller

Christmas was to become a family tradition for many years.) By then, Emily-Jane was sixteen months old and we were expecting our second child, who was due 21 June, which was around two months before her second birthday. Our second child actually arrived late on a Sunday night, at 11.15 pm on 4 June. It was almost a dream birth; I did better and felt more in control. She was born very quietly, and both Malcolm and I had a concerning few moments when she didn't start breathing straight away and the doctor and sister took her over to the other side of the ward. I am not sure exactly what they did, but thankfully, after what seemed a long silence, we heard a small splutter and a little almost apologetic cry.

Annabel Rosemary was tiny and neat and had Malcolm's beautiful blue eyes. He and I both felt so blessed to now have two little girls. Two perfect little girls! We couldn't believe it.

Mum had been staying with us that weekend and was planning to come again the following weekend in case the new baby came early. She and my brothers had recently moved to the Central Coast and were now living in Avoca, and we had just driven her to Hornsby to catch the train back home. We were barely back in our own home when labour began and we had to ring Mum (who had also just arrived home) to arrange for one of my brothers to drive her back to Newport. Our neighbour, Wyn, came in to stay with Emily-Jane until Mum arrived later that night.

Two little girls with Aunty Hilda

I had just finished knitting the new baby's homecoming layette. This one was a 000 size. The one I made for Emily-Jane was way too big for a newborn and fitted her best at around four or five months. I hadn't realised how small new babies were.

Unwrapping the new baby (in her tiny 000 layette) on her first day home. She was like a little doll

My father's birthday was 5 June, and I had secretly hoped that if the baby came early it would arrive then. I also thought it would be nice if it arrived on 19 June, Malcolm's father's birthday. I knew both he and Malcolm would be quite chuffed. However, once labour started, any thoughts of trying to hold off until the fifth, let alone the nineteenth, completely disappeared.

It was another joyous homecoming. Once again, I was so fortunate to have help. Mum was with me for the first week and Malcolm's parents for the second. I think Father (Malcolm's dad) loved that he got to be in charge of Emily-Jane while Mother and I attended to the baby.

This was a truly happy time. Our two little girls were such a blessing, and both were

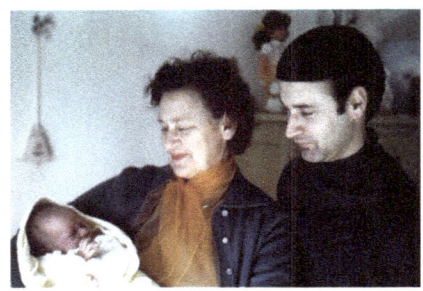

Grandmother Johnston and Uncle Alistair (Malcolm's brother) with baby Annabel

very good babies. They were also the first babies of the next generation on both sides of the family, so everyone celebrated them.

I knew Malcolm's parents would love to show off their little grand-daughters, and as it happened our church was between ministers, so we decided to have the new baby's Christening at their church, St David's in West Strathfield. All the family who could come were there, including Aunty Hilda who came over from Adelaide. My oldest brother had recently been married. His wife was expecting their first child and was not very well, so they couldn't come.

Both families celebrating Annabel's christening at Malcolm's family church, St David's. Malcolm's father was very proud to be the one holding the baby. (I think Mum gave her to him.) Photo taken by Malcolm. (l-r) Danny, Chris, Alistair, Mother, RRJ holding Emily-Jane, Aunty Hilda, Mum, Father holding Annabel

Winter walk with Mum carrying Annabel

It was a very big day. We had to leave Newport at about 8.00 am for the service at Strathfield at around 9.30 am – bath, feed, dress both babies, spare clothes and so on just in case. Then everyone came back to Kerensa for lunch (and probably dinner as well, I can't remember).

The night before, in between icing the cake, I had been finishing off a little, white, knitted cape that was fringed with angora for Emily-Jane to wear. Malcolm spent a lot of time tidying up the still nascent garden and sweeping the paths, as well as borrowing some chairs so everyone would have a seat.

It was a precious family day.

This was the time of the Sprouts. These years were exciting, busy and wonderful. As the Sprouts were appearing, and I was busy with them, Malcolm was continuing to do things around the house and garden. He was also working and was, at various times, in charge of departments at Pittwater High School, Meadowbank High and Narrabeen High. He was always promoted quickly, but promotion was neither his guiding principle nor his ambition. He loved being constructive and making things, and he always wanted to keep working in the areas he enjoyed and for which he saw such practical outcomes: technology, engineering science, technical drawing, woodwork and metalwork (thus our lovely wrought iron, which over the years he extended to make Kerensa safe for inquisitive creeping crawlers).

With my two precious babies!

Proud father and grandparents with two little girls

Emily-Jane's second birthday, with Uncle Alistair and Uncles Dan and Chris in background

He was a true artisan, who wanted to keep the old skills alive and respected them, demonstrating their relationship to the new. He also kept up his involvement as a musician, playing in bands and orchestras, including Willoughby Symphony Orchestra, Warringah Concert Brass, Harbord Diggers Big Band and various smaller church and community bands.

Malcolm loved the beach and the surf. There were only a few days each year that he didn't walk up and over the hill to 'our beach' (Bungan) at least once and, very often, when work permitted, twice. In summer, when we could, we went over early in the morning and then late-ish in the afternoon. The beach was so beautiful at those times. If the tide was just going out, the wet sand reflected pools of rose-pink, lilac and mauve and amethyst, in sleek, perfect iridescence.

With Annabel

We also, as soon as Annabel became more mobile, started taking the girls to the beach. We didn't go so much to Bungan, as getting down to it required negotiating a steep slope. Our daily trips there came a little later, when the children (or at least most of them) could manage the bushy track. In the earliest days, when at least one might still be in a stroller, we went to Newport or Mona Vale or, quite frequently, Clareville,

The girls and Mum on the sand at Newport

a pretty and quiet little beach on Pittwater. We were great walkers and went for long, long walks with a stroller that could, if need be, accommodate another little person when legs just got too tired. It would be only a few years later that I would occasionally have three little people crammed into that stroller by the end of a long walk. I'd pack some sandwiches and drink bottles and fruit and we'd have fun choosing the place and time for refreshments. It was quite a workout, though that word was not really in common parlance or practice at this time.

Our two little girls

And I was pregnant again. This was not quite as easy as the first two, and I spent some weeks, first at about five and a half months and then at about seven months, in hospital, as there was a threat of miscarriage or premature birth. Luckily, the outcome was safe and well: a beautiful little boy arrived (with a bit of help as he was settling in), on the actual day he was supposed to (27 November). He is the only baby I carried full term.

Because of the good ending, it is safe to tell a now-amusing story associated with the first sudden trip to hospital at about five and a half months. My doctor had told me a few days earlier when contractions started that sometimes brandy could help settle them down. Mother (Grandma Johnston) and Father J were staying with me at the time. Malcolm was at work and Mother despatched Father to buy a bottle of brandy. Sometime later, after he returned, the pains started again, and we decided I should try the brandy cure. I'm making light of it here, but I was really frightened; this baby was already precious to me. I lay as still as I could on the bed and tried to keep my breathing normal and regular whilst Mother opened the bottle and poured the brandy. I think we discussed quantities, but neither of us knew for sure and the doctor hadn't specified. We were both (very unfashionably then) teetotallers.

We decided, to be safe, to make it just a small kitchen glass, which Mother brought up to me and which I drank quite quickly to get it working faster.

Well!

My first ever alcoholic drink, probably over 150 millilitres of brandy – the very best, the bottle shop person had told Father – downed, burningly, in a few sips. The rest of the afternoon is a blur. But, whatever else the brandy did, it didn't stop the contractions.

The ambulance was called. It arrived but couldn't get up our drive because the slab of concrete at the very end had only just been poured and it was all roped off. And I couldn't walk. So I was stretchered down and around the still wet concrete and into the ambulance and taken to hospital. I have no real recollection of any of this except how nice and very white the new bit of drive looked.

Drive laid to letterbox

The second time I was in hospital during this pregnancy was during the opening of the Sydney Opera House. This time they kept me there until they thought the baby was big enough to be okay. My tummy was measured every day with a rather gruesome-looking metal device. On 1 November, Malcolm took me home and the baby relaxed comfortably. In fact, too comfortably. In the end, twenty-seven days later, they had to start the induction process to get him going. They didn't need to complete it, however. He was on the move.

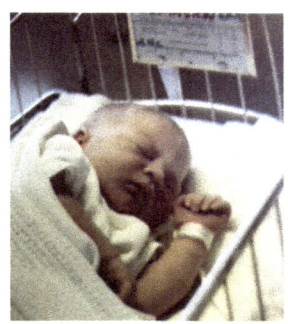

Our beautiful son, Malcolm Ross

When he emerged, he was so beautiful: much bigger than the girls and very finished-looking. After my two dainty girls, who were just under seven pounds, at over eight and a half pounds he was a big baby. He also had no problems feeding and slept long and comfortably.

Immediately after he was born, I remember Malcolm and the doctor, who was stitching me up, having an animated discussion about Hornby train sets. I did try to make a few comments here and there, but they were talking well and truly above my head (literally). I was at that point irrelevant, and felt rather miffed but incredibly happy that our son – Malcolm Ross – was safe. And years later, setting up that Hornby train set in our lounge room was fun for everyone (especially Malcolm the Elder!).

Our first Christmas with three little Sprouts – Malcolm Ross about four weeks old, Annabel about eighteen months. Emily-Jane about three years and three months

So we had three little ones. Everyone was so happy. Mother and Father had another little Johnston and were delighted that we called him Malcolm, just as I am delighted now that he and his wife, Helen, have a son they named Malcolm. And Mum was delighted that we added Grandma's family name of Ross. So he is a heritage bearer for both sides of the family.

Three little ones so close together was a joy, but a busy one. All through this I was very involved in teaching Sunday School, serving on New South Wales syllabus committees (honorary) and doing a little bit of private tutoring. I was also interested, if not much involved, in the wider church. This was the period of Union, when Methodists, most Presbyterians and most Congregationalists came together to form the Uniting Church of Australia. I had originally been baptised in the Anglican church and married a Presbyterian. When we came to Newport, we had searched around and chosen St Paul's Presbyterian in Mona Vale as our church 'home'. We often also attended, on Sunday nights, the Mona Vale Methodist Church. They were a dynamic and interesting crowd, with bright and lively services and a great band, which Malcolm was immediately invited to join. Later, I was asked to join their singing group, the Chorale.

Involvement in this church, which had regular monthly special 'public outreach' services in an often-crowded village hall and a charismatic minister, as well as Malcolm's musical performances, led to my writing of skits and playlets and sometimes acting in them (between pregnancies). This was a very exciting period, with an endless cast of interesting people (some well-known, like singer Julie Anthony, and one soon to become world famous, James Morrison). But that program sadly fizzled out some time in the late eighties.

A special note about James Morrison. He was a young teenager when I first knew him, and on one occasion we cast him in a short play I had written (today we would call it a rap) about hypocrisy. I asked him to sit on a high block and 'rap out' the words. All the other kids were part of a chorus. From memory:

James:

When the old man says 'Now listen Son,
There's a lot of things that can't be done:
Don't take drugs, you'll only regret!'
As he puffs away at his cigarette.
Have the moral strength to just say 'No'
When one of your mates says 'Have a go!'

Kids' Chorus:

Help us! Help us! We don't know what to do!
We're part of a modern-day scientific world!
Oh, what's a kid to do!

I remember that James just 'got it'. I gave him the words and told him to sit on the box and maybe swing his legs as he rapped the words, which he did, straight away, brilliantly. He was such a champ. And he has spent his life helping other young talented musicians, as well as

Malcolm Ross in his first car, and the children on the beach

touring and playing his magic trumpet all over the world. His mother, Jess, a beautiful local school teacher and dance teacher, taught probably thousands of young people, including my own daughters, the joys of moving their bodies to music.

When Malcolm Ross, whom Emily-Jane had christened Manny-Ganks (it was her just-three-year-old interpretation of 'Malcolm Ross', and he remained 'Manny-Ganks', 'Manny' or 'Ganks' for years) was about eighteen months old, we found that another little Sprout was on the way. Perhaps I should note here (later rather than sooner) that the night before our wedding was the first time Malcolm and I actually discussed children. I was a bit surprised when Malcolm (one of two boys) said that he thought maybe one child would be quite nice. Then he asked me how many I wanted. Remember this was well before anyone (that I knew, anyway) was talking about population control. In fact, the opposite was true in Australia; the catchcry was 'populate or perish'! It was also well before widespread talk of the depletion of world resources. So, I said the truth, that I loved babies and would like six of our own. Malcolm was very quiet for a while. It was, in retrospect, rather an awkward silence. Then I said: 'Perhaps we could compromise.' This he agreed to, very enthusiastically. The funny thing is, when we had our first, Emily-Jane, she was just so beautiful that he himself said: 'Perhaps we should have another.' And the same thing happened after Annabel, then after Malcolm Ross and then after Sarah. To be honest, however, not so enthusiastically after Robert Charles, because our family felt so complete then, with two sons and three daughters. I joked to Malcolm later that our compromise was my six minus his one.

Anyway, that was a very happy Christmas. And on 20 January, in high summer, our third daughter arrived: upside down, but fortunately a textbook breech birth. There had been all sorts of dire warnings, and I had an audience of half the hospital at the birth, or so it seemed when I opened my eyes and saw them all pressed around the labour ward walls. I promptly shut my eyes again. My legs were also in stirrups (first time), and I just had to retreat into my inner sanctuary to escape the image of what it must look like.

Sarah Elizabeth was bright eyed, and with three older but very small siblings she soon (very soon) started to stake her place in the family hierarchy. She seemed to start smiling and responding very early on. She also had a very determined and independent spirit from the

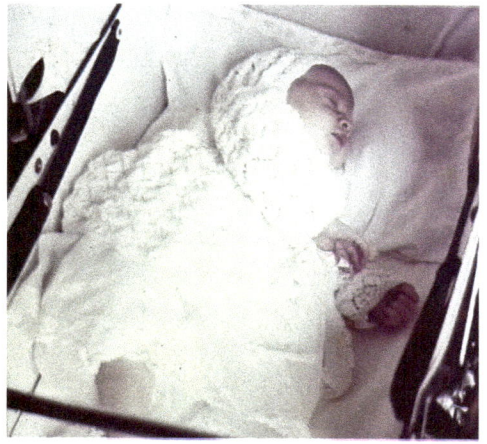

Sarah Elizabeth

beginning. As she grew older, she did things none of the others would have dreamed of doing. She peeled a loose strip of wallpaper off the bathroom wall: not to be destructive, not even to see what was under it, but because, as she told her very cranky father, she knew 'it would feel so satisfying to peel the loose hanging strip of wallpaper down as far as it would go. And,' she added, 'it did.' She had a joyous nature, was thoughtful, loved words and unselfishly loved her family and had an immense loyalty to each one. She rescued wildlife – big and small, from ants to possums and birds – fostered three little fluffy ducklings, loved our chookies, and to this day will turn her car around to rescue any injured animal she sees along the roadway.

I always feel that we have a bonus child, a sort of 'buy four and you get one free'. That perfect, wonderful bonus is Robert Charles, a gift that arrived on 31 May. All the kids loved him. He was a real, live living doll to them. There is a photo of the girls in their beds with dolls and teddy bears all around them and, if you look closely, a real live baby in the dolly's cot. He accepted all their ministrations (most of them tender) with equanimity. He had arrived after a sad few years. We had earlier lost the vibrant Aunty Hilda as well as Malcolm's father, who was such a steady rock. The new baby's second name was 'Charles', after Malcolm (Malcolm Charles Ferguson) and his father (Charles Thomas). I was able to tell Father before he died that if we had another son we would do this. His response was: 'You've got enough children!' It was a view both he and Mother had expressed more and more vigorously about every child after Annabel. But they were softies and loved each one as they came along.

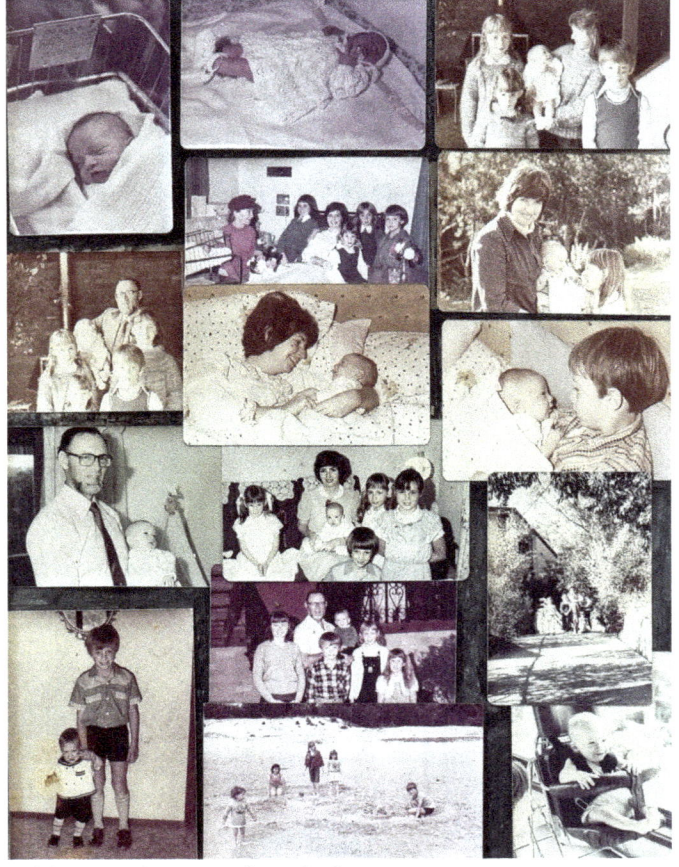

Celebrating Baby No.5, Robert Charles

The new baby was 'Robert' because we had both always loved the name (despite its popularity) and its rich Scottish associations. I also knew it was one of my father's favourite names. Sometimes I think Robert Charles was sent to help us through this difficult period. It was only a few years later that we were to lose my beautiful and talented young mother, Dorothy Patricia, 'In the midst of life'. It's part of being in a family, isn't it? It's part of being human, part of loving. But it's so hard to live through.

So, Robert Charles was a beautiful bonus, a beautiful gift. He was an amazing baby from the very beginning. He survived his siblings' mostly loving attention and was quickly and easily packed up when I had to take the other four here, there and everywhere: kindy, school, drama, various practices, music, dance, cricket, church groups, Cubs and Sea Scouts. If I had to pick him up when he was sleeping, which was often, he would resettle comfortably and with equanimity in his car seat. He truly made our perfect six minus one!

Both Mum and Malcolm's mother loved and enjoyed this new little grandson, who despite being a fifth child seemed to be no trouble. He did everything early: took his first steps in front of us all at just on nine months and was talking fluently from about eighteen months. I think it was because the kids all loved him so much and he loved being part of them, so he was determined to catch up and be like them.

Our family

We had already extended the house, building two small bedrooms and a rumpus room. This extension comes off the kitchen (but on the lounge room level) and runs along the northern wall. A dear builder friend, Eric, constructed it to lock up stage and Malcolm finished it off. This made it affordable. Annabel and Mal had excitedly moved into the new bedrooms. When Robert grew into a bed, Malcolm built a wonderful double bunk to accommodate him in Mal's room. (Many years later, Mal used it for his own two sons.) So Robs, only about two or three, moved in. He was desperate to be with his big brother. But the room was quite small, and when Mal got older, Malcolm made another room under the

Mal's own two sons, Malcolm Luke Allinson and Toby Charles Havilland, inherit his and Robert's bunk bed (made by Malcolm)

back deck and lined it to become a big bedroom for him. It opened onto the lower level off the utility room and had its own little ensuite. The house has also accommodated a number of visiting others, from both close by and overseas, for weeks, sometimes months. I have loved the way, at various times and to meet various needs, we turned the dining room into a bedroom and made sure the sunroom always had a divan ready for an expected or indeed unexpected guest.

I have tried to limit my desire to celebrate and revisit that lovely time and include lots of photographs. There were so many epochs and adventures and firsts: first day at kindy, first day

Newport Primary School Centenary – with Robert

at school, first day at high school; summers full of beach adventures with a loving and patient father who took them over to 'our beach' it seems, in my memory, every day; swimming and swimming lessons every holidays with local celebrity and my very good friend the novelist Colleen Klein; picnics and about seven years of caravan adventures every holidays. We eventually outgrew the four-bed van that was given to us by Uncle Basil. The kids when small slept two to a bunk – one each end. Robs getting beyond babyhood coincided with the first four getting too big to fit. But what adventures we had squeezed in: South Australia, the Flinders and Victor Harbour, the Snowy Mountains, the bush, the Mount Macedon area of Victoria, Armidale and New England (because of Judith Wright), Queensland, the Gold Coast, Sea World, and so on. We had one holiday that had a terrible ending because all the children caught a violent tummy bug. But from the perspective of the now-time, even that seems an adventure! (Can we find a suitable spot to pull the van over before the next child throws up again?) There were first days at Cubs, at Scouts and at Guides. At the first Guides camp, the tents were all washed away in a big storm and Annabel's brand-new uniform and fancy clobber were covered in thick gooey mud. (This was, strangely enough, also the last Guides camp she wanted to attend.) There was church and Sunday School every Sunday, and so many associated fun activities: camps, youth groups, dinners (some big ones at our place, with borrowed tables set up in the lounge room), play nights, sleepovers, picnics at the Basin, hikes and concerts. There were play days and Book Weeks and all sorts of festivals. There were birthdays and parties. And there were Christmases, for which we now always had a real tree, some years driving up to a Christmas tree farm in the foothills of the Blue Mountains to choose it. There was a shift from large EH and HQ Holden station wagons (DOM and EIBy, the 'Brown Bomb') to a briefish flirtation with a bright blue Mini! Then, when we had a fifth child and brought Malcolm's mother to live next door (Wyn, our neighbour, had moved on, and Mother was so lonely and faraway in Strathfield; it was good for everyone), the bronze

Urvan (MCX 819), which was spacious and fitted all eight of us comfortably. What fun we had piling people (and their friends) in for trips and holidays.

Ah, what memories!

Like Judith Wright's Old Dan in 'South of My Days', I 'shuffle the years like a pack of conjuror's cards'.

Like Old Dan, I now have seventy years of stories; I have seventy years 'hived' in me 'like old honey'.

Those years with the growing little Sprouts, with all their ups and downs, comings and goings, for me were the Golden Time.

As parents (I know I am speaking for Malcolm as well as myself, perhaps not so much in terms of the poetic response, but definitely in terms of the emotion generating it), the simple but lovely words of e e cummings quoted at the beginning of this chapter express what filled and spilled out of our hearts as we looked at our small children (especially, to be honest, when they were fed and washed and sleeping):

I carry your heart[s] with me (I carry [them]in my heart).

Each child in my mind has various lines from prose or poems or songs associated with them.

Emily-Jane Melinda: John Donne, 'Meditation 35' (1623)

These famous lines relate to her overflowingly generous spirit as well as to her loving and lavish responses to the world and to others in it.

> *No man is an island, entire of itself;*
> *every man is a piece of the continent, a part of the main.*
> *If a clod be washed away by the sea,*
> *Europe is the less, as well as if a promontory were,*
> *as well as if a manor of thy friend's or of thine own were:*
> *any man's death diminishes me, because I am involved in mankind,*
> *and therefore never send to know for whom the bell tolls,*
> *It tolls for thee.*

Annabel Rosemary: David Malouf, from 'For Two Children' (*Poems 1959–1989*)

These lines seem to reflect in its gentle waves her warm and sensitive embrace of beauty, her keen perception and attention to detail ('reflect us tiny'), and her imaginative soul.

> *Across the lake the small houses*
> *appear to be real, and to imagine themselves somehow*
> *painted on the view and leaning toward*
> *their shaky selves in water, taking the sun*
> *for granted, stretching their timbers, half asleep*
> *in a dream of such apparent permanence*
> *that we hire a boat and would row across to visit,*
> *or walk there if we could, watching fishes*
> *snap their tails beside us and the mirror scales*
> *reflect us tiny on their backs.*

Malcolm Ross, our third child and first son: John Masefield, 'Sea Fever' (the first two verses)

This poem not only expresses our son's great love of the sea, it also expresses his spirit, his love of nature and his undemanding outlook. I even see in these lines the lilting rhythm of his walk.

> *I must go down to the seas again, to the lonely sea and the sky,*
> *And all I ask is a tall ship and a star to steer her by,*
> *And the wheel's kick and the wind's song and the white sail's shaking,*
> *And a grey mist on the sea's face, and a grey dawn breaking.*
>
> *I must go down to the seas again, for the call of the running tide*
> *Is a wild call and a clear call that may not be denied;*
> *And all I ask is a windy day with the white clouds flying,*
> *And the flung spray and the blown spume, and the sea-gulls crying.*

Sarah Elizabeth, our third daughter: G. M. Hopkins, 'Epithalamion' (the first seven lines) This poem expresses her great love of using words differently to express deep thoughts and her creative perception and passion for the world and everything in it.

> *Hark, hearer, hear what I do; lend a thought now, make believe*
> *We are leafwhelmed somewhere with the hood*
> *Of some branchy bunchy bushybowered wood …* [line 4 omitted]
> *That leans along the loins of hills, where a candycoloured, where a gluegold-brown*
> *Marbled river, boisterously beautiful, between*
> *Roots and rocks is danced and dandled, all in froth and water-blowballs, down.*

Robert Charles, our second son: A. B. Paterson, 'Clancy of the Overflow' (stanzas 3 and 4) He went adventuring into the bush, to Dubbo and beyond, as a jackeroo, and later also travelled into Mongolia. The rhythms of country and space and distance are in his vision and in his blood.

> *In my wild erratic fancy visions come to me of Clancy*
>   *Gone a-droving 'down the Cooper' where the western drovers go;*
> *As the stock are slowly stringing, Clancy rides behind them singing,*
>   *For the drover's life has pleasures that the townsfolk never know.*
>
> *And the bush hath friends to meet him, and their kindly faces greet him*
>   *In the murmur of the breezes and the river on its bars,*
> *And he sees the vision splendid of the sunlit plains extended,*
>   *And at night the wondrous glory of the everlasting stars.*

Annabel anticipating Robert, who arrived the next day

The talisman of family

> Talisman: an inscribed ring or stone, thought to have magical powers and to bring good fortune.

This chapter about our little Kerensa Sprouts has been about motherhood, parenthood and, most of all, *familyhood*. Children's lives are made up of family: mothers and fathers, grandmothers and grandfathers, aunts and uncles and cousins, indeed, all sorts of enriching connections. We each carry the talisman of family, both the good and the not-so-good, within us: in our memories, in our thinking places, in our judgements, even in our dreams. And as Sprouts grow into their own lives, other families grow into them, seed into them, sending new shoots and seedlings of allegiances, thoughts, ideas and experiences. These may sometimes be challenging – they sometimes were for me – but they are also re-vitalising, refreshing, energising, horizon-expanding and strengthening. They may disrupt, but they may also affirm.

It is not for me to tell the stories of the grown-up Sprouts; they can tell their own stories. Just to say that I am so proud of each one. So I want to close this chapter with part of a poem by Maya Angelou, the thoughtful American poet and memoirist. Although this is addressed to the poet's mother, it is a poignant expression not only of motherhood but of *life* – its cycles and its different roles that we sometimes choose and that are sometimes thrust upon us. It expresses how I feel (and felt) about my mother, and it tells, with such honesty, how family relationship can fluctuate and how perspectives shift and alter, blend and harmonise. It is perhaps another version, more tender, more hopeful, more loving, of Shakespeare's 'seven ages of man'. As Jaques says in *As You Like It*:

> *All the world's a stage,*
> *And all the men and women merely players;*
> *They have their exits and their entrances,*
> *And one man in his time plays many parts.*

I want to thank my mother again for all she passed on to me, and which I, I hope, have passed on to my own children and know they will pass on in their own ways to the next generations.

From **'Mother, A Cradle to Hold Me'** by Maya Angelou (1928–2014)

It is true
I was created in you.
It is also true
That you were created for me.
I owned your voice.
It was shaped and tuned to soothe me.
Your arms were moulded
Into a cradle to hold me, to rock me.
The scent of your body was the air
Perfumed for me to breathe.

A Mother's Heart

Hold him tight, Lord, keep him growing,
    Keep him safe below my heart,
Make me now a perfect vessel,
    Let him have a perfect start.

Hold him tight, this different wonder,
Hold him tight, this precious son,
Watch him grow and reaching outwards,
    Watch him walking, watch him run.

Reaching up to kiss him nightly,
Standing on the bunk below,
Watching for his coming home times,
    Help me, Lord, to let him go.

Now he leaves in search of something,
    Home alone his little brother,
Yet I glimpse his eager dreaming,
Oh, the pain of being a mother!

Hold them tight, those years of growing,
Hold them tight, and watch him grow,

Hold them tight, those precious memories,
Hold them tight – but let him go.
    RRJ
    (Written for our elder son, Malcolm Ross)

Mum with Malcolm and me

9. Revelations

9.1 Preamble

My father had the heart of a crusader and the soul of a poet. He was a dreamer, an idealist and an intrepid champion of causes he believed in.

He loved my mother passionately and she adored him. She continued to mourn him until the day she died (some thirty years after his death).

He was very tender and protective with me, as a daughter and as a little girl. (I turned twelve in the year he died.) He was sterner with the boys, my brothers, but very proud of them and clearly delighted to be the father of three sons.

He was courteous and knowledgeable. He seemed, to us, to have travelled all over the world.

He was acutely perceptive and at the same time an impetuous adventurer. And he was both clever and sometimes impractical.

He loved cooking but disliked gardening, except for his little plot of radishes and the very long row of *Pinus insignis* he planted along the quarter mile of road frontage that included Oasis, Cameo, Grandma's spare block and Dorset Cottage. In a very modern role reversal, he looked after much of the cooking and Mum did most of the gardening. This suited them both very well.

He was generous to a fault but not very good with organising finances.

He had an absolutely beautiful speaking voice. Sometimes, on a Sunday afternoon, sitting in the afternoon glow of our lounge room at Oasis, he would read aloud to Mum an interesting article from the newspapers and I would stop what I was doing just to listen to his voice.

Yes, he was widely travelled and crammed a great deal of adventure into his scant fifty-seven years. But from the time he first landed in Australia in 1921/1922, he became intensely loyal to his new country and thoroughly, deeply committed to Australian causes.

He campaigned and fought for Australian content in Australian cinema and in Australian films, writing to leaders and trying to stand up to powerful American monopolies. He composed country and western songs celebrating Australian geography and history. His song 'The Overlander Trail' was well-known and was recorded by many leading artists, including, among others, Buddy Williams, Slim Dusty, Wayne Horsburgh, Lindsay Butler, Col Edmonds, Smoky Dawson and Reg Lindsay. A more recent version was recorded by Lee Kernaghan, with choruses by Slim Dusty, Reg Lindsay and Smoky Dawson.

His 'Eureka: The Stockade Song' is less well known and deserves to be re-recorded; the surviving rendition is old-fashioned. But the melody is appropriate and the lyrics are so very pertinent to Australia's story, as well as being particularly relevant to the story of my father. Written in the late 1940s, it describes an event that has become a national legend. The courage of the diggers in standing up for their mining rights is now celebrated by many as the birth of Australian democracy.

'Eureka' is expressive of my father's spirit: romantic, sometimes perhaps even quixotic, but determined to fight against the odds and to do what he believed to be right for Australia. It appears at the end of this chapter: a fitting end-piece to his story.

December 1922 Olympic Films 'New Australian Productions'

9.2 Childhood

Infant Joy

'I have no name;
I am but two days old.'
What shall I call thee?
'I happy am,
Joy is my name.'
Sweet joy befall thee!

Pretty joy!
Sweet joy, but two days old.
Sweet Joy I call thee:
Thou dost smile,
I sing the while;
Sweet joy befall thee!

William Blake

My father at about three

My father, in many ways, remains a mystery to me; but I loved him, and my mother loved him passionately.

I knew my father as Royston Frederick Darling, born in Hayle, Cornwall in England, son of Rose Isabella Reay-Edwards, an English girl from an upper middle-class very artistic family that some claim to have been related to Arthur Wellesley, the Duke of Wellington. It was whispered that the relationship was on 'the wrong side of the blanket'; Wellington had many extramarital liaisons, and the name Wells or Welles does appear in various family chronicles. Some of the Edwards branch believed that Wellesley had an affair with Lady Ann Mann, who became pregnant with his child and who was subsequently persuaded to marry Wellesley's friend (their ancestor), William Edwards, to preserve her reputation.

Rose Isabella, my paternal grandmother, with her first son, my father

These chronicles and the stories they tell add to the confusion. We have found that they are often based on family hearsay and are vague and sometimes incorrect. I wish we could have asked my father about it all. He, of course, played his own part in not only influencing but retelling.

My father's mother, Rose Isabella, sang, played the piano and other instruments and also composed music. When I was born I was named after both her and my mother's sister (Aunty Hilda), whose second name was Mary. As children, we knew about our paternal grandmother, Rose, who had died in childbirth just before our father left home and ran away to the Great War. When we started meeting his family, decades later, they all stressed how much Rose was loved and how creative and musically talented she was; they told us that she had, among other things, composed a lovely waltz, the 'Trance Waltz' (what a pretty and romantic name) and a version of the hymn 'Nearer my God to Thee', which was published by the International Music Publishing Company in Durban.

My father, at around seventeen

Right here I need to pause and explain. Sometimes I am not quite sure about what we as children learnt and when; indeed, I am not always completely sure of the order of things. And insertions and corrections are very much reflective of my learning of my father's story.

According to my recollection, my father never ever mentioned any of Rose's compositions. He certainly did not say anything about them to me or in my hearing. He himself became a published and recorded composer, although of a very different type of music, and for some years he was very successful. Indeed, my mother received considerable royalties for years after he died. As children we loved playing his records and dancing around and singing to them. I've described this in Chapter 3.

So, why didn't he tell us that his mother also composed? Rose's compositions were not revealed to me until years later, when I was grown up, married and had my own children. Only now, in researching this, have I come to understand why he didn't talk about them to us, as I will explain a little later.

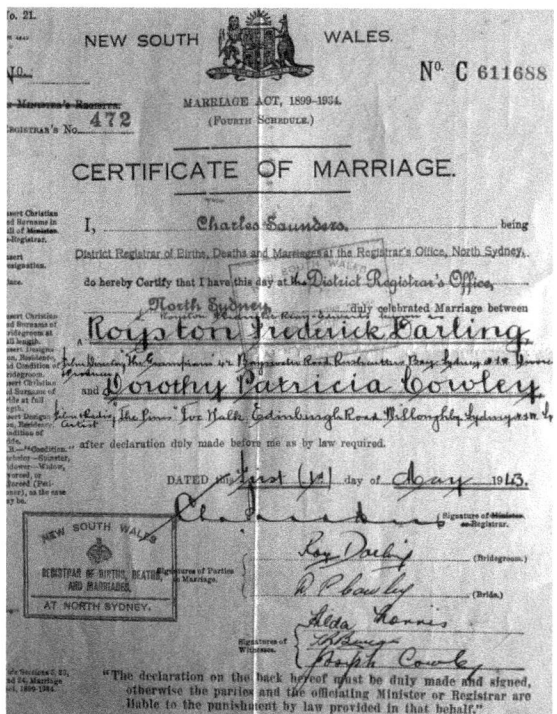

Marriage certificate: Dorothy Patricia Cowley to 'Royston Frederick Reay-Edwards, known as Royston Frederick Darling'

I'll try to order this chronologically: what we knew at the beginning and then what we found out later, which of course changed much of what we thought we knew. Known and unknown are tangled and interwoven and not straightforward.

I have described my parents' marriage in Chapter 1. My father was a film producer. My mother, Dorothy, met him whilst making a commercial; she was very young and still attending acting school at Doris Fitton's Independent Theatre and was already having some professional success. But this marriage to Dorothy all happened decades after his early years in Sydney as 'Roy Darling'. And there was another hidden story, which was not revealed until many years later and which Dorothy was never to know.

Until I was in my thirties, my mother, brothers and I believed my father was the son of Frederick Reay-Edwards and Rose Welles. On the marriage certificate, my father is named as 'Royston Frederick Reay-Edwards, known as Royston Frederick Darling' and described as a 'Film Director and Producer'. Mum (Dorothy Patricia) was named as a 'Film and Radio Artist'.

Mum obviously knew about my father's change of name and, as I have already mentioned, I somehow became aware of it as a child. I found it interesting and remember doodling my signature as 'Rosemary Ross Reay-Edwards'. The change of name, therefore, was not a secret. Why did he later discard that name? The story I was told then was that my father changed his name in South Africa, where, in his early days of film-making, he had played the part of a 'Roy Darling'. People began calling him by that name and it stuck.

But this was all to come a little later.

9.3 Frederick George Reay-Edwards (c. 1915 to c. 1920)

So, Frederick George Reay-Edwards, or a version thereof, probably came into being about 1915, when my father ran away from home and enlisted as a British subject in the Great War. As a child, I knew about him running away to war. I knew it was because he was very upset with his father, whom he blamed for his mother's death. Later I found out that Rose had died giving birth to her ninth child in October 1914.

Pte F.G.R. Edwards SAMCC

I don't remember my father telling me anything about his father. I knew that my father had put up his age to enlist and that he had at some point joined the South African Motor Cyclist Corps (SAMCC). Unfortunately, all SAMCC pertinent records, which were apparently kept in London, have been lost. His British war medals tell us he enlisted in the name of Frederick George Reay Edwards. This was probably the name he used from when he ran away from home in early 1915.

My son Robert, an historian, has pointed out that it looks like 'Frederick' was in uniform in his stamped passport photo prior to the trip from Bombay to Durban South Africa in July 1917. We still don't know the name of the corps from which he was earlier 'invalided from field service'. We think it was probably from Durban that he joined the South African Motor Cyclist Corps.

The South African Motor Cyclist Corps (World War I)

The Mesopotamian Campaign

The British Empire and the Ottoman Empire fought in Mesopotamia from 1914 to 1918. The Allied forces included British and Indian troops and some Australians and New Zealanders. My brother recalls my father telling him that he fought in this campaign at the Siege of Kut where he was shot in the leg and sent

An SAMCC dispatch rider of World War I

home. I don't remember hearing that story. But I remember another, which may be related. As small children, my father loved us doing what he called 'pulling his toes' (a sort of foot massage). I have a dim memory of him telling me that a white scar on his leg was caused by a bullet made out of nails and wire. There are reports that this was a common practice of the Turks when they ran out of real bullets during the Mesopotamian campaign.

Robert tracked my father's early movements:

> It looks like the passport was renewed in September 1921 at a British Consulate General office. It may not have been used for international travel between at least 1919 and 1921 because it may have lapsed. It looks like it was renewed twice on the same day in September 1921 (perhaps you had to pay the renewal fee twice if it had lapsed for two periods without being renewed). This was done at the British Consulate General office in Lourenco Marques, Portuguese East Africa (now Maputo, Mozambique).
>
> In September 1921 it initially looks like he went from South Africa to New York USA. However, after closer inspection it could be an endorsement, like a travel visa, to go to 'New York via South Africa'.

C. S. Forester's The African Queen (1935) is inspired by the East Africa Campaign of World War I. I remember seeing a copy of this book at home as a child

145

The South African Motor Cyclist Corps and the Campaign in German East Africa (WWI)

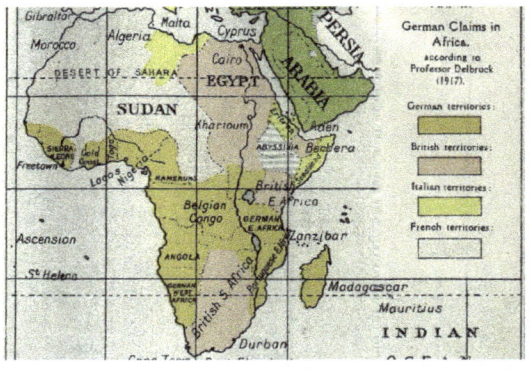

The South African Motor Cyclist Corps was formed in January 1916 under the command of Colonel James Fairweather. Four hundred motor cycles, with leather gun buckets mounted on the forks for carrying rifles or signalling equipment, were sent out from the UK. They were adapted to carry 140 lbs of kit besides the rider.

Germany took the East Africa Campaign very seriously. It was where aircraft were first used as spotters in naval warfare and where the entire crew of the German cruiser Königsberg were awarded the Iron Cross. Two gunboats were carried 3,000 miles into the war zone at Lake Tanganyika overland from Cape Town by railway and then dragged in turn by traction engines and hundreds of 'porters'.

The South African Motor Cyclist Corps delivered equipment and despatches into the war zones, often travelling long distances over very difficult terrain and having to pull their heavy machines over sand and up hills.

This endorsement was issued at the same office as his passport renewals. The signature looks like the same person on both the 'New York' page and the 'Renewal' page, plus there is the same Lourenco Marques stamp, as well as the faded blue text stamp which signs off saying something like 'Acting British Consul General, Lourenco Marques'.

There is no typical United States of America eagle entry stamp, unless there are other documents I haven't seen. Inconveniently, there is no entry stamp into Australia and I can't seem to locate any passenger arrival record at the Australian National Archives online search under that name or other known names between September 1921 and July 1922. It is possible he planned to go to the USA but was suddenly able to hitch a ride to Australia and just did that instead. I also couldn't readily find his name in the online USA Ellis Island arrival register.

His marriage certificate in Australia names him as 'Frederick George Reay-Edwards, known as Royston Frederick Darling'. So he must have used documents with that name to prove his identity in Australia, even though he had publicly started using his stage name Roy Darling as soon as he arrived or beforehand in Africa or elsewhere. As you know it was quite common for stage and screen players to take a different name that would look snappy on a billboard, e.g. Cary Grant was originally Archibald Alec Leach. His daughter's name is Jennifer Grant.

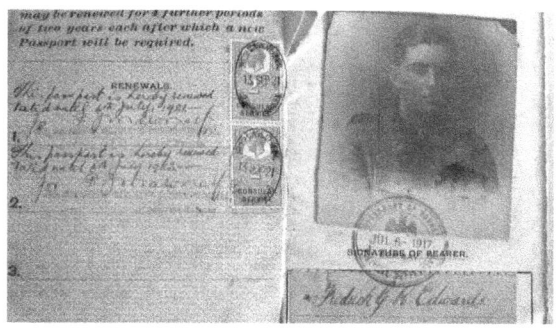

As Robert says, while it is possible Frederick went to New York, it seems improbable since he is confirmed in newspapers as directing a movie in Sydney in July 1922. It would have been a very short trip. More significantly, I don't think any of us ever heard him talk about a trip to the States.

So, whilst there is some uncertainty about his activities between 1915 and 1921, we can be sure that by 1922 he was in Sydney, New South Wales, Australia, making his mark.

9.4 Royston Frederick Reay-Edwards known as Royston Frederick Darling (c. 1922 to 1956)

My father is mentioned as 'Roy Darling' in Sydney newspapers of October 1922, and I will refer to him as 'Roy' from now on. Clippings at that time record that 'his services have been procured as directing producer' for Olympic Films, 'a new Australian producing Company'. They also note that he has been involved in the movies *King Solomon's Mines* (1919) and *Prester John* (1920), both of which were filmed in South Africa/East Africa, where he was an assistant producer.

So, it is apparent that Roy spent time in South Africa and that very soon after the war it was here that he somehow became involved in theatre and film-making. (A recent academic paper notes the leading role being played in the film industry around this time by South African film-makers.) Some family rumours have him also going to New Zealand for a short period. There is also some evidence that in South Africa he may have been, in some way, involved in the filming of wildlife and wildlife safaris (or perhaps observing or acting in them as an extra). Other reports note that in 1919 he directed a documentary in India called *Beasts in the Jungle*.

This interest in wildlife fits in with some of my childhood memories. He truly respected the large animals of Africa and the East. As very young children we all knew about, even if we didn't actually witness, his passionate and indeed angry reaction to the deplorable conditions of the elephants in their enclosure during the early days at Taronga Park Zoo in Sydney. Indeed, I feel as if I have a strong early memory of being at the zoo with both my parents when I was very small (no more than five) and wanting to go for a ride on the elephant. I can see in my mind's eye even now the row of people and children lined up and waiting against a stone wall and a dark bank of trees and, although the memory is only hazy, recall my parents being very upset when they saw the heartbreakingly resigned slouch of the elephant trudging back to unload and reload its human cargo.

Did I hear the anguish of my mother, who loved animals, as well as the anger of my father at such exploitation of this proud and gutsy creature of the bush, of the veld, of the jungle? Or is that a gloss of memory or perhaps of retelling? I'm not sure. But we left the zoo soon afterwards. I do know that I no longer wanted a ride; even as a small girl I had glimpsed the horror and despair of that beautiful shackled animal, dragging chains and confined to a monotonous few steps up and down a concrete track. Afterwards, my father wrote several urgent letters to Sir Edward Hallstrom, then chair of the Taronga Zoological Park Trust, complaining about the conditions in which the elephants were kept.

Many years later, I was taken by South African academic colleagues on a wonderful and mind-enhancing tour of Kruger National Park where we stayed overnight. I'll never forget the sights and sounds of that amazing time. We were fortunate enough to see, roaming free, at least one member of all of the so-called Big Five (rhinoceros, buffalo, elephant, leopard and lion). The lioness was very close and intent on mothering her small cubs, little fluffs the colour of honey curled up in long grass that seemed, in that bush palette, just one shade paler than her offspring. I also saw beautiful elephants, strong and free, insistently pushing their way through the wild, waving their trunks around exuberantly, and I was transported back over decades of time and the spaces of continents and fully and profoundly understood why my father was so upset.

So, as a youngster of about twenty-one, and before the many revelations that were still to come, Roy already had an intriguing past.

9.5 Roy Darling's crusade

Young Roy became a leading crusader, however incongruously, in the beginnings of an Australian film industry. The name 'Frederick George Reay-Edwards' was changed to 'Roy Darling' soon after (or just prior to) my father's arrival in Australia, probably around 1920. As noted earlier, this is the name in which Roy married my mother (Dorothy Patricia) on 1 May, 1943.

Roy kept a scrapbook, which I knew about and had seen but was never actually encouraged to go through. It is now in the possession of one of my brothers and is around one hundred years old. I asked my brother to digitise the scrapbook, which he has done. We now all have a copy. While I sometimes saw bits of it as a child, I have now been through it all for the first time.

What really amazes me is that Roy, this young man in his very early twenties, with his Oxford accent and genuinely British, rather old-fashioned (even then!) courteous manner, became such a passionate, perhaps even aggressive, crusader for Australia, for Australian history, for Australian music – country music! – and for Australian film.

From my father's scrapbook, 1 October 1922

The National Film and Sound Archive of Australia in Canberra lists most of Roy's achievements. The remnants of film are not in a wonderful condition and they are not the best examples of his film work. Much was, very sadly, lost years ago in a flood in my mother's home on the Central Coast. Royston, the oldest of my three brothers, fortunately took what was left to the National Archive. But his music, which came later (in the late 1940s), is memorable and evocative. 'The Overlander Trail' has been very popular, as noted in Chapter 1, and has retained its popularity, with frequent re-recordings. The only recording of Roy's 'Eureka: The Stockade Song', however, which was performed by Buddy Williams, does not do the music or the lyrics justice. I would love to see it re-recorded. It deserves to be. It feels a particularly appropriate song for both Australia and for Roy, indeed so much so that I've used it as an endpiece to this chapter.

Roy directed his first Australian film, *The Lust for Gold*, in 1922, financing the enterprise with his own money. The film secured only a limited release. According to reports, because of the difficulty in obtaining screenings, he lost all the money he had invested in it. This began his long-running battle against powerful international monopolies that sought to discourage the production and screening of Australian moving films.

His second feature film, previewed under the title *The Boy of the Dardanelles* and later exhibited as *Daughter of the East*, was, as the numerous clippings show, not only an Australian story, but 'first and last an Australian production'. The film was shot around Sydney in mid-1923, with its battlefield scenes played out at Maroubra Beach. It was financed by a Greek businessman who was committed to showing how Greeks had contributed to the British war effort during World War I.

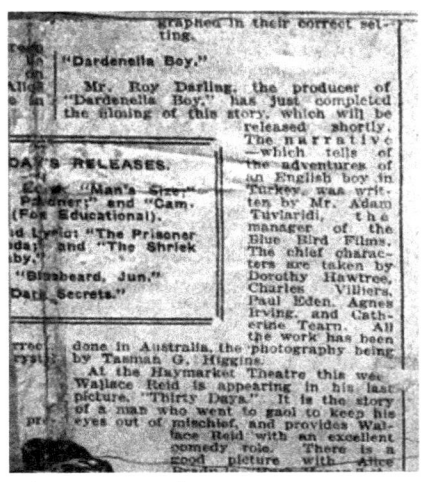
Sydney newspaper clipping, 23 June 1923

Again it was a struggle to get the 'photoplay' (as it's referred to in the press clipping here) released, but Roy eventually succeeded in making a deal with Paramount Pictures.

This film was made in Australia on the cusp of the transition from silent movies to 'talkies'. It is an important part of Australian cinema history, not so much for what it was, but for what it represented. Although it did not do well at the box office, *Daughter of the East* helped to develop an Australian awareness of the possibility of, and an Australian appetite for, films made in Australia and with Australian content.

My father's scrapbook contains many clippings from these early years and they tell an enthralling story. From the beginning, and more-or-less out of nowhere, Roy and his various partners demonstrated not only a passion for encouraging Australian film-making, but also an entrepreneurial spirit in seeking ways to do so. As shown in the clippings here, he somehow managed to get his film into screenings with a film starring Hollywood screen goddess Gloria Swanson (*A Society Scandal*); in some of the advertisements *Daughter of the East* is tucked

9. Revelations

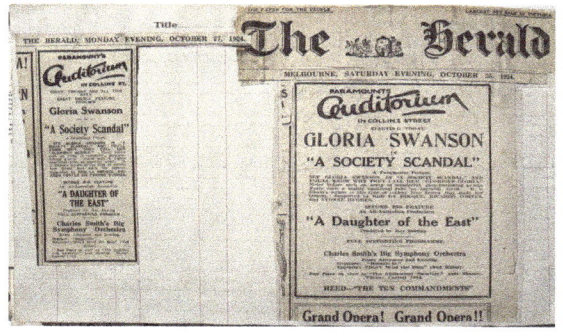

'A Daughter of the East' – Produced by Roy Darling

away in the bottom corner, but in others it is much more conspicuous. I imagine much negotiation would have been needed to make this happen, particularly when faced with negative and unhelpful (and powerful) opposition.

Roy ran all sorts of special showings and invited political and community leaders to attend. He and his partners appear to have been cluey in inviting influential people to their various screenings. The correspondence shows the excitement of, for example, the Dickens Society when invited to a special showing of the Dickens classic *Little Dorrit*. Roy had an impressive correspondence, of which now only traces remain. He wrote to the principals of Sydney's elite high schools and colleges to invite them and their students to attend. When I came across these letters in the scrapbook, I had a strange feeling: this is what we had done, half a century later, at the University

'Moving picture manufacture in Australia is advancing rapidly … Mr Roy Darling has been engaged by the company as producer … Mr Darling directed and produced 'A Daughter of the East', which was released by Paramount at the Globe Theatre Sydney and at the Auditorium in Melbourne. He was responsible for the recent film controversy for the advancement of film production in Australia, which caused such a stir amongst the American Film Exchanges in this country'

of Technology Sydney (UTS) Centre for Research and Education in the Arts, of which I was director. We organised dramatic productions (with tutorials) of texts on the senior syllabus that were performed by university students for school audiences. We also produced, with students, multiple shows for primary schools, including one very successful musical play on road safety, which was sponsored by the Road Traffic Authority and which was attended over several weeks by thousands of primary students (see Ch 10).

After *Lust for Gold* and *A Daughter of the East* and the various struggles and battles Roy had in order to obtain both financial backing and screening rights, he became a vocal advocate for changing government policies about film rights and the need to oppose the increasing power and influence of self-interested American monopolies on distribution. In fact, he started and appears to have become a leader in a campaign towards advocating for these changes.

The struggle that was to dominate the next twenty-five or so years of his life had begun.

The Royal Commission on the Moving Picture Industry in Australia, 1926–1928

The fight was now on to produce Australian films with Australian content that Australians could actually go and see, and Roy was playing a leading role.

In early 1925 he started bringing interested parties together and arranging meetings with leading political figures. After insistent lobbying, this led, in 1926, to the establishment of a royal commission to inquire into the moving picture industry in Australia.

Roy was among other leading directors called as witnesses to give evidence to this inquiry. They were also considerably concerned about a proposed amalgamation between Union Theatres Ltd and Hoyts Ltd that would make it even more difficult to secure screenings.

During their appearances at the commission, the various witnesses recounted dubious practices that both discouraged local filmmaking and exploited it. The newspaper reports copied here encapsulate and indeed foreshadow the long battle that they, and many who followed later, would have to wage in the fight to claim the right to produce and screen Australian content.

The comments made to the minister included: that film supply houses which used to be Australian-owned were now American-owned and American-controlled, that a first-grade Australian picture had no chance in the local market, and even when the American combine consented to show an Australian picture they 'froze' it. Suggestions to the minister included:

Advance Australia

that all theatres in Australia should have to screen a certain percentage of Australian films, that American imports should be limited to eighty-five per cent and that first-grade Australian films should receive an *ad valorem* bonus out of the entertainment tax, and that Australian producers should not have to ask American permission to show Australian films.

Street photograph of Roy Darling c. 1920s

> **Mr Raymond Longford,** an Australian producer, gave evidence on the need for developing an inter-imperial film market. Australian films had not been screened as frequently as might have been desired, he said.
>
> The chairman: In reading the evidence of Mr. Stuart Doyle, I notice he says he has screened ten of your productions in his theatres. Do you say that is not a fair showing?
>
> Mr Longford: I do. Mr. Doyle has not screened that number.
>
> Witness added that picture exhibition was largely in the hands of a combine. He considered that all theatres in Australia should be required to screen a certain number of Australian films.
>
> https://trove.nla.gov.au/newspaper/article/16422603

> *The Sydney Morning Herald* **Mon 20 June 1927 p.14**
>
> **FILM INDUSTRY**
>
> **GERMAN PICTURES.**
>
> **Preference Over Australian**
>
> Giving evidence on Saturday before the Royal Commission which is inquiring into the film Industry in Australia, **Mr Roy Darling**, an Australian producer, declared that German films were able to obtain a screening at Australian picture theatres where Australian productions could not.
>
> He said that he knew of a picture coming to Australia under the guise of a British production in which all the actors were Germans and the leading lady was an Austrian. He did not think it fair that foreign-made pictures of this kind should be screened in preference to those made in Australia.
>
> Witness went on to describe his experiences with local distributors and his difficulties in arranging for screenings of pictures which he had produced. In 1922 he made "The Lust for Gold", but was unable to secure a release, and lost £900 upon it. In 1924 he made "The Daughter of the East", for which he obtained a screening only after considerable trouble through Paramount Pictures, and his receipts amounted to £50.
>
> Other producers had been treated unfairly by Union Theatres, Ltd., which controlled the majority of the theatres in Sydney. **He understood that an amalgamation between Union Theatres, Ltd., and Hoyts, Ltd., was contemplated.**
>
> **If it were accomplished there would be no possible chance for Australian producers to secure screenings**. [my emphasis]
>
> The Inquiry was adjourned to Brisbane.
>
> https://trove.nla.gov.au/newspaper/article/16385685

Newspaper reports of the time reflect enthusiasm to address these concerns, but the results of the commission were disappointing. Unfortunately, these problems and issues would continue to dominate Australian moviemaking for at least the next twenty-five years and arguably are ongoing. As Ray Edmondson wrote in 'The long shadow of 1927' (part of an online publication, *Re-evaluating the Royal Commission into the Australian Moving Picture Industry, 1927–28*, Volume 9, 2015, Issue 3, pp. 230–240):

Despite their hopes, the Commission's work would not advance the fortunes of so many of the significant industry figures who gave evidence and placed their hopes in it. Instead they would soon, effectively, disappear from the scene as the 'talkie' era took over. Australia's biggest silent epic, *For the Term of His Natural Life*, was released in 1927. The creation and the fate of this mammoth production, directed by American Norman Dawn, is in many ways a metaphor for the Commission's deliberations and ultimate outcome: **the cultural cringe which accompanied the eclipse of Australian talent by overseas practitioners, the slow contraction of Australian production, and the destruction of its silent heritage.** [my emphasis]

In the same publication, in a piece entitled 'American combine: Australasian Films Ltd., and block bookings', Stephen Gaunson writes:

> With the Commission established, in part, to explore the accusation of an American combine ruling the exhibition industry, and stunting the local production sector, the real question was whether the Commissioners would be persuaded to make recommendations to wrest the powers from America, and consequently redirect the local exhibition industry's dependence on Hollywood movies. https://www.tandfonline.com/doi/full/10.1080/17503175.2015.1087122

The commission was held at a crux time for moviemaking: sound was now about to take over the old silent movies. Brian Yeceis claims that this provoked further aggressive moves by powerful American companies seeking to overwhelm local producers and **ensure American monopoly not only in product but in technology** [my emphasis]:

The Daily Telegraph, 11 Feb 1925

> The 1927–1928 Royal Commission on the Moving Picture Industry in Australia sought to strengthen the domestic film industry's competitiveness against foreign investment, technology and manpower. Although it concluded before the wide-scale rollout of sound exhibition, it began collecting evidence after the coming of sound had already begun to make waves. Beginning in 1924 and continuing beyond the Commission, agents of the US De Forest Phonofilms company, primed the local market for sound through a series of publicity events. Their activities led the local trade

press to dub the Australian Phonofilms franchise as the instigator of a 'Talkie War', challenging the Commission's ability to curtail the expansion of human capital and technology from the USA. Within a year of its conclusion, agents from the US Western Electric company arrived in Australia to wire the major capital city theatres with sound. Initially, this strengthened Hollywood's foothold in ways that the Commission was anxious to avoid. Hoyts Theatres intensified the 'Talkie-gear war' by backing the 'Australian-made' Markophone as a competitor to the US Fox–Movietone sound system. Hence, while the Commission failed to achieve its aims, local pioneers took action by innovating rival sound systems with local technology, engineering and showmanship. (pp. 253–270).

So, it was a time of controversy and powerful deals, proposed mergers and monopolies. It was also a time of great change; the film-making industry and cinemas were undergoing a radical technological transformation as they moved from silent movies into 'talkies.' Roy obviously maintained his advocacy and correspondence. We don't have copies of his letters but do have some replies.

During this period Roy married for the first time and had a daughter, whom he spoke about to Mum and occasionally mentioned to me. I liked that her name had the same melody of syllables as mine: three syllables in the first name and one syllable in the middle name. However, the marriage became very unhappy and eventually ended in divorce. The divorce appears to have been acrimonious. This was, of course, years before the 'no-fault divorce' and guilt had to be attributed for the legal process to continue. To my knowledge, my father never saw his first daughter again. Mum told me on several occasions, however, that Roy had very much wanted me to be a girl to help fill the gap made by the loss of his first daughter. Mum, on the other hand, made no secret of the fact she had wanted a boy so that she could have called him after our father.

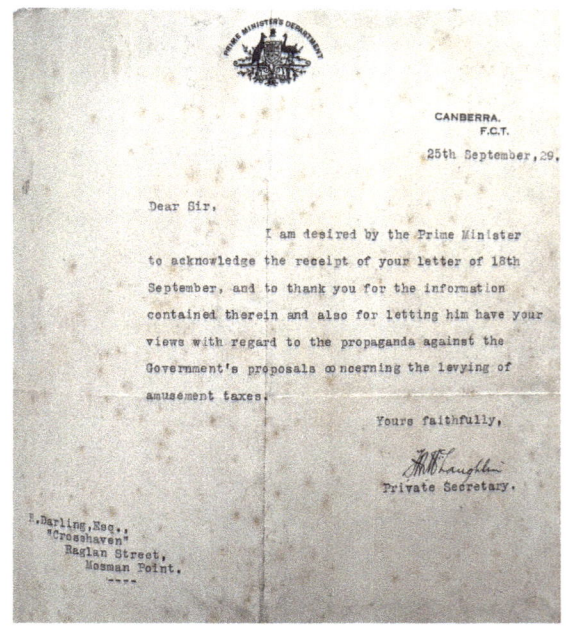

None of this, of course, helped Roy's case when, years later, he sought to marry seventeen-year-old Dorothy Patricia. As noted in Chapter 1, the family opposition to the match was very strong. Her father, Joseph, and siblings, Hilda and Les, attended the wedding and were witnesses, but her mother, my precious Grandma, did not. Yet Mum and Grandma, who called me her 'Little Apricot', remained close and depended on and loved each other all their lives. In another strange twist, that I was to learn many years later, for different reasons there had also been vigorous family opposition to Roy's own parents' marriage.

Roy had helped his first wife's family with a subdivision of what is now the sought-after 'golden triangle' of Newport. We didn't know this at the time, but it was very close to *Kerensa*, which Malcolm and I built in 1968 and moved into in April 1969. Rather amazingly, Malcolm, who bought the block years before we met, had selected land only about a kilometre away from that subdivision, in which Roy had helped name some of the roads. Hollywood Road is among those that survive to this day. He and his first wife also lived (or at least holidayed) there for a period. Mum told me he used to love fishing off Newport Reef. He also did this later, when he and Mum lived for a short time at the Rock Lily in Mona Vale, which he had purchased. But it worried her as Roy, apparently, couldn't swim.

Roy's struggle against the powerful forces seeking to control and indeed inhibit independent Australian film-making continued. He and other Australian producers continually found obstacles in their way: difficulties in obtaining distribution and screening rights and even in getting hold of the continuously upgraded technologies of the flourishing and developing industry.

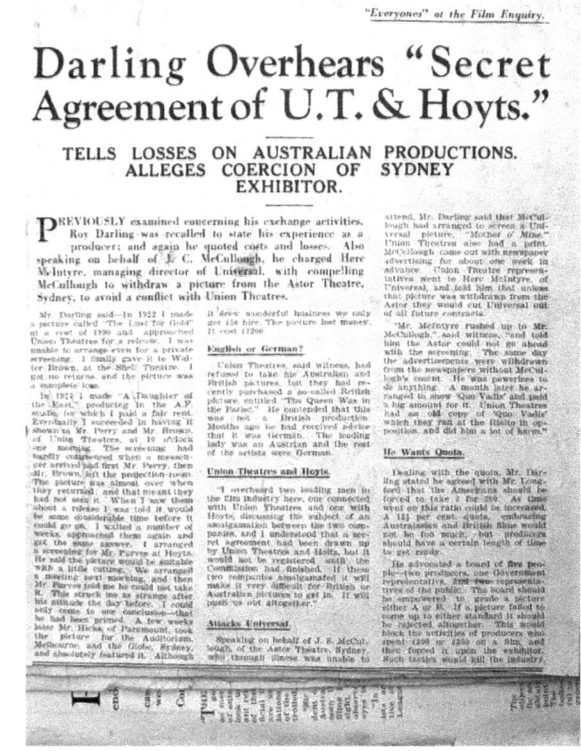

The ongoing crusade for Australian content and production

Professionally, he was now working mainly on documentaries, educational films and commercials. He made two short films: *The Hand that Rocks the Cradle* (1942) and *He Chased a Chicken* (1946). He did not attempt any further feature films until 1947, when he began filming *The Intimate Stranger*. This movie was financed by Endeavour Film Productions Ltd, which had been created by a group of businessmen with the intention of producing one feature and four shorts a year. It was based on a novel by William Lynch.

Advertising described it as:

> Completely unlike anything attempted before … the most interesting film project yet undertaken in this country … the characters are real people, with the authentic ring of the present day. The story unfolds against a background of the more Bohemian sections of Kings Cross and the idyllic seclusion of the Pacific coast near Palm Beach.

Well-known radio actor John Saul was to play the lead, Paul Garner, 'a strangely complex personality' who gets involved with an 'alluring model', Kitty (Georgie Sterling). The rest of the cast was mostly taken from popular radio actors, including Sydney Wheeler and Lloyd Lamble. Screen tests for young actors were held at Supreme Sound Studios in February 1947. June Dally-Watkins also worked on the movie doing make up.

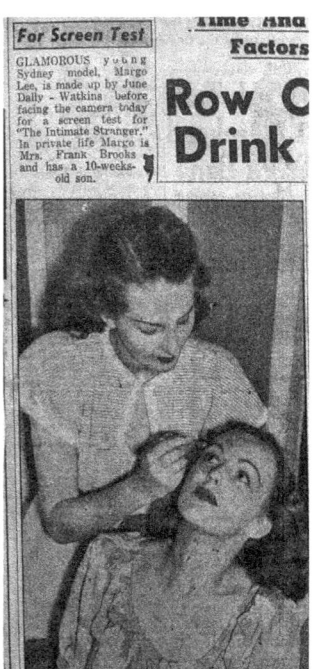

The Intimate Stranger (unfinished film)	
Directed by	Roy Darling
Produced by	William Lynch
Written by	William Lynch
Based on	novel by William Lynch
Starring	John Saul
	Georgie Sterling
Cinematography	Carl Kyser
Production company	Endeavour Film Productions Ltd
Release date	1948 (intended)
Running time	Incomplete
Country	Australia
Language	English

The Intimate Stranger was a proposed Australian feature film from director Roy Darling. The film was never completed although some scenes were shot and the cast included some of the country's finest actors. It was billed as a 'psychological drama'. (*Wikipedia*)

The Sun, 12 Feb 1947. June Dally-Watkins, later to become 'Miss Dally', was the make-up artist for the screen tests of Roy's 'The Intimate Stranger'

From The Film Weekly, 24 April 1947

Unfortunately the proposed movie was to be made during a time of considerable turmoil in the film industry, with Actors Equity fighting Ealing Studios, Columbia Pictures and Charles Chauvel over minimum weekly wages for actors. The union sought to increase this from £18 a week to £20. Producers of *The Intimate Stranger* had their pay rates approved by Equity and the actors were able to continue with stage and/or radio work provided it did not interfere with the film's production schedule. Filming began in April 1947 in North Sydney, with William Constable as art designer. However, the times were inauspicious and the movie ran out of money and was never completed. (*Wikipedia*)

The Second World War 1939–1945

In 1939, Australians, all too soon, had to prepare for a global war again, and this one would come frighteningly close, with Japanese midget submarines actually in Sydney Harbour. Indeed, from February 1942 through to November 1943, the Australian mainland and Australia's domestic airspace, offshore islands and

coastal shipping were attacked at least 111 times by Japanese aircraft. Most Australians at the time did not know how serious the bombing of Darwin actually was. (Baz Luhrmann's film *Australia* dramatically portrays this.)

Whereas Australia's involvement in World War I emerged out of loyalty to Great Britain and the Empire, in World War II there was a much stronger and more personal fear and desire for defence. Roy, at forty-one, made enquiries but was not accepted into the Citizen Military Forces. So he swung whole-heartedly into the war effort and began arranging artists and shows.

'Keep Smiling', supporting the war effort

Roy on set, sitting in director's chair

The Tatler Theatre, Sydney (later, as seen here, the Paris)

The Tatler Theatre (1935–1950)

The Australian Picture Palace, which was situated in a prime position overlooking Sydney's Hyde Park, was designed by Walter Burley Griffin and opened in January 1916. In 1935 it was renovated and renamed the Tatler Theatre; in 1952 it was renovated again and renamed the Park Theatre; two years later it was renamed (again) the Paris Theatre. In 1981 the theatre was, very sadly, demolished.

Roy's ongoing struggles to obtain distribution and screening rights for both local and overseas films had developed in him a desire to have his own theatre. Earlier, he had demonstrated interest in several suburban theatres, including the Kings at Spit Junction. In the later forties he successfully leased a city theatre, the Tatler, on the corner of Liverpool Street and Wentworth Avenue.

> *Joseph Benedict Chifley (1885–1951)*
> Sixteenth Prime Minister of Australia 1945–1949. Roy wrote to him (13 August 1947) about American companies stifling Australian film and cinema (see Ch 1).

These were tumultuous years. The government was considering drastic cuts in Australia's expenditure on American motion pictures. The distributors met with Prime Minister Ben Chifley. When 'Austral American Productions' came to an exclusive arrangement with Warner Brothers to release only Warner Bros films, the Tatler reopened as a first-run theatre. But three years later, now limited, it had to switch to revival screenings.

And there was more trouble. On 28 August 1947, *The Film Weekly* reported: 'Australian film production today lies dead in the blood-running gutter'. (See clipping). The problem was Britain's imposition of a seventy-five per cent tax on imported films – not only on American films but also on those made in Australia.

The last two paragraphs in this press report state:

> Roy Darling, Director of Endeavour Film's *Intimate Stranger* disagreed that the tax would cripple Australian production and claimed it is possible to make good films cheaply enough to get their cost back in Australia.

Roy went on to say (as quoted):

> More important to Australian producers than the new tax … is the position of raw stock. If American raw stocks are cut, the English firm, Ilford, may not be able to supply both Britain's and Australia's needs. (*The Film Weekly*, 28 August 1947)

The Film Weekly, 28 Aug 1947

The struggle was ongoing and about to become bloodier. In 1942, the Federal Government had brought in the Entertainments Tax Act, which by 1948 added up to thirty per cent to the cost of adult cinema tickets. However, tickets to live theatrical entertainments paid twenty-five per cent less than film screenings. Further, after World War II, cinema patronage declined as the cost of living rose both in Australia and around the world. It was a bleak period. The famous Rank Organisation of Britain announced a loss of over £3.5 million for 1949 and began closing down almost all its production studios. The big Hollywood studios were also affected and had to make drastic cuts. The Tatler Theatre's average takings fell dramatically.

'Live' Theatre returns

In November 1949, when it became almost impossible for Roy to obtain screening and distribution rights and faced with high taxes, rising costs, falling revenue and flagging audiences, Roy terminated film screenings and took the radical step of turning the Tatler Theatre into a venue for live theatre and staging plays and live revues. There were two shows a day, at 3.00 pm and 8.00 pm. They featured tap dancers, ventriloquists, fan dancers,

Chinese magic acts, vocalists, balancing acts, contortionists and jugglers, all with the added attractions of the Charlie Steel Orchestra and ballet (the 'Tatler Lovelies').

The move was immensely popular and at first very successful. 'Legitimate theatre booms in Sydney', trumpeted the press.

The critics of the day also applauded the move, as this celebratory article (see following) by David McNicoll shows. Note the last paragraphs, which are quoted below.

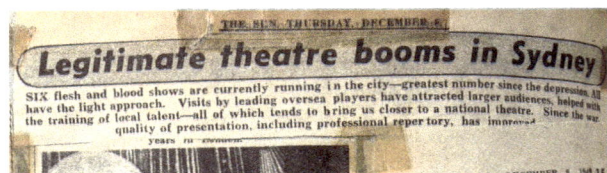

The Sun, 8 Dec 1949

> ***Daily Telegraph* 1 December 1949**
>
> ***Seven stage shows pack 'em in – it's like 1899 again***
>
> ****The 'legitimate' stage in Sydney has made a comeback …***
>
> As audiences fell off, the movie magnates in their plush offices felt the draught.
>
> Some of the results are very recent – sackings of theatre orchestras, other economies effected to save money.
>
> But while the cinema feels for the first time the chill wind of public depression, the live theatre is experiencing its greatest shot in the arm.
>
> Today you have The Royal, The Minerva, The Palace, The Empire, The Tatler, The Independent – all playing to packed houses. It's like going back to 1899 again.

Despite this praise and applause, this was a very difficult period in social history. A post-war sense of depression continued and was pervasive, and after a while the novelty of live theatre started to wane. By early 1950, desperate to keep his theatre afloat and egged on by less courageous (or less foolhardy) voices, Roy announced that out of respect to his patrons he would not put up his theatre prices but would instead pay the government's entertainment tax into the theatre's general revenue. Further, he would seek to have the Commonwealth of Australia's Entertainments Tax Act of 1942 and Amendments of 1944 and 1946 repealed.

The NSW Chief Secretary, Claude Matthews, retaliated by banning the Tatler live shows, claiming concerns about safety issues as the reason.

Live Shows Banned at Tatler Theatre

> The Chief Secretary's Department has ordered the Tatler Theatre, Liverpool Street; to cease live shows. He says the management is committing a breach of the Theatres and Public Halls Act by not having an exit on the right-hand side of the theatre. The penalty for this breach, if a conviction is obtained, is a fine of £100 each day after receipt of the department's letter closing the theatre.
>
> Mr. Roy Darling, director of the theatre, said yesterday that he would continue with live shows. If the department succeeds in its order, more than 60 artists and employees would be thrown out of work. Mr. Darling said the Tatler had three fire exits on the left-hand side. 'It has more fire exits than many other city theatres which are presenting flesh and blood shows,' he added.
>
> Mr. Hal Alexander, Actors Equity secretary, said his association would support Mr. Darling. (*The Sunday Herald*, 11 December 1949)

Roy was fined a total of £120 on three charges of failure to pay entertainment tax in March. He was also fined £200 for not paying tax on his employees' wages. This soon got him into further trouble with the Chief Secretary, who said the current production was in defiance of the law because the temporary A-class licence issued some months before was on the understanding that alterations would be made in the interests of safety. The theatre was built as a picture theatre (and was originally given a B-class licence for this purpose) and did not have a wide enough stage or the backstage facilities required by live performers.

Roy told the court that he had lost £7,000 during the last nine months and that he was in the process of negotiating for a stage play, which he hoped would be a financial success. That play, *Rusty Bugles*, by Sumner Locke Elliott (who was later to become famous for *Careful, He Might Hear You*), had been produced by the highly-respected Doris Fitton at the Independent Theatre and had enjoyed a long successful run at the King's Theatre in Melbourne.

Sadly, it was only going to bring Roy more trouble.

Rusty Bugles

Rusty Bugles depicted the life of bored soldiers in a Northern Territory army camp. The play had already survived a series of skirmishes with state chief secretaries and censors; Doris Fitton had to rewrite and replace some of the words in her original production at the Independent. In Melbourne, the Chief Secretary of Victoria insisted on the replacement (with 'ruddy') of many of the seventeen occurrences of 'bloody' in the first act.

Rusty Bugles was an interesting choice of play for the Tatler. No doubt there were pragmatic reasons for it, but such a choice seems to demonstrate a progressive spirit that belies its times. In a study of 'Great Australian Plays after World War II', Professor Julian Meyrick, Professor of Creative Arts at Griffith University, describes *Rusty Bugles* as a comedy-drama that up until *Summer of the Seventeenth Doll* six years later was 'the best known and most successful Australian play of its day'.

Rusty Bugles theatre advertisement

The play is set in the Northern Territory during the summer of 1944 within an army supply depot. Professor Meyrick describes what he calls its 'revolutionary features': the characters are the story, and its language is what *The Sun* called 'unladylike, but beautifully lusty, and one hundred per cent Orstyrlian'.

Cartoon by Mercier

Lusty indeed! The chief secretary sent the vice squad along to opening night. Meyrick writes:

> The language of *Rusty Bugles* is not only remarkable; it is remarkably assured. While British dramatists were stuck in the tar pit of what critic Ken Tynan scathingly called 'the Loamshire play', Locke Elliot was idiomatically portraying the realities of class and region. In so doing, he advanced Australian drama by more than an addition of one good play …

Australian drama is a fugue drama, at once part of

the larger body of Anglophone playwriting and radically distinct from it. *Rusty Bugles* is an important link between the plot-based realism of the 1920s and 1930s, exemplified by companies like The Pioneer Players, and the radical explorations of the Australian voice that characterise 1970s writers like Jack Hibberd, David Williamson, Alma de Groen and Dorothy Hewett ...

It is a great thing to write a play about human affection that has little affectionate dialogue in it; a play about war that has no fighting in it; a play about Australia with no self-consciousness, stridency or nationalist bathos. https://theconversation.com/the-great-australian-plays-speaking-orstyrlian-in-rusty-bugles-69642

Doris Fitton wrote the introduction to the 1980 re-publication of the play (which restored all the original language):

I consider *Rusty Bugles* to be *the* war play, at least for this country. *Rusty Bugles* was based in reality, in people that Sumner knew; and based on the little things, however trifling, that happened from day to day in this isolated ordnance camp.

He had written the play, he told me, as a protest against bureaucracy: in memory of hundreds of men up there rotting in an ordnance depot who had wanted to be on active service to their country. Of course, it is a long time ago that we first presented *Rusty Bugles*; but I still believe it to be the best Australian play ever written.

Did Roy perceive all this? Seventy years later, I just don't know. The music he was also writing about this time – 'The Overlander Trail' and 'Eureka: The Stockade Song' in particular – is so patriotic, so Australian in tone, it is hard not to see them as an expression of battling for a cause you believe in and keeping on, even against the odds. *'Come on men/It's our turn'*, he wrote in 'Eureka: The Stockade Song', *'Men of every nationality/Fought against the troopers to be free'*. *'We're on the Overlander, Overlander Trail/Where only sheer determination will prevail'*, he wrote in 'The Overlander Trail'.

But the fight for Roy was almost over. The NSW Chief Secretary, who had expressed concerns about the Tatler's exits, also insisted that the offending adjectives were removed. At first there were full houses and good reviews, but the controversies continued, leading to financial losses. Roy had lost the battle and in September 1950 the Tatler Theatre closed down. And, almost six years later, Roy suddenly died.

Defending the Stockade (from Roy's Eureka: The Stockade Song)

Diggers everyone and what care we
Burn our permits let the troopers see
We are going to fight until the end
For the right we must defend

To some, Roy was a crusader, to some, in taking on the powerful American conglomerates, most likely a madman. Contemporary reports were both admiring and disparaging; and several of the later ones are ill-informed. He had many people onside, including, as previously noted, Hal Alexander, the secretary of Actors Equity. He had an enormous amount of support, both from actors and the general community.

I was barely five years old and didn't know any of this at the time and indeed have only found out much of it in the writing of this memoir. I can't imagine how Mum – a scant twenty-four years old when all this happened and with three very small children – survived. I do know she had incredible support from Grandma Elsie and the rest of the family, and she never ever stopped loving him; she loved him through thirty years of widowhood. She never spoke about this 'Tatler period' to me, but one of my brothers tells me that she did speak to him. It was a hard time. But Mum, for all her quiet softness, had a core of steel where her loved ones were concerned. Sadly, we have been without her now for many years. On her recent birthday I wrote this to my family:

> Today is Mum's, Grandma Darling's, birthday. I've just been looking out at the sky and thanking God for her – and saw little streamers of blessings she has brought to all of us: love of course, loyalty, awareness of life as a spiritual experience, the 'eyes of her mind' that saw beauty all around her, a sense of the dramatic in the everyday, tenacity and the willingness and energy and determination to work hard, a far vision that always saw what could be in what is. I see bits of these, strongly, in all of us, and am grateful.

Roy was jaunty and fun and emotional and sentimental; he was extremely clever and smart and creative and quick and eloquent and impractical and sometimes, perhaps, unwise. I hope I have portrayed him here truthfully, fairly, compassionately and, most of all, lovingly.

AN OPEN LETTER TO EXHIBITORS AND OTHERS WHO MAY BE INTERESTED IN FILM PRODUCTION IN AUSTRALIA

Gentlemen,

The way is open for us to make <u>Our Own Pictures</u> for <u>Our Own Theatres</u> to show to <u>Our Own People</u>.

The American Film Combine is already within measurable distance of being brought to its knees. Probably the most powerful monopoly Great Britain and this country has seen is on the verge of elimination.

Arthur Rank set the ball rolling ... the serious position in Great Britain, though regrettable ... carried it on.

Some years ago a showman said ... "the Australian Exhibitor doesn't amount to the squeal in the Chicago Meatworks."

<u>Exhibitors</u> ... why remain "The Marionettes of the Movies?" In the first place, you do not buy on an "open market." You hire ... which makes a vital difference. You do not even hire on an "open market," for you have no say as to what pictures come into the country. Your hiring is done on a "local market" in which you are allowed to select the "exchange." When you make your choice you shed your freedom.

<u>Get behind the Australian Film Production Industry</u>. It needs your co-operation and help to build it into something worthwhile.

<u>Why be dependent upon another country to keep your theatres running?</u>

<u>Archer Whitford</u> once offered £100,000 towards the erection of studios to foster local productions, provided the Government allocated a similar amount for this purpose. The Government at that time refused the offer.

There are other "<u>Arthur Ranks</u>" and "<u>Archer Whitfords</u>" in this country if they will only come forward.

Men like <u>Merv. Murphy</u>, of <u>Supreme Sound</u>, and engineers at <u>Cinesound</u> have proved that good equipment can be built in this country. Sound, lighting and even cameras have been made here in Australia. These things have been accomplished on very little capital.

"The Overlanders," "Smithy," and "A Son Is Born" ... ample proof that good films can be made <u>here</u> in our <u>own country</u>.

One good producing unit could turn out four films a year at an average cost of £10,000 per film.

With your <u>co-operation</u> and <u>financial aid</u> it would not be long before fifty units could be in constant production.

<u>Support</u> the <u>Film Production Industry</u> in this country, gentlemen, it is certainly worthwhile.

Roy Darling
Master Tele Film Productions,
8A CASTLEREAGH STREET,
SYDNEY

Letter printed in The Film Weekly, 11 Sep 1947. 'Eureka: The Stockade Song' was published c. 1948

I like that in the midst of all this tumult of activity there is so much evidence of small acts of kindness and generosity.

☐   DAUGHTER OF THE EAST : [FRAGMENT]   (1924)   Director: Roy Darling
Details of individual titles can be found under Contents.
Media: Film   Produced as: Feature Film

☐   THE HAND THAT ROCKS THE CRADLE   (c. 1942)   Director: Roy Darling
From a story by Elizabeth Lang.
Media: Film Produced as: Short

☐   HE CHASED A CHICKEN   (c. 1946)   Director: Roy Darling
A short film featuring country singer Buddy Williams.
Media: Film   Produced as: Music

National Film and Sound Archive of Australia

Title No: 127649
Title: DAUGHTER OF THE EAST : [FRAGMENT]
Alternative Title: THE BOY OF THE DARDANELLES : [FRAGMENT]
Production Date: 1923
Release Date: 4 October 1924
Produced as: Feature Film
Category: Silent film
Media: Film
Summary: A World War I romance with action on Gallipoli and return to Australia after the war. General notes: The picture was written and financed by cafe proprietor Adam Tavlaridi to show the positive contributions of Greek people to the British war effort. Filmed in and around Sydney with battle scenes staged on the sandhills at Maroubra. Trade previewed in 1923 as "The Boy of the Dardanelles" but released under its changed title the next year. Original length unknown, surviving footage 66 feet of 35mm (25 secs at 18fps). Access copies: 35mm, 1/2 inch video.
Country of Origin: Australia
From National Film and Sound Archive of Australia

Works by Roy Darling: from the Australian Music Centre archive

Bib ID: 6569832
Format: Manuscript, Music [notated music, volume]
Author: Darling, Roy, composer
Description: [between 1944 and 1950?] Scores.

Full contents:
- Darling 1. Coo-ee oo-ee oo-ee : (mountains of blue)
- Darling 2. Dear little lady o' mine
- Darling 3. Dreaming
- Darling 4. Home once again
- Darling 5. I don't care
- Darling 6. I don't care
- Darling 7. Kokoda trail
- Darling 8. Life's symphony : (Aussie-land, home of mine)
- Darling 9. Manda Amanda
- Darling 10. Murray my river of stars
- Darling 11. The Overlander Trail
- Darling 12. Proudly the stars look down
- Darling 13. Silver wings across the sky
- Darling 14. Smokey Eyes
- Darling 15. Those Sunday blues
- Darling 16. When the echo answered yes
- Darling 17. When the moonlight kissed the bay.

"Dear little lady o' mine," "Dreaming," "Home once again," "I don't care," "Kokoda Trail," "Proudly the stars look down," "Silver wings across the sky," "Smoky eyes," "Those Sunday blues" and "When the moonlight kissed the bay" arranged by Hilda Bevege. This collection contains manuscript music and Australian Music Centre reproductions.
[NB Hilda Bevege was, of course, Mum's sister, our 'little Aunty Hilda'].

'"**Dear Little Lady of Mine**" comes from the 1948 Australian short movie *He Chased a Chicken* which Buddy starred in. The movie was produced by Roy Darling who wrote this song. There were two other songs in the movie, "The Overlander Trail" & "He Chased a Chicken". The two latter songs were released on Regal-Zonophone but "Dear Little Lady of Mine" never came out on record. This would certainly be one of the earliest, if not the earliest, 'music clip' made in Australia. The clip is also of major significance in that there is very little such material of this vintage of any of Australia's great entertainers. At the time of the movie Buddy was 30 and one of the biggest names in Australian entertainment. He would have been touring Australia with his big-top rodeo & circus at the time. At this stage Buddy had released about 60 songs on Regal-Zonophone since his first recording in 1939. Enjoy one of Australia's greatest all time entertainers, Buddy Williams "The Yodelling Jackaroo" from a golden era of a great career.' From YouTube (Garry Coxhead)

Description Sydney : Boosey & Hawkes (Aust.), c. 1964
1 score (27 p.) ; 28 cm.

Full contents

- Ballad of the drover / words by Henry Lawson ; music by Hal Evans
- The shearers' jamboree / arr. by Hal Evans ; words and music by Eric Tutin
- Overlander trail / arr. by Hal Evans ; words and music by Roy Darling
- A bush Christening / words by A.B. (Banjo) Paterson ; music by Hal Evans
- What makes it snow /words by A.B. (Banjo) Paterson ; music by Hal Evans
- Over hill-top and hollow / arranged by Hal Evans ; words and music by Stanley Robinson
- A song of wind /words by Will Lawson ; music by Hal Evans
- Eureka: The Stockade song arr. by Hal Evans ; **words and music by Roy Darling**
- Lightning Ridge / arr. by Hal Evans; words and music by Roy Darling.

Note: The composition of 'Eureka: The Stockade Song' is incorrectly attributed here to Buddy Williams, who recorded but **did not write** the song.

https://catalogue.nla.gov.au/Record/1785602

In good company: Henry Lawson, A. B. Paterson, Will Lawson, Roy Darling

9.6 In the beginning

But wait – there's more!

So that is the story of Roy Darling, the producer, theatre owner and film-maker. My father. That is all fascinating enough. I've already said I didn't know much of this story until I began researching for this memoir. And that's true. But we, as a family – all of us, none of us – knew or even suspected what would be revealed, many years after his death, about his early days.

We knew that Roy's mother was Rose Isabella Reay-Edwards. We thought we knew that he was born in Cornwall. We knew that he had been married before and that he had had a daughter, whose name I knew.

Roy, as I wrote in Chapter 3, died very suddenly at home in August 1956. He had only just turned fifty-seven years old. A few years before, in August 1953, his family made contact. Apart from a short visit to his mother's brother and some cousins in England at the end of the Great War, he had not seen any of them since leaving home in 1915. They had been looking for him for many years, they said. We knew nothing of this nor anything about them. The only family person I ever remember Roy talking about was his mother, Rose Isabella, whom he had loved very dearly. (And we now have, in a new generation, a beautiful Isabella Rose.)

We assumed, I suppose, that the family were all living in England. He was, after all, English, wasn't he? It was a surprise, then, when one of his sisters succeeded in tracking him down, we discovered she lived in New Delhi, India. Apparently, his father, who we later found out lived to be ninety, had been desperately seeking his older son's whereabouts for years, and so the whole family had been trying to trace where he was and what he was doing. In a letter dated 23 July 1953, his sister explains that she tracked him down through a friend who was visiting Sydney and who had seen his name in a Sydney newspaper in connection with the well-known film producer, Chas E. Blanks.

This letter, even though half of it is destroyed (itself revealing: presumably it was torn in half by Roy) is very interesting. Her brother is addressed, without any enquiry or explanations, as 'Roy'. Somehow they already knew or had known that he was in film-making. They were aware of his change[s!] of name and that he was now going by the name 'Roy Darling'. Later, I was told by several new-found relatives that when they had discovered he was in films, some years before, they had thought he might be Errol Flynn.

The sister who made the initial contact was, I was told, my Aunty Zen, who was married to a high-ranking army officer, Edgar Lewis. The family seemed to be dispersed around the world. Zen was living in New Delhi in India, another sister was living with her daughter in Canada and a cousin owned a huge coffee plantation (five square kilometres) in Kitale, Kenya. All of this seemed rather exotic to us at Oasis, in our little country village about sixty-five kilometres south-west of Sydney.

My father was, apparently, very unsettled after his family made this contact. A few years after, Mum told me and also repeated to several of my brothers that after his sister, Aunty Zen, had been in touch, he became very upset and said there was something important he had to tell her (Mum). Mum, who would have been in her late twenties at the time, said she just held him close and told him: 'If it's going to upset you so much, darling, don't tell me. Or tell me later on, when you are feeling better.'

He never did tell and Mum never knew.

Neither did any of us until about twenty-five years later.

We did know, rather vaguely, that we had this far-flung family around the world, but we still saw England as the core of our locus of place. These years were Oasis years: one of our happiest times. A little after becoming aware of this aunty and her family living in India, another aunty and her family living in Canada and an 'uncle' (second cousin) living in Kenya with his family, when I was about eleven – and just before my father died – encouraged by Mum, I started writing letters. First of all I wrote to Aunty Zen and her daughter, who had the lovely nickname of 'Gypsie'. After my father's death, I became pen friends not only with Aunty Zen and Gypsie, but also with 'Uncle' Ron in Kitale (a great letter writer) and two of his children, Joy and David. This correspondence, though intermittent at times, was to go on for years.

So, at this stage, I was more-or-less in a regular – every few months – correspondence with at least three members of my father's long-lost family. We now thought we knew almost everything about them – and, of course, him.

But we didn't.

And they were all, deliberately or tacitly, very, very discreet.

As we have seen, 'Roy Darling' came into existence somewhere between South Africa and Australia, and this identity lasted until 21 August 1956 when he died. We will probably never know all that happened, but this is what we do know.

Royston Frederick Reay-Edwards, known as Royston Frederick Darling (c. 1920–1956) was, as noted earlier, the name in which Roy married my mother (Dorothy Patricia) on 1 May 1943. But now I come to the messy bits of overflow and edits, where what we knew as children was infiltrated with what we subsequently discovered. As noted earlier, I am not always completely sure of the order of things.

Although Aunty Zen was the sister who made initial contact, it was another sister, Hunsia Mary Lewis, and her daughter, Zarina, who were the first official paternal relatives to actually come to Australia to visit us. (I was to become quite close to my cousin Zarina, who lived in Calgary, Canada, and many years afterwards, when I was speaking at a conference there, she took me on a beautiful tour to Banff National Park and Lake Louise. So lovely. And it snowed, extravagantly and magically.) These were the first members of my father's family any of us (the Australian clan) had ever met, save for one. Years earlier, as noted in Chapter 5, David Edwards, the younger son of 'Uncle' Ron, who owned the coffee plantation in Kenya and who had become one of my many pen friends, immigrated to Australia as a 'ten pound Pom'.

Dave was young and, although initially very pale, had an aura of overseas glamour. Aunty Hunsia, however, was grey and elderly and rather like an extreme version of Agatha Christie's Miss Marple. We had been sent a few photos, but when Hunsia and Zarina arrived they didn't bear much resemblance in the flesh to the images we had seen, which were small, black and white snaps that had been taken when they were much younger. Hunsia was sweet and loving and a little fussy. Her daughter, Zarina, was charming. She was both spiritual and practical and rather exotic. They came in the late '70s and stayed with Malcolm and me for several weeks. The plan was for them to then go to other members of the family, including Mum and my brothers. From the time we picked them up at the airport, the whole visit seemed to have a mysterious aura of impending import. I knew not why.

I will never forget their second night, when after dinner this aura intensified into a sense of secrecy and imminent disclosure. It had been such a busy day – several days in fact – preparing for their visit: working out beds, stocking up food and making meals. I had very small children and had to get them all bathed and into bed before we four adults settled down after dinner in the lounge room with our cups of tea. As we did so, they announced they had some important family news to tell us.

I don't know what I was expecting, but I was certainly not expecting this story, which they told in such a convoluted way – no doubt trying to be sensitive – that it was hard to understand. To me, it made little sense. Malcolm probably followed it better than I did. Whereas I had to continuously rejig the stories I had grown up with, he had no such impediment to understanding.

9. Revelations

I think Hunsia and Zarina might have started by checking what I actually knew (or thought I did). I was relatively blithe as I told them.

My father was born in Cornwall (and thus 'Kerensa'). No, they said, he wasn't.

My father's family were all English (and thus my love for all things English, especially landscape and literature). No, they said, actually they weren't.

My father's 'real' name was not Royston Frederick Darling – I already know that! It was, I said, Royston Frederick Reay-Edwards. No, they said, it wasn't.

Then it was Frederick George Reay Edwards. No, they said, gently, it wasn't.

The family had grown up in England. No, they hadn't.

My father had gone from England to South Africa. Well, yes he had gone to South Africa from England as a child, but he had not started life in England.

Where was he born then? I asked. He was born in Budapest, they replied.

I was left reeling on the inside but calm enough on the outside. Then came the clincher:

My father's father was not an Englishman as we had always assumed. (I don't remember actually being told that; it was just understood.)

So what was he? I asked.

Again, their answer was vague and convoluted. (Or it was to me.) Afterwards, Hunsia and Zarina told me they were worried that Malcolm would be upset. But he wasn't. He was, in a way, more interested than I. If I remember correctly, I went off to bed quite early. I couldn't take it all in, and we had planned to take our visitors, along with our little children, to the zoo the following day. This was not so much to show our visitors the animals (in retrospect quite ironic) but to show them the wonderful views of the city and Sydney Harbour, which are the backdrop of Taronga Park Zoo's setting. But it would be a big day, and I still had to pack what the children (one not yet a toddler) would need for the day.

In a nutshell, this is a summary of what they told us, in that very roundabout way. My father was not born in Hayle Cornwall in the UK as we had thought, but that in fact he was born in Budapest, Hungary (his younger sister was born in Hayle; perhaps he thought he was born in Cornwall); that he was not really Roy Darling, which I knew, but that he also was not Royston Frederick Reay-Edwards; that he also was not Frederick George Reay Edwards; that his mother was indeed Rose Isabella Reay-Edwards, an English woman, but that his father's name was not Frederick George Reay-Edwards, as we thought; that his father's name was actually Mirza Ziauddin Akmal, and that he, Roy, was born Jelal Frederick George Reay Akmal.

Mirza Ziauddin Akmal

Learning about another grandfather has been a process, and not always an easy one. (Grandfather Joe as a seafarer from the Isle of Man had seemed quite exotic, but it had nothing on this!) That evening, long ago in our 'Kerensa' lounge room, was difficult. So many new facts had to juggle around and indeed dismiss and replace some of the old. And some things have only become clearer over the years, even quite recently.

My paternal grandfather

At the time of meeting Rose Isabella Reay-Edwards, Mirza Ziauddin Akmal (Zia) was a distinguished linguist, fluent in many languages, employed at the School of Oriental Studies in London, which by the 1890s was awarding degrees. He wrote many articles on Hindu legends as well as on the origins of the Hungarian nation. In later years he worked for a cigarette manufacturer and became general manager and technology expert of the Hyderabad Deccan Cigarette Factory, established 1930. (I find myself wishing it was not a cigarette factory, but it was.) I marvel, and still wonder, at three aspects of this story:

1. The unlikely alliance

Rose and Zia's subsequent marriage took place at St Mary's Church in Kilburn, near Hampstead, on 29 January 1896. They had met in London and the union was bitterly opposed by both families. I've been told by several people that Rose saw Zia walking past her home and said to her mother: 'That is the man I am going to marry.' This, to me, is either exaggerated or quite amazingly prescient; I don't know which. The ensuing match certainly wasn't anything either family desired; indeed, Rose's family believed she had been 'mesmerised' by the clever (and very 'other') Zia.

Further, and to make matters worse, Zia apparently hated the English, and family oral history suggests he was a direct descendant of the last of the Moghul emperors, who were deposed in 1857 by the establishment of the British Raj.

As an aside, it is interesting that many of the later Moghul emperors had strong Persian and Indian *Rajput* social ancestry. (*Rajput* are multi-ethnic clusters originally descended from warriors.) Akbar (the Great) was half-Persian and interested in religion, philosophy, art and science. He encouraged religious tolerance and accommodated India's majority Hindu population, abolished the poll tax on non-Muslims, translated Hindu literature and participated in Hindu festivals. Shah Jahan (in Persian شاہ جہان, literally 'King of the World'), was three-quarters *Rajput* and a great patron of architecture. He commissioned many monuments, including the Taj Mahal in Agra.

> *The British Raj extended over almost all present-day India, Pakistan, and Bangladesh, except for small holdings by other European nations such as Goa and Pondicherry.*

2. The faith heritage

> **Mirza Ziauddin Akmal**
>
> **Excerpt from the 1938 edition of *Who's Who in India***
>
> From the age of 17 to 39, a globe trotter with a love for adventure. Lived in London during the Sinn Fein outrages; visited Turkey during the Turco-Greek war of 1897; Hungary during students' riots; Cuba during the rebellion of 1899; and South Africa during the Boer War and the Zulu rebellion. For many years a cigarette manufacturer, abroad and in India. [At the time of this article] he was General Manager and Technology Expert of the Hyderabad Deccan Cigarette Factory. A believer in the militarisation of the British Empire as the only safe-guard of world peace, and a writer of pamphlets and books on the subject.

I have always known that Grandmother Rose was a committed Christian. In researching for this chapter, I discovered that the church in which Rose and Zia married was a Catholic church, St Mary's near Hampstead. They were both of age and apparently Zia's guardian and uncle, a lawyer who was supervising his nephew's studies, approved. This no doubt explains why the children all attended Catholic schools.

I have long been a reader of the works of some of the famous Church fathers, whom I admire: St Augustine, St Jerome. It was written a little later (in the early seventeenth century) but I also have long admired the little book written by Brother Lawrence, *The Practice of the Presence of God*:

> We ought not to be weary of doing little things for the love of God, who regards not the greatness of the work but the love with which it is performed.

Indeed, this became and still is a sort of mantra or refrain for me. I also read and learn from the more recent spiritual writings of Evelyn Underhill, Carlo Carretto and Henri Nouwen, among many others. The Catholic Church kept Christianity alive for fifteen hundred years, up until the time of Luther and the Reformation. Whilst I am not a Catholic (and resist labels anyway), I am a committed Christian, and faith in God and a deep interest in the Divine has been and is at the core of many of our lives.

3. The creative heritage

Zia was also a poet. The creative heritage, along with the faith heritage, runs strongly through all the diverse branches of family. My cousin Azim, himself a former (and internationally famous) musical child prodigy, recently sent me this:

> **Of Man and God** by Mirza Ziauddin Akmal, trans. Azim Lewis Mayadas
>
> Original poem in my paternal (Azim's maternal) grandfather's native language, Urdu, from Lahore in India's Northwest Punjab in the days of the British Raj.
>
> **Khuda Aur Insan**
>
> *Insan aur khuda ki purani kahaniyan*
>
> *Hain irtaqa'e nav'i bashar ki nishaniyan*
>
> *Joon joon chiragh-i-'ilm ki barhti hai roshni*
>
> *Pahchanta hai apni haqiqat ko admi*
>
> **Of Man and God**
>
> *Of Man and God there are*
>
> *Tales of Old*
>
> *That Signs of Mankind's*
>
> *Ascent unfold:*
>
> *As Light from the Lamp of*
>
> *Knowledge grows*
>
> *So Man the Truth of his*
>
> *Being knows.*

Again, I am moved that a sense of the spiritual and awareness of the Divine seems to run so strongly in all our threads of family.

Back to that night at Kerensa

We of course had had no inkling of any of this. However, Roy's Catholic education and Christian upbringing does help to explain many of his later kindnesses as 'Roy Darling'. His mother's influence was very strong, not only on him but also on other members of the extended family I later met.

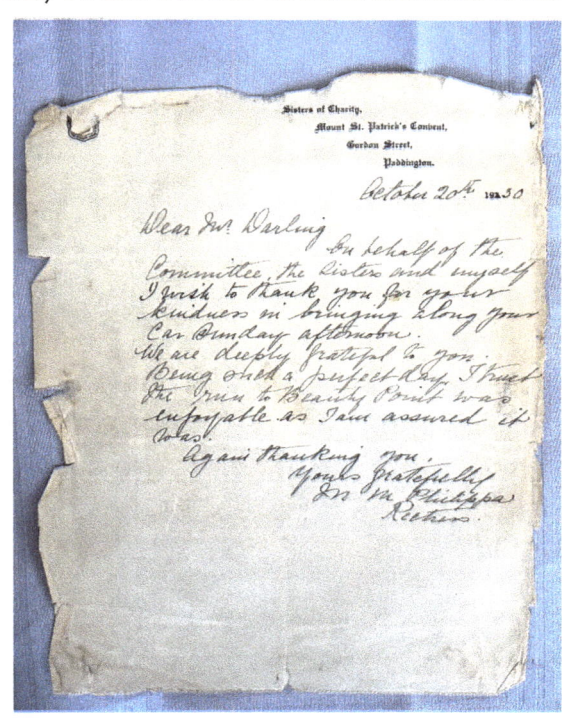

Rose Isabella, my paternal grandmother, is indeed a fascinating figure: clever and artistic and very musical, a lovely soprano who played not only piano but violin, cello and harp. I am impressed by her determination; in 1896, she not only defied her family to marry Zia but went with him across half the world, leaving the culture and refinements of London behind. She died far too young (at forty-two), but the reports of her influence and the tragedy of her loss are still talked about down through the generations. I am proud to have been named for her and proud that there is now a precious granddaughter who bears her name. Rose is an authentic part of the English heritage that we all knew about (or thought we did).

As noted in Chapter 7, the Cornish name for my new home with Malcolm was chosen because my brothers and I had always understood that our father was born in Cornwall. So did Mum. She told me how much he liked Newport – where we live now and where he lived for a time (before we came on the scene) – because it reminded him of the beach in Hayle, Cornwall. He told her that was where he had been born; but in fact, that was where his first sister was born, which is no doubt why he remembered it. He was, however, as his more recently sourced birth certificate irrevocably shows, born in Budapest, Hungary. After his marriage to Rose and ostracised by both families, Zia accepted a position as an English professor in Budapest. He was a remarkably fluent speaker of many languages and well-read in literature. He was also clearly an adventurer and was later to become a clever businessman.

Zia and Rose were invited to spend their honeymoon overlooking the Danube River at the home of the artistic Baron and Baroness Czobel, friends of Zia's uncle. Zia's linguistic skill was attested to in Budapest by Professor Vamberg Armin. Because of his fluency in many languages, a family story suggests that Zia later worked in the early 1900s as a private secretary to Kaiser Wilhelm II, during which he was present at a secret meeting between the Kaiser and Czar Nicholas II on the Baltic Sea.

After Budapest, the little family returned to England, where both Zia and Rose joined the Language Institute. Rose also continued her musical studies and singing. Then a chance encounter with a resident of Durban, South Africa, inspired them to emigrate. A few years later, after the birth of their second child (a daughter, Zohra Miriam Charlotte, born in Hayle), they did so. On a hill in Durban called the Berea (the Brear in family annals), they bought a large, pretty house that was just up from the beach and refreshed by cool sea breezes. They called the house 'Villa Medina', after the holy city in Saudi Arabia. And here I must insert a comment about another of the little 'coincidences' (?) that have been glimpsed in the new landscapes revealed and traversed as part of this *passeggiata*.

There have been several references to the Durban house, all stating that it was named after the ancient Arabian city of Medina. During one of my spot researches, I found that the city of Medina was constructed in or on an oasis. An oasis! Our father and mother named their first real home together 'Oasis'! I have always thought that name was Mum's idea. It was she who explained

Villa Medina, Napier Road, Durban – Roy's childhood home. Zia standing on the front steps with his oldest child, Jelal, and several daughters. Rose on the left coming up the back steps to join the family

it to me as a place of refuge: our little private and safe protected place. But now I wonder. Did my father also think back to that lovely old family home in Durban? Was it a secret link, a tentacle of memory for him that reached across the many years from his long-ago childhood? I'll never know. But it adds another fascinating layer, a poignant nuance, to their story. And to our story.

Despite parental ostracism, Rose must have remained close to her sister Charlotte ('Aunty Char'), because later Charlotte left England and came to live at the 'Villa Medina' to help Rose with the growing family. It was here that Zia bought Rose a piano, which she loved, and which all the children learnt to play, along with other instruments. There are many reports in the family about the musical evenings held at their home. The oldest son, who was to be my father, grew up at Villa Medina having twice-weekly violin lessons and was also to become captain of his school cricket team. And it was most likely at Villa Medina that Rose, very moved by verses written by the Norfolk MP Sir Robert Price about a dream he had of being on board the doomed ship *Titanic,* used his words (after seeking his permission) to compose her version of the hymn 'Nearer, My God to Thee'. This was published in 1912 by the International Music Company in South Africa.

Remember how I wrote earlier that my father never mentioned his mother's musical

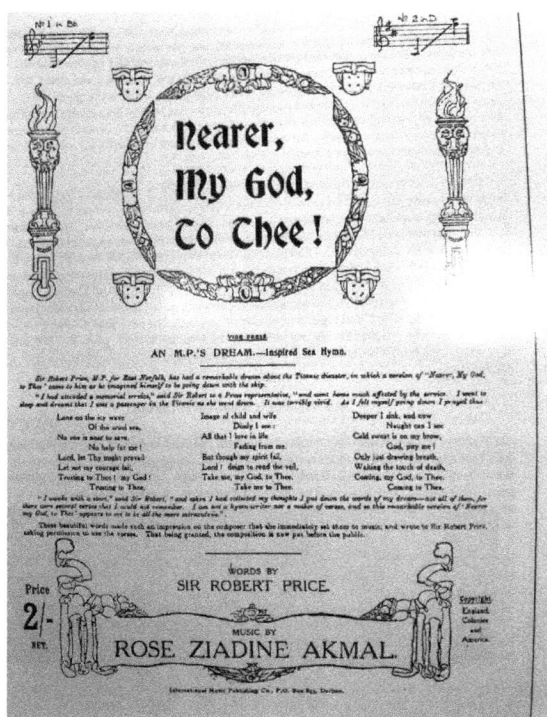

success to me? I suppose it was because, had we ever looked it up somehow, we would have seen and wondered at Rose's married name. Sad that he couldn't tell us.

Music was very much a part of life at Villa Medina. All the children were musically talented and classically trained. And the son of one of Roy's younger sisters, Zenobia, became an internationally acclaimed pianist. This son, a 'child prodigy', was Azim Eric Lewis, who years later became the general manager of the Florida Philharmonic Orchestra. In another amazing family synchrony, later still he became the managing director of the National Guild of Community Schools of the Arts, Engelwood, New Jersey.

Zen describes one of their family musical evenings at Villa Medina in her booklet of family history, *A Tale of Three Continents*. In a charming scene, she writes how Jelal and Zohra (the two eldest children) were allowed to attend and perform at these functions, while the younger girls watched from the stairs:

> We three sisters used to sit on the hall staircase from where we could see the guests and hear the music being played. Also, Aunty Char would tell our maid to serve us cold drinks and snacks up there.
>
> On this particular occasion, which was my mother's birthday, the guests requested their hostess [Rose] to play, as the last item on the evening's program, Beethoven's 'Moonlight Sonata' because there was a full moon outside. She played it beautifully. One of the guests drew the lace window-curtains aside so that the moonlight could shine on her at the keyboard, and then put off the lights.
>
> I shall always remember with nostalgia that lovely scene.

The family of Mirza Zia Akmal and Rose Isabella Reay Edwards are: Jelal Frederick George Reay (born Budapest), Zohra Miriam Charlotte Reay (born Cornwall), Yasmin Amelia Reay, Zenobia Rose Reay, Hunsia Lucy Reay, Zarina Isabel Reay, Anwar Kenneth Hugh Reay and Roxime Reay.

Because this Passeggiata, written so many years later in a different country, is composed around a motif of homes and gardens and artistic culture, it is interesting to see some of the names which Rose and Zia chose for their children. Born during the last few years of the nineteenth century and the first decade of the twentieth, all were given an Indian first name and an English second name; I like the meanings of some of the Indian names.

Jelal Frederick George Reay – Jelal means greatness, superiority, or renown. It is interesting that the name he was apparently given in South Africa, and was to go by for most of his life, was Roy, from Old French for 'king'.

Zohra – means 'flower blossom' in Arabic

Zarina – of Persian and Slavic origins, means 'golden', 'dawn', or 'daybreak'

Yasmin – of Persian origin, means 'flower', 'gift from God'

Anwar – means 'luminous'

In faraway mid-century Australia, my parents on both sides taught me to love flowers and the sacred beauties of nature, and to treasure and respect words and their meanings.

Tragically, Rose Isabella died from complications in childbirth bearing her ninth child, a stillborn son, in 1914. Some time before, Zia had moved the family from Durban, firstly to Bombay and then to Azimabad in North India. After Rose's death, the children were all placed in Catholic boarding schools. Jelal's school was in Bombay. Jelal, now about fifteen, blamed his father for his mother's death and, grieving and angry, did not return home when expected. One aunt (Hunsia Lucy) cried as she told me, sixty years later: 'Jelal, my very handsome big brother, just didn't come home. Our father was frantic.' Then Zia found out through Aunty Char (Rose's sister), with whom Jelal had apparently been in contact, that Jelal was not going to come home: he had put up his age, enlisted, and run away to the Great War.

Zia and children, probably Jelal, reaching for his hand

In my end is my beginning

As T. S. Eliot wrote, and as I have already quoted, 'In my end is my beginning'. And so it is with Roy/Jelal. Here is where I end his story, with the young, good-looking, talented, promising elder son – artistic, musical, creative, a leader among his peers, captain of his school cricket team – who one day just didn't come home, who ran away not only to the Great War, but to a new identity, indeed, new identities. These would take him to a new life, into (surprisingly, ironically) a national activism on behalf of a young country he had probably scarcely heard of and into an industry which at this point, in 1915, he surely would not have known much, or indeed anything, about, that indeed was still in its birth pangs.

Roy's father, Zia, in later life. He and Jelal/Roy never saw each other after Roy ran away in 1915

It is here, in this ending, that Jelal Frederick George Reay Akmal, beloved son of Rose and Zia, disappears. He was to live a short but tumultuous life, far away from those with whom he had grown up at Villa Medina. The people he was then to love most in the world – his young and beautiful second wife, Dorothy (his 'Smokey Eyes') and the four children born of that marriage – would not know anything of this beginning, nor even suspect any of it, for decades. He was never to tell us; he died so suddenly, so abruptly.

Jelal Frederick George Reay Akmal, born in Budapest, grown in Durban, schooled in Bombay, died on a frosty August night in a tiny village on the edge of another ocean, in another country and bearing another name.

Political/historical contexts of family history

Creative heritages – which we all have – are exciting to explore. Ours reveals a fascinating and intriguing mental landscape that makes me wonder about the symmetries and asymmetries of nature and nurture. As I wrote in a family email:

'I admire the early literature of Persia, and the great mystical writers of India, and the evocative Irish poets and the proud Scottish storytellers. I think my Manx grandfather was probably steeped in the famous Icelandic sagas of the sea.'

Completely coincidentally, our first little Kerensa kitten was called 'Shah'. We had him for almost eighteen years.

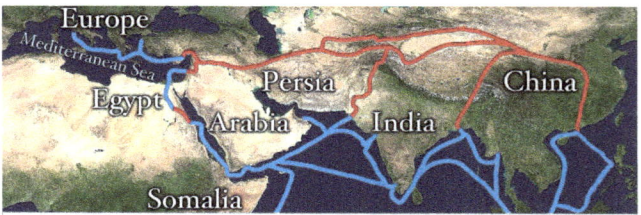

The Silk Road – *an ancient network of trade routes. What a magical name! I like this map for its grand yet simple sweep.*

Indian Partition (1947)

This marked the end of British rule, the British **Raj**.

On 14–15 August 1947, the subcontinent of India was partitioned (divided):

- the new Dominion of Pakistan came into being [East Pakistan later became Bangladesh]
- the following day, 15 August 1947, India became the Dominion of India; an independent country
- Dominion of Ceylon (now Sri Lanka) and the Union of Burma (now Myanmar) also gained independence in 1947–1948.

Pakistan became a majority Muslim country, and India became a majority Hindu but secular country. The name Pakistan means literally 'a land abounding in the pure' or 'a land in which the pure abound' in Urdu and Persian. It references the word کاپ *(pāk),* meaning 'pure' in Persian and Pashto.

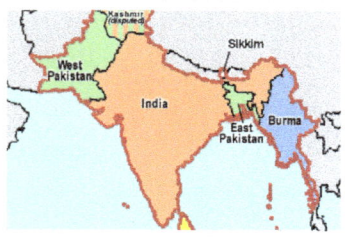

Rumi (1207–1273 AD) was a Persian theologian and scholar who became famous as a mystical poet. His work focuses on the opportunity for a meaningful life through personal knowledge and love of God.

Rumi was an experimental innovator among the Persian poets. 'This combination of mystical richness and bold adaptations of poetic forms is the key to his popularity today,' (Mojaddedi). It is said that people of all religions came to Rumi's funeral in 1273, because, they said, 'he deepens our faith wherever we are.'

Rumi celebrated love and believed God is welcoming to all.

The Persian Empire

The Persian Empire was one of the most powerful empires of the ancient world. At its height, it encompassed the areas of modern-day Iran, Egypt, Turkey, and parts of Afghanistan and India. Most scholars agree that North-Western India including North Punjab was part of the Persian Empire. The Empire emerged under Cyrus II, who became 'Shah', or king, of Persia. 'Cyrus was unlike other emperors because he showed mercy toward the cities and kingdoms he conquered. He was known to spare the life of a defeated king so that the king could guide Cyrus in successfully ruling over the captives' subjects. Cyrus also practised religious and cultural tolerance toward conquered people.'

Malcolm was always with me as I discovered more and more about my father's life. Here we are with our little grand-daughter Evelyn and Lee Kernaghan, who recorded a new version of Overlander Trail with 'pioneering greats Smoky Dawson, Reg Lindsay and Ray Kernaghan'

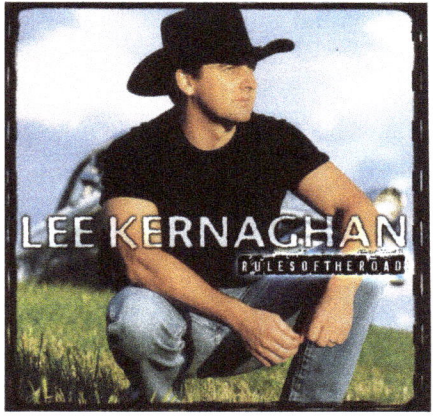

11. OVERLANDER TRAIL

Roy Darling (Boosey and Hawkes) with special guests Smoky Dawson, Reg Lindsay and Ray Kernaghan.

Overlander trail was first recorded by Buddy in 1946 for the Regal Zonophone label. It was the culmination of several vintage Buddy years which began after his recuperation from serious injuries he sustained on active service in the Pacific during World War 2.

It was an honour for me to record Buddy's old song with pioneering greats, the legendary men, Smoky Dawson, Reg Lindsay and my dad Ray Kernaghan

Wagon wheels are rolling on
And the day seems mighty long
Clouds of heat dust in the air
Bawling cattle everywhere

They're on the overlander overlander trail
Where only sheer determination will prevail
Men of Aussie with a job to do
So they'll stick and see the cattle through
And though they sweat and curse
they know they surely must
Stick on the trail that winds ahead
through heat and dust
All sons of Aussie and they will not fail
They're on the overlander overlander trail

Soon the journey will be won
In spite of heat and blazin' sun
Land where friendships never fail
Overlanders on the trail

They're on the overlander overlander trail
Where only sheer determination will prevail
Men of Aussie with a job to do
So they'll stick and see the cattle through
And though they sweat and curse
they know they surely must
Stick on the trail that winds ahead
through heat and dust
All sons of Aussie and they will not fail
They're on the overlander overlander trail

Roy's lyrics in Lee Kernaghan's album sleeve

Eureka: The Stockade Song

(This must be re-recorded!)

Ballarat we hear
In a bygone year
Beckoned young and old
In a search for gold ...

1854 Eureka days
Burning sunshine and a golden haze
Heat dust rising as the wagons rolled
Onward in the search for gold

Ballarat the ending of the trail
From the goal the seekers could not fail
Wheels stop rolling and they settle down
There to build a mining town

Very soon troopers came
From then on things weren't the same
With the law on their side
Miners' claims were all denied

Men of every nationality
Fought against the troopers to be free
Built upon a hill a great stockade
There a final stand they made

'We must live or die', was the miners' cry,
This they really meant, singing as they went,

Marching onward up to Bakery Hill
No more bowing to the troopers will
For our freedom we're prepared to fight
For we know that we are right,

Diggers everyone and what care we
Burn our permits let the troopers see
We are going to fight until the end
For the right we must defend

Come on men, it's our turn
Troopers soon must surely learn
Safe within our stockade
There's no need to be afraid

Marching onward up to Bakery Hill
We can't lose if we have got the will
Keep on singing as we march along
The Eureka Stockade song.

> 'On 30 November 1854 miners from the Victorian town of Ballarat, disgruntled with the way the colonial government had been administering the goldfields, swore allegiance to the Southern Cross flag at Bakery Hill and built a stockade at the nearby Eureka diggings.
>
> Early on the morning of Sunday 3 December, when the stockade was only lightly guarded, government troops attacked. At least 22 diggers and five soldiers were killed.
>
> Eureka is a significant event in the development of Australia's representational structures and attitudes towards democracy and egalitarianism.'
> https://www.nma.gov.au/defining-moments/resources/eureka-stockade

10. A Well-Watered Garden

Often I sit, looking back to a childhood
Mixt with the sights and the sounds of the wildwood,
Longing for power and the sweetness to fashion
Lyrics with beats like the heart-beats of passion –
Songs interwoven of lights and of laughters
Borrowed from bell-birds in far forest rafters;
So I might keep in the city and alleys
The beauty and strength of the deep mountain valleys,
Charming to slumber the pain of my losses
With glimpses of creeks and a vision of mosses.

From 'Bell-birds' by Henry Kendall

10.1 Teaching again

Well, here we are, heading towards the final chapters and the last stops in our *passeggiata*. This is really a wrap-up of what we did – and what I did – after the Sprouts grew into their own lives. Of course they overlap and spill into everything, as they and theirs all do and will do always. They are at the core of me and of their father.

My first real foray back into the paid workforce was a job that was both perfect for me with the children and undemanding, but it was this experience – teaching English at the Sydney Japanese School, which was relatively close by at Terrey Hills – that was actually the catalyst for what I did a little later. My hours were 9.30 am to 2.30 pm five days a week, which meant I could drop my children off at school/kindergarten and pick them up afterwards. This was important to me.

I really enjoyed these years. I started learning Japanese and made many friends. It was such an interesting cultural experience that after a few years we moved Robs there for his primary schooling. During that time he became fluent in Japanese and knowledgeable and appreciative of the Japanese culture. Much later, after graduating with his first degree, he obtained a position teaching English at a language school in Kyoto and spent over a year in Japan.

The Japanese School had a language festival each year, when each class put on some sort of a performance in English: a little play or song or skit. Before long, I was asked to turn this assortment of random presentations into a more coherent script, with rehearsals and a big, sung, all-in-together finale finish. This is sort of what I had been doing for our church Christmas presentations (which later became interdenominational shows in the Village Park, Mona Vale, that continued for some years and are still held today in a different form). I chose popular songs for these events, sometimes writing my own words to make them appropriate for whatever theme or occasion the school was celebrating, with a fine disregard for any copyright laws, of which we were all then largely unaware.

But I was aware, and increasingly so, that the way we were teaching English – in a sort of hybrid 'teaching as a second language' and 'teaching as a foreign language' (most of the students returned to Japan) – could perhaps be better informed. At the very least, I wanted to explore the theory.

One spring day, and I have never forgotten this, I was driving down the long, wattle-fringed Boorailie Road to the school, revelling in the beauty of the golden puffs against the bright blue sky, when I suddenly had a flash: I would return to university to undertake postgraduate study. I decided to research what courses were available. I had actually never stopped studying, but I had not had any previous desire or plan to formalise this until that moment.

Now a tumble of events happened. I looked up English as a Second Language (ESL) courses, which led to several phone calls with Macquarie University – a 'newish' Sydney institution to which I had never been but which wasn't so very far from where I was working in Terrey Hills. I discovered Macquarie University offered a Master of Children's Literature degree that enabled me to include an ESL subject. It sounded fascinating. So I enrolled, graduated with a master's degree and was then invited by my supervisor to enrol in a PhD, which I did. A little less than three years later (in record time according to my supervisor, Professor John Stephens), I obtained my doctorate.

A year or so before this, a nice thing had happened. Judy, my dear girlfriend from undergraduate Sydney University days, had been doing some part-time lecturing at UTS. She phoned me and said: 'Rosemary, there's a job going at the University of Technology Sydney and you should apply.' This was before mobile phones and smartphones, and the only way I could see the advertisement was to go and buy the paper, which I did. When I read the ad, I phoned Judy and said I didn't think the job was for me. It seemed to be about the 'new English curriculum', of which I knew nothing; we didn't follow NSW curricula in the senior years at the Japanese School. 'It's about much more than that,' she told me. 'I know it's for you. It's about literature and inspiring students.'

With students and staff in Apia, Samoa

So I applied. When the date of announcing the shortlist came and went without any notification, I was very disappointed; I didn't realise until then how much I wanted this job. We had been away visiting family in Canberra all week and came back to no messages and no letters. We were unpacking the car and five children and washing after a week away, and I slipped upstairs and looked out our small ensuite bathroom window, praying for a sense of acceptance. It was by now about 5.30 pm. Then the phone rang. It was my young cousin, Janine, who was on a working holiday with her boyfriend, Mark, both of whom had recently arrived in Australia from England. We had been corresponding, but for various reasons we had not yet met. She told me an amazing story. She had taken a short (three days from memory) temping job at UTS in the Human Resources Unit, and late that afternoon, her boss, sitting at a desk near her, had said: 'I've been trying to ring this woman all week to let her know she's been shortlisted, but there's never any answer!' Janine had glanced across at the letter her boss had pushed aside and then looked again: she recognised the shape of my signature. Her boss passed over the letter, and Janine said: 'She's actually my cousin. Would you like me to try again later tonight?'

Well, the boss agreed, so Janine did and got on to me. I've always thought how truly amazing that was: that my young cousin, who was on a working holiday in Australia and whom I had not at that stage even met, was there, on that day in that place at that moment, and that she noticed and recognised my signature on a letter on an adjacent desk.

I was fortunate enough to get the job. It was only a twelve-month half-time contract, but I didn't care. For me (as I later wrote in a short poem) 'It was Oxbridge, at the end of Eton Road'.

That initial contract ran into a three-year full-time contract, at the end of which there was another little miracle. The dean called me into his office one Friday, asking me if I had a CV and, if so, requesting that I put it on his desk on Monday morning. I agreed, and he said: 'We're going to give you tenure.' Just like that! I couldn't believe it.

This all led to a rich and largely unpremeditated professional focus. I was still teaching, but teaching adults, and now I could turn my deep and consuming interests in literature, language and education – and indeed life – into real research, exploring and sharing, and, of course, writing.

Malcolm was incredibly supportive of this. Years later, as a professor, I several times had mature-age women come to me in tears because their husband was angry about them studying again. Malcolm was the opposite; he was truly happy for me. We both shared the quality of being totally absorbed in what we do – reading and writing, making and creating, continually seeking to find out more and to do better.

A wonderful literary trip to the UK. (The reason I missed my PhD graduation.) This is my favourite picture of Shakespeare's church, Holy Trinity, Stratford-upon-Avon. Here he was baptised, married and buried. A larger version of this photo hung for decades on the wall in my work office

And so began my wonderful years at the University of Technology Sydney. Here I found close, like-minded friends, endless challenges and mind-enhancing opportunities. And when I completed my PhD, I didn't attend my graduation ceremony at Macquarie University, because I was given the chance of undertaking a literary tour of Great Britain, with my first international invitations to speak.

I loved university life. It was rich, diverse, inspiring, creative. I loved the teaching, especially the mature age master's and higher degree research students. Undergraduate lectures, generally to about 120 students in a large lecture theatre, appealed to my sense of the dramatic. I borrowed (from my dear storytelling friend Barbara) a special hooded red 'storyteller' cloak to don when introducing a new text and learnt how to play with the lights in order to induce a particular atmosphere: anticipation, fear, excitement, wonder. Students told me that some of their friends from other courses would sneak in to the back of the theatre for the last quarter of an hour or so of my weekly lectures, just to observe this performance. I like to think that perhaps they also learnt something about motivation, creating interest and enriching a learning environment by using story to bring knowledge alive. Some colleagues also dropped in, a few of whom probably thought such antics were not quite seemly, but most appeared to enjoy it.

I also started accompanying education students to Thailand (and later to Laos and Samoa) on their international practicums. These were excellent experiences; they not only broadened the world-view of the students, but also, as some later wrote to me, gave them valuable practice in teaching speakers of other languages. When they began their own teaching and found themselves in Sydney schools, they were to discover that sometimes eighty-five per cent (or more) of their students did not speak English at home.

It was here that I learnt – and experienced – the fallibilities of that 'new English curriculum' (now discontinued) mentioned in my job interview and the unfortunate way in which traditional grammar had been generally eliminated from NSW schools. These students, practising teaching English to Thai (Laotian, Samoan) students as a foreign language, just did not have the grammatical vocabulary, let alone the

Afternoon classes in English grammar in Vientiane, Laos

With the Thai Head of School Education at a function in Bangkok, Thailand

With Malcolm at the bridge on the River Kwai

With dear colleagues in Apia, Samoa

knowledge, to do so. Indeed, everywhere we went, and as it is in most countries of the world, schools taught grammar using basic traditional grammar vocabulary.

So, every afternoon we would return to our accommodation and I would teach a speed course to my third-year university students in elementary grammar. These experiences were very hectic, and often we had problems to be sorted out either with students or with our host schools. I was usually away on these stints for about a month. Mostly I was on my own, but it was often possible for Malcolm to join me for the last week or so. This was nice for us both and meant that he could get to know the friends I had made, several of whom later visited us at Kerensa.

Celebrating a great storyteller with a great storyteller: with Barbara at Robert Louis Stevenson's home in Samoa

With Malcolm in Thailand

10.2 Adventures with CREA

With some clever colleagues, we set about reviving and giving new life to a small university centre, the Centre for Research and Education in the Arts (CREA). This had been started by Dr John Lloyd, who was to become a dear friend and whose scholarship and musicianship I very much admired.

Now began some of the most exciting years, both for my colleagues and for myself, and, so they tell us, for some of our sparkiest and most creative students as well. We introduced a tumble of activities: arts dinners with well-known and topical speakers, such as Aden Ridgeway and conductor Simone Young, seminars and fora, holiday programs, drama camps and writing camps, UTS Young People's Theatre Company and the Creative HSC program.

At this time we were situated on the Kuring-gai campus. The university wanted, as I was told, 'to highlight UTS Kuring-gai'. So we did. Our programs generated both significant excitement and considerable publicity. Our student performers loved it. Some said it was the highlight of their university life. And schools enjoyed it as well. CREA initiatives brought over 25,000 school students to activities on the UTS campus during just under ten years. Primary schools in their enthusiastic hundreds came to pantomimes, plays, music and musicals in our beautiful large theatre. There would often be lines of school buses stretching all along Eton Road.

The Creative HSC program was particularly successful for secondary students and made the most of all our resources and facilities (a great Drama Studio and a large theatre, the Greenhalgh). We would consider the texts senior students were studying for the Higher School Certificate. Then, with my wonderful creative friend Associate Professor Barbara Poston-Andersen and supported by our colleagues Dr Paul March and Dr Lesley Ljungdahl, we would adapt these into a script, often with an unusual twist. Our UTS students performed these scripts in 'user-friendly' productions that were very popular with both public and private schools. And just to cap it off, between us we produced all sorts of original handouts and study notes for both students and teachers. These productions included:

Senior high school students arriving for a CREA production of HSC texts

> *Fool for thy Love: Hamlet*
>
> *Antigone and the Fall of the House of Oedipus*
>
> *The Fatal Flaw: Macbeth and Othello*
>
> *History and Hysteria: The Crucible*
>
> *Mary Shelley's Monster: The Story of Frankenstein*
>
> *Pride and Prejudice*
>
> *Away*
>
> *Masquerade: Shakespeare's Hidden Women*

We always looked for community support and collaboration; for example, a play on road safety for primary schools was sponsored not only by the Road Traffic Authority of New South Wales, but also by three local councils.

Alongside all the literature and drama, we were also featuring music seminars, including performances and lectures under the inspired leadership of our colleague Dr Robyn Staveley.

This performance represents collaboration, co-operation and community.

The Road Safety Officers of three local councils, Ku-ring-gai, North Sydney and Warringah have worked with the Centre for Research and Education in the Arts at all stages of this project.

UTS Faculty of Education students are performing the play and have contributed ideas. The director is a post-graduate student in the Master of Arts in Children's Literature and Literary program at UTS.

Road safety is an issue that is of utmost importance to us all. UTS is a progressive university which seeks to serve its community. We feel privileged to have been a part of this project.

Dr Rosemary Johnston
Director
CREA

◆◆◆
BOOK NOW FOR
A CULTURAL CELEBRATION OF
ITALIAN FOLKTALES
1, 3, 9 December 1999 – 10am, 12:15pm
Friday 3rd December – 7.00pm

Year 2000 Performances

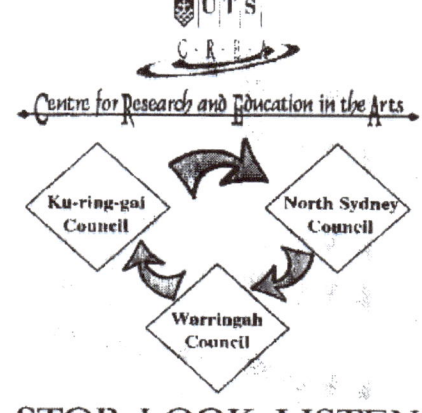

STOP, LOOK, LISTEN
Santa in the City
A Performance about Road Safety

With the support of the
Road Traffic Authority (NSW)

CREA Performances for primary and secondary schools. This one was about road safety. Sponsors included three local councils and the Road Traffic Authority, which contributed funds and lent us road signs and equipment. We also presented pantomimes and children's plays, all of which were both enthusiastically acted by our university students and enthusiastically attended by schools. Performances for secondary school students focused on senior texts and were accompanied by tutorials and study notes. They were much appreciated by teachers

In between all this, our international programs continued and grew. I learnt how pleasant it is to be able to invite like-minded people to become part of a team that has a worthy purpose. Because I believed in what we were doing, I felt comfortable asking others to contribute their expertise. Thus we were able as a centre to attract wonderful staff and exciting patrons, to whom I am forever grateful (they willingly agreed). These wonderful people gave us a real presence in the university and a sense of significance.

In Regensburg, Germany

Thailand Board meeting with the Princess of Thailand; RRJ opening as Vice President of FILLM (Fédération Internationale des Langues et Littératures Modernes)

With philosopher John Ralston Saul in Canada

Media requests for comment on education and literacy/literary issues. This ABC team came to my home

10.3 The adventure in Finland

My first international invitation to speak fortuitously led to further invitations. I was elected to various executive boards: that of the US based Children's Literature Association (its first Australian Board member); of the inaugural Australian Children's Literature Association for Research (ACLAR); and of the International Research Society for Children's Literature (IRSCL) as secretary. I also became associate and then vice-president of the *Fédération Internationale des Langues et Littératures Modernes* (FILLM), which is affiliated to UNESCO.

In 1999 I was invited to spend about nine months in Finland as H. W. Donner Research Chair, Åbo Akademi University, researching the teaching of literacy and literature. This was a shared venture of the university and the Finnish Ministry of Education. The project was led by Professor Roger Sell, who approached me at a conference in Exeter and issued the invitation.

This sounded exciting. I would be given travel costs, accommodation, a generous salary and, best of all, I could bring my husband. I was granted leave from UTS, and in early January 2000 Malcolm and I embarked on a wonderful Nordic adventure that was not only intellectually enhancing, but also personally fulfilling for both of us.

Malcolm outside our home in Finland. We had the ground floor apartment on left with the white door opening straight onto the courtyard. Yliopistonkatu 24D 55 20100, Turku

After Christmas, we went, as usual for our holiday at Soldiers Point, to stay with the family in the lovely waterside unit that belonged to Alistair, Malcolm's brother, and his partner, Stephen. It was a particularly beautiful few weeks: perfect weather, perfect water, and lots of swimming and water activities, which Malcolm loved. On return we had only a short few days turnaround in which to pack for being away for months in a very different climate – indeed, in a Nordic country. As we raced around washing and packing and sorting out, Malcolm became quite reluctant about our proposed adventure. It was just glorious at Kerensa as well, and he was swimming at our beach (Bungan) each morning and late afternoon. However, we were eventually on the plane, first to London, then to Helsinki and then to Turku. We had packed our warm jackets in the carry-ons, but we did not really notice the change in hemisphere and northern January weather until we arrived in Turku, where Roger met us to take us to the apartment he had organised.

One of the first of many meals and research team get-togethers at Tia and Roger Sell's beautiful home. Great hospitality!

What a wonderful adventure! Our apartment was right in town and had its own white door (complete with a brass plate with our name on it) opening straight into a courtyard and directly opposite and just over the road from Turku's answer to our David Jones, which had a food department in the basement. We could wake up on Saturday morning and one or both of us could stroll through the courtyard and across the road and buy beautiful fresh baguettes and some favourite cheeses and strawberries to bring back for breakfast. The university and my new office were just a walk through the town away and opposite the lovely old cathedral, where we attended both services and many magnificent music recitals. Malcolm, advised by both Roger and Tia (Roger's wife who became a great friend), joined several choirs.

I walked through the cosmetics department of the store (Stockmans) each morning to get to work. And each morning I allowed myself to test a small squirt of one of the perfumes. (Towards the end I felt I needed to do it rather surreptitiously.) Once or twice one of the girls would smile and say: 'See what you think of this one.' (Or words to that effect.) Walking to work in a cloud of pretty scent and with snowflakes landing on my arms was a pleasure.

Although I did have to purchase, with Tia's help and despite ideological misgivings, a Finnish fur coat. All the women wore one; it was really, really cold!

But our apartment was snug and warm and amazingly easy to keep clean: wooden floors and sparsely furnished. There was a study with a desk and spare bed (where Alistair slept when he came to stay with us for a holiday in spring); a bedroom with a 'double' (two single beds pushed together and made up as one), a wardrobe and a dressing table; and a sitting/dining room with couch and armchair and a small dining table with four chairs. The kitchen, which had a front window looking out over the courtyard, was equipped with four plates, spoons and so on, and two saucepans, a neat frying pan and a coffee maker. It was all we needed – plenty – and so easy to look after; I loved it.

Roger had gathered an amazing team for his project, and I learnt so much about the seriousness of Finnish research and scholarship, particularly in relation to education. I was working with so many interesting and dedicated people and was able to do a great deal of writing.

With Malcolm in Finland

After a while, Malcolm and I started going away for weekends, especially when I could take a flexible extra day. We went by train to Sweden (and woke up and the carriage was on a large boat!) and also to St Petersburg. (I had a student there; it was incredible to visit.) And we flew to Berlin, Oslo, Paris and Prague. I loved Prague; it was like a fairytale. We especially liked the Strahov Library, which is part of the monastery. We came across it on our walk up to the castle.

We relished the winter, the snow and watching the snowflakes land on the trees and on each other; we relished the spring, when the town square, empty and cold and bare through winter, started to fill up with stalls and all sorts of wares, tasty and otherwise; we relished the summer, with bunches and bunches of beautiful flowers filling the air with scent for miles around. It was in Finland that I fell in love with tulips. I'd liked them before, but now I found them incredibly beautiful, almost a metaphor for the Nordic world: sparsely coiled and bare in the cold, opening up into such fragile and tender beauty as the warmer weather comes.

There were many wonderful adventures in Finland, but our holiday in Äkäslompolo, deep in Finnish Lapland, was one I will never forget. Äkäslompolo is located about two hundred kilometres north, heading towards the North Pole. We went there in March, as we were told that was the best time to see the Northern Lights. Alas, we didn't see them, but what we did see was entrancing.

We stayed in our own little cabin topped with several feet of snow. Like many Finnish homes, it had its own sauna, which was fantastic. The high point was the day we went for a long ride of several hours on skidoos, led by a guide who told us he took us deep into the Arctic Circle. We each had our own skidoo with heated handles, which I really appreciated. Later our Finnish friends informed us that they had never been solo on a skidoo going so far into the forest; they always had a guide actually riding with them on the same skidoo. We didn't know any better! Our guide sailed on in front, Malcolm followed and I brought up the rear. This was all right until I skidded on a slope and was scared to try to move back lest I fell down further into the huge mounds of snow concealing goodness knows what. I called out to Malcolm, only a few feet in front, but he couldn't hear me. I could scarcely hear my own voice; it was so muffled by the deep snow all around us. There was a moment when it was like one of those nightmares when no one can hear you scream. Luckily, Malcolm looked back and saw my predicament and came to yank my skidoo back up onto the track.

On a skidoo in the Arctic Circle

A fairytale landscape

In Stockholm at the Astrid Lindgren (Pippi Longstocking) monument

It was snowing softly all the time as we rode through the fairyland forest, being led

Tia and Roger and another family function at which we were always welcomed

deeper and deeper into a magic landscape of huge puffy meringues of snow, with flakes floating down on us from the dripping firs all around. We both looked pretty puffy ourselves, dressed in several layers of our own warmest clothes topped with a much-padded all-in-one suit that was given to us by the skidoo proprietors. The clothes made us both look like bouncy round balls.

We paused for lunch at a small wooden hut where the guide made us a deliciously sweet hot chocolate. (I don't usually like sweet things but this was just perfect: a hot mug in an isolated wooden hut in the middle of a magical and snowy fairyland forest.)

What a wonderful adventure! And what a wonderful professional experience. I had many local invitations to speak, both in Finland and in Sweden and Norway, meeting interesting people wherever we went. We travelled by train to Sweden (where I had been asked to run some professional workshops) and woke up, as mentioned earlier, on a boat but still in our sleeper on the train. Amazing! We went away on weekends to other countries – something Australians can't usually do. We revelled in having the rest of Europe just a few hours away. Malcolm bought a bike and went riding all around Turku and exploring the countryside whilst I was at work. But most of all we just

Some of the Nordic press (note photo of front page where I'm positioned next to Friedrich Nietzsche!)

loved Finland. I learnt so much about this noble little country of about five million people, perched so precariously, it felt to us, right next door to Russia.

What makes it all work so well? It's readily observable. I saw it everywhere. Finland values education, values its teachers, makes sure they are all extremely well qualified and that they keep up to date. And it values its universities. The essence of Finnish high standards in education is just that: teachers are socially valued, esteemed, respected and they live up to it. I went into many schools whilst there and saw pride – pride in the schools for their teachers and pride in the teachers for their schools. It's a pride less focused on self and more focused on an idea of national excellence that serves the country so very well. Everyone has a part in it. Everyone is a bit of it. And the children are the beneficiaries. They feel valued as well.

10.4 Working against disadvantage

The experience of being in Finland re-ignited – not that it had ever gone out – my desire to work with children who, through no fault of their own, were in circumstances not conducive to developing productive futures. They were and are often labelled as 'disadvantaged'. Of course, they were/are, but labels do not help. There are many facets to 'disadvantage'.

As noted in an earlier chapter, I had started this work whilst a university student myself, working with Barney's Club at St Barnabas, Broadway, opposite the Sydney University campus. Glebe in those days was a very different place to the upmarket area it has subsequently become. Now on the staff of a university, new worlds of opportunity opened for me in which to pursue this passion.

I had done much reading and research and was interested not only in the esoteric but in the practical. If we were working with a particular group as part of our research, I wanted to make a practical difference to that group, not simply observe it and write about it.

The first thing to do was to obtain funding, and I started looking for experts who could help and would be willing to collaborate. I wrote my first application for an Australian Research Council (ARC) grant, calling it *New Ways of Doing School: Mixing story and technology to generate innovative learning, social and cultural communities*. This project was designed to 'develop innovative mixes of story arts with multimedia technologies to create a new sense of place, learning community and belonging for children in remote and urban regions'. We gathered a strong team: academics Professor Larissa Behrendt and Professor Ross Gibson, Rev Bill Crews, founder of the Exodus Foundation, and Mr Stephen Harris, then principal of Northern Beaches Christian School. And the application was successful!

In a very real way, this first project remains at the moral core of everything I tried to do as a researcher: seeking to give, in the glorious diversity of 'multicultural Australia', all students – whatever the cultural heritage, whatever the social background – a sense of belonging, a sense of a shared 'my place' of thinking and ideas, of dreams and hopes and possibilities. The remote programs involved us sitting alongside and simultaneously being learners and teachers, engaging and encouraging, sharing together. We had used the idea of 'talk-story' – teaching and learning through telling stories – but we quickly developed for ourselves the even more important idea of 'listen-story' – teaching and learning through listening – listening to the stories of those who had lived and worked in these communities, in some cases for all their life.

Some of our early research recommendations are still, sadly, relevant. What became clear very quickly was that challenges could not neatly be categorised as 'educational'. School attendance, for example, pertains to health, housing, government policies and political decisions, overcrowding, parenting practices, employment opportunities (or not), school organisation, teachers, pedagogy, histories, geographies and difficult social problems. Recognising this and as an outcome of the *New Ways* research, UTS grew and developed the Centre for Research and Education in the Arts, which later evolved into the International Research Centre for Youth Futures, as an interdisciplinary meeting place for researchers across the disciplines to work together with a broader scope (not only arts related) of issues pertaining to young people.

Our first patron was the lovely Thérèse Rein, wife of then Prime Minister Kevin Rudd, who lent her charm and presence to many of our programs. Our second patron, who generously supported our activities and graced our functions for years, was then Governor-General Quentin Bryce (now Dame Quentin). What a brilliant yet down-to-earth gift she was (and is) to our nation! Then we were blessed with the support of our third patron, the charming Kerryn Baird, wife of Mike, who was Premier of New South Wales from 2014 to 2017 and the son of Judy and Bruce Baird, dear friends of many years.

With Thérèse Rein, wife of then Prime Minister Kevin Rudd

Launch of Centre Board at UTS, so many wonderful, supportive people: (l-r) Gregor Ramsey, Amanda Bell, Leon Parioissien, Thérèse Rein, RRJ, David Hannaford, Vicki Jack, Paolo Totaro, David Gallop, Mike McCluskey. (Absent: Peter Browne, Cherrell Hirst, Neil Jackson, James Morrison, Theo van Leeuwen)

A little later, Ken Jolly, then chair of Scholastic Australia, also joined our board. This group of people were magnificently supportive for many years.

Paolo Totaro and Gregor Ramsey encouraged our endeavours, and me personally, for many years

> Our Centre patrons were Thérèse Rein, wife of the then Prime Minister Kevin Rudd and a successful business woman, and Dame Quentin Bryce, then Governor-General. A little later, we were also fortunate to have Kerryn Baird, wife of then Premier of NSW, Mike Baird, as our patron.
>
> We were truly blessed to have the support of these three wonderful women as patrons of a university centre dedicated to overcoming disadvantage and supporting young people, a mission in which they all truly believe.

25 October 2010
Professor Rosemary Johnston, Chancellor Vicki Sara and Vice Chancellor Professor Ross Milbourne, greet the Governor-General on arrival at the Building Literate Nations Forum at UTS. This followed on from weeks of field work in the Pilbara (WA), Yorke Peninsula (SA), and Galiwin'ku (NT) and led to later work in Lockhart River (QLD)

Centre Board Meeting at the Governor-General's residence, Admiralty House: (back row l-r) Leon Paroissien, Neil Jackson, Gregor Ramsey, Attila Brungs, Amanda Bell (front row l-r) Mary Spongberg, RRJ, Quentin Bryce, Vicki Jack

There were a number of recommendations and comments submitted in our final report on this first grant (2010). The most urgent of these was to address health issues. For example, we were horrified at the prevalence of *otitis media*, which impedes hearing and can appear (and is often misinterpreted) as disinterest or even rudeness. We suggested there should be specific training for community health workers in the 'Breathe Blow Cough' programs and compulsory modules in Indigenous health education for pre-service teacher education students and police officer cadets. (I met with state health and federal education ministers to discuss this.) We also recommended reconsidering and implementing bilingual education. English is not a first but a second or even a third language for many Indigenous children. Bilingual education is appreciated in communities and seems to work. Other recommendations and comments included: End NAPLAN in remote schools at least, as it only compounds feelings of disadvantage and deficit and does not help in 'closing the gap'; offer support and real incentives for teachers to work in remote areas for longer periods; encourage and train teachers and health workers from within communities; approach education holistically and use business not just to provide funding but to provide expertise; and consider innovative and creative pathways both in and out of school.

Rawa Aboriginal Community School, Western Australia

Working with communities in Newman, Punmu and Kunawarritji in the Pilbara and Desertlands of Western Australia, in this first of three ARC grants, provided both the idealistic and formal beginning of subsequent similar projects: *New Ways Old Ways: Personalising Education to Meet Local Community Needs* (with Rawa Aboriginal Corporation, Kanyirninpa Jukurrpa Pilbara and Department of Education and Training WA and supported by the Martu peoples of the Pilbara); *The Dreams Projects* (in various iterations and with many collaborators over different times), which sought to address the needs of both regional and urban Indigenous youth; *The Widening Participation Projects* and *Sky High Projects* (providing opportunities for young people in disadvantaged areas to find and explore new options and possibilities for futures); and *The Literacy Projects* (expanding the idea and promise of literacy into a concept of deep literacy – building imaginations and minds that help to generate creative and civil societies). This nest of projects conceptualised literacy not only in terms of skills, but, as noted above, in terms of the idea of literate imaginations and of thinking as being reflective of its most profound aspect.

Indeed, literacy became a core area of research and *Literate Australia* a core project. Literacy pertains traditionally to the critical skills of reading, writing, speaking and listening, but my idea of 'deep literacy' extrapolates it into what these skills seed and grow: learning about others, learning about self. Deep literacy is nuanced with identity and place; it is a creative ability that, as I have written, 'generates imaginative understandings of relationships to others and relationships to difference that profoundly influence personal and communal behaviours'. We worked both with remote and regional Indigenous communities, as well as with diversely 'disadvantaged' city communities. Our city programs, in particular, were aimed at 'showing and telling': exposing students to wider horizons of *what is* in order to inspire ideas of what perhaps *could be*. All our programs were about opening doors that might have been seen as closed, nourishing thinking and promoting both capacity and aspiration.

These projects led to the Building Literate Nations National Forum, held at UTS, with the opening address delivered by the Governor-General. The forum was cross-sectoral and interdisciplinary. It was attended by: the chancellor, vice-chancellor, deputy vice-chancellors and senior academics (deans, professors) from across the disciplines; Indigenous educators from three states; the NSW Minister for Education and Training; several other Members of Parliament; Hon. Bruce Baird; Dr Gregor Ramsey; Father Chris Riley (Youth off the Streets); Rev Bill Crews (Exodus); Mr David Gallop (National Rugby League); Dr Cherrell Hirst (ex-chancellor QUT);

high level representatives from the Australian Broadcasting Corporation, the Smith Family, Oxfam, the Indigenous Literacy Project and the office of the NSW Police Commissioner; education providers; Mr David Hannaford (Tresillian); and CEOs of large corporations, including Gilbert+Tobin, Anchorage Holdings, Woolworths, Apple and Microsoft.

As a continuing part of all this, a little later I was also fortunate to be able to have several one-to-one meetings with Peter Garrett of *Midnight Oil* fame (although his minder/assistant was also present), who was then Minister for School Education, Early Childhood and Youth in the Rudd government. The meetings were held in his beautiful office overlooking the harbour. He was both frank and encouraging, but I sensed a degree of unspoken frustration; I think he is a doer and felt constricted by the actual politics of his portfolio.

All these projects were highly collaborative and only worked as well as they did because of the wonderful teams with whom we partnered: Professor Larissa Behrendt and Professor Ross Gibson, Dr Paul March, Dr Lesley Ljungdahl and Dr Robyn Staveley among many. I was fortunate also to be able to employ creative and skilled young people, some newly-minted PhDs, as part of our teams working with students in school-based projects. Rachel, Nicola, Sarah, Sandris and Karen all worked with us for many years and others brought their wealth of talents for shorter periods. Robyn was our research assistant in the early days and Libby was an expert and thoughtful personal assistant later. And I also had the ongoing support not only of my husband, but of our children. Indeed, some lovely synergies evolved and some of the projects became, for a period in the early days, family affairs. The first of these involved my daughter-in-law, Helen (Mal's wife), who brought her skills to work with me as my research assistant. Soon after, a spot opened up for another part-time assistant and my daughter Annabel joined us. This was the time when we were doing many CREA drama performances with the students (one play going on, another one in rehearsal, another auditioning), and Annabel became a mixture of technology expert and wardrobe mistress. This meant concocting costumes out of very little. She had recently graduated with a design degree from UTS. Helen moved on whilst we were in Finland, and a few years after we returned, Robert, who had just finished his master's degree after a summer program at Harvard, became the Centre Research Officer. At that time I was doing a lot of travelling around the country and into isolated communities, and he came with me as part of the team, writing, researching and arranging all the logistics. He was a wonderful support; indeed, they all were. What a challenging and truly exciting time it was.

Brief pictorial synopsis of New Ways research

Rawa (via Newman, WA), Punmu, Kunawarritji (WA), Yorke Peninsula (SA), Galiwin'ku (NT), Lockhart River (QLD)

This represented a partnership consisting of the Puuya Foundation, Lockhart State School, Lockhart River Parent and Community Engagement (Chair Greg Pascoe and Co-ordinator Barbie Chippendale), with the support of the Lockhart River Aboriginal Shire Council (Mayor Rodney Accoom, Deputy Paul Piva and CEO Peter Opio-Otim).

Lockhart River Team

Denise Hagan (CEO Puuya Foundation), John McSweeney (Principal Lockhart State School), Veronica Piva (Puuya Board), Barbara Chippendale (PaCE) Miss Yolanda (Deputy Principal Lockhart State School), Rosemary Johnston, Lesley Ljungdahl, Nicola Sinclair, Robert Johnston.

The program was attended well, response from both school and community was enthusiastic, and one of the outcomes was a video clip and song celebrating local vocabulary, environment, history and experience, and evolving out of the words and images contributed by students. It was built around an old song remembered by and sung by one of the community elders.

This has now been adopted by the community as its school song and is a creative output of the project – *Oh Lockhart 2012* www.youtube.com/watch?v=k8mVc2Sbcag

Lockhart River (Far North Queensland)

Sky High, Dreams, Literate Australia: Urban and Regional Projects

Making it work for all stakeholders (and giving begets giving)

Clipping from local paper 27.2.13

- Sailing day with Jesse Martin on Sydney Harbour
- The *IMC Sky High!* project impacts the community and the school enhances its image
- This activity related to the importance of team work, observation and tenacity
- It was only made possible by University, corporate, and community collaborations:
- Four yachts, with Captains and crew, from the Cruising Yacht Club of Australia, were loaned to the project; four qualified lifesavers donated a day of their time, as did IMC and UTS student volunteers, and the UTS team.

Archibald Prize Finalist Ben Hedstrom during one of our Sky High! workshops, and one of his works above

10. A Well-Watered Garden

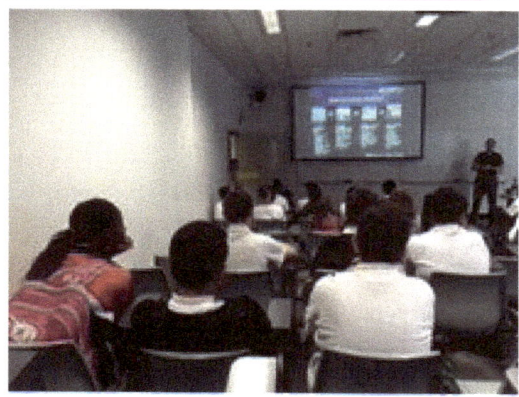

Coding, visits to the Sydney Opera House, music studio sessions, forensics lab, art and cooking classes – just some of our various projects and activities

Be bold, be curious – UTS social justice program helps students to aim high – 8 June 2016

- Students who are finding school life challenging for personal and social reasons are part of a research project aimed at promoting educational achievement.

- The Sky High! program works with students from more than a dozen western Sydney high schools to expose them to new experiences and ideas.

'What's physiology? Has anyone heard that word?' asks science postgrad student Hayley.

Quick as a flash, the answer comes back. 'It's about the human body,' says a young girl.

As 30 young western Sydney high school students mill around lab benches in the UTS Science faculty, their mentors get down to business, attaching blood pressure cuffs to arms and electrodes to foreheads.

The students are soon learning the difference between systolic and diastolic pressure as the cuff tightens and loosens; others monitor what happens to their brain activity when they perform simple mental arithmetic.

The students are participants in Sky High!, a two-year donor-funded social justice program for students in years 7 and 8 which is run as an action research project by the International Research Centre for Youth Futures at UTS. It's a long way from another ordinary day at school – in fact, for several students their visit to UTS is the first time they've travelled to the city.

Professor Rosemary Johnston, director of the centre and leader of the program, says schools choose students to take part because they are seen to have the potential for academic achievement but may be held back by a range of circumstances. 'We work closely with our participating schools to select students who will really benefit from exposure to new environments. Some students are finding school life challenging for complex and varied personal and social reasons,' says Professor Johnston.

'Sky High! is a valuable way to support the great work teachers are doing and the aspirations parents have for their children. The program encourages students to complete their schooling, and is designed to grow literacy, participation, engagement and confidence.

'Our research into the program's impact shows that exposing students to wider options and exciting ideas – and people – leads them to be bolder and more curious about their own potential.'

The research centre works with more than a dozen schools, but today's visitors are from Ashcroft, St John's Park and Cabramatta high schools. Their day also included a visit to the Data Arena in the Faculty of Engineering and IT. Marianela Hernandez, a teacher at St John's Park High School, says she is always striving to engage parents and the community to support the students in activities such as the Sky High! initiative. 'A visit like this one to UTS is often a student's first connection with a university because no one else in the family has gone on to higher education,' Hernandez says.

Quizzed about what they might do in the future, the students have a range of goals: zoology, says one; flight attendant, says another; join the army, says a third.

Dr Sarah Loch, project development manager at the International Research Centre for Youth Futures, says students visit UTS with open eyes. 'We organise a program that is diverse and focused on the future. We cannot imagine the types of careers these young people will enter after school, but we do know that we want them to see themselves working or studying in areas that will bring life satisfaction,' says Dr Loch. Dr Nicola Sinclair, the program's event manager, says they are currently working with more than 150 students. 'All of these young people will take different ideas from each workshop. Our aim is to open doors to the unexpected,' she says.

In coming months, the students will participate in a moot court in Hyde Park Barracks, attend a trial at the Downing Street law courts, attend a UTS music workshop, attend and participate in play readings at Riverside Theatre, spend a day cooking and learning about nutrition, go backstage at the Sydney Opera House, and learn about coding with employees in a large corporate city office.

Byline: Fiona McGill
<http://newsroom.uts.edu.au/news/2016/06/be-bold-be-curious-%E2%80%93-uts-social-justice-program-helps-students-aim-high>

The Literacy projects and Kid's Proms

- **Exposure to excellence**
- **Shifting horizons of thinking, possibilities and aspiration**
- **Enriching experiences**

The Australian Centre for Child and Youth is an interdisciplinary centre that integrates technology, research, teaching and practice in fields pertaining to the culture and well-being of children and youth – including education, health, family, law, community and policy.

Director Professor Rosemary Johnston says that literacy goes far beyond the basic concepts of reading and writing.

'We are thinking in terms of deep literacy, which sets up inner connections and grows minds, generating imaginative understandings of relationships to others and relationships to difference, that will profoundly influence personal and communal behaviours,' she says.

Interview at Australian Parliament House, Canberra, addressing literacy and disadvantage

'Bright Futures' – UTS Holiday programs for young children. These had different foci. This one was science and robotics/electronics. We capped numbers at twenty, employed an inspiring instructor and charged reasonably. The team helped. It was vibrant and wonderful and beautifully showcased UTS.

This was a July week, students waiting in Building 10 for others to arrive

> There are so many dear people at UTS whose intellects have both inspired and challenged me, and whose support and leadership helped to enhance and enlarge my university experience, creatively and excitingly. I have already mentioned some but want here particularly to acknowledge Professors Mary Spongberg, Theo van Leeuwen, Attila Brungs, Christine Deer, Diana Slade, Larissa Behrendt, Alan Davison, Ross Milbourne, Shirley Alexander, William Purcell, and Tony Blake.

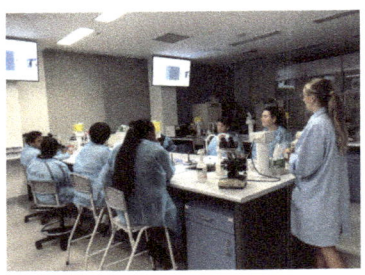
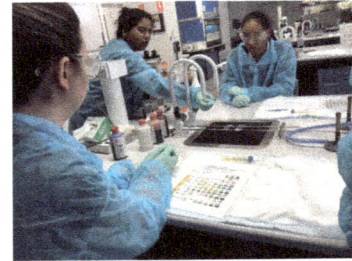

This is a project that we launched but that was unavoidably interrupted. I hope it may inspire other thinking and doing. I believe in its potential.

> **Digital encylopedia tells a new story of learning for schools – 11 Aug 2016**
>
>
>
> **The NSW Premier and Minister for Education have launched a UTS-developed digital encylopedia for schools that will encourage schoolchildren to tell their own stories and those of their communities.**
>
> Encouraging schoolchildren to tell their own stories, and those of their communities, is at the heart of an innovative online educational resource recently launched by the NSW Premier Mike Baird and Minister for Education Adrian Piccoli. *Australopedia,* a digital, multimedia encyclopedia built by students as part of their normal school work has been developed by the UTS International Research Centre for Youth Futures to be introduced initially in a group of Sydney high schools along with remote Indigenous schools in Western Australia and Queensland.
>
> '*Australopedia* gives these schools the opportunity to model what will become a national endeavour,' said Director of the Centre and creator of *Australopedia*, Professor Rosemary Johnston, who has been developing the idea for several years. 'This is a new model for project-based, interdisciplinary, self-directed learning and real-world collaborations with families, local school communities, businesses and organisations,' Professor Johnston said. 'It will encompass stories and oral histories from local citizens and local heroes, explore the local impact of real-life issues and apply STEM (science, technology, engineering and maths) and STEAM (STEM+arts) knowledge to possible solutions. It will also discover local Indigenous histories, legends and languages and give a platform for appreciating, protecting and enhancing the local environment.'

Speaking at the 3 August launch at NSW Parliament House, Minister for Education Adrian Piccoli said the curriculum developed by the Board of Studies worked for the vast majority of students, but not 'for every single student. That's why it is important that there are other paths for students, other opportunities to engage them in learning and for them to see its relevance and importance,' Mr Piccoli said.

(l-r) UTS Vice-Chancellor Professor Attila Brungs, NSW Premier Mike Baird, Mrs Kerryn Baird, Professor Rosemary Johnston, Minister for Education Adrian Piccoli and Minister for Planning Rob Stokes at Australopedia launch, NSW Parliament House

Premier Mike Baird said *Australopedia* would give schools in regional and remote communities an incentive and mechanism for students to enjoy being at school, to connect them to their community and to students at other schools. 'I think this program has the capacity to connect them, to promote their story, their community, their organisations … I think through that the kids will enjoy school more and be inspired to keep going,' Mr Baird said. The Sydney high schools inaugurating *Australopedia* are already part of the International Research Centre for Youth Futures Sky High! social justice program, supported by IMC Financial Markets and Asset Management.

UTS Vice-Chancellor Attila Brungs told the *Australopedia* launch that the IMC Sky High! program was an exemplar for the kind of collaboration between universities and business 'that I'd like to see more of.'

'It is an authentic real-world partnership that fosters collaboration and brings together researchers, community and industry,' Professor Brungs said. 'Initiatives like Sky High! have helped participants to develop and realise their potential, to encourage aspirations and to inspire continuing participation in education.'

<http://newsroom.uts.edu.au/news/2016/08/digital-encylopedia-tells-new-story-learning-schools>

11. Requiem

Requiem: An act or token of remembrance

I am always deeply moved by the music of 'Requiem' by Andrew Lloyd Webber. I was introduced to it by Ella Johnston, a dear cousin of my husband's father. It is heart-rendingly sad, and heart-rendingly beautiful.

At this place in my *passeggiata*, I realise that permeating the whole latter half of the book and indeed the greater part of my life is the presence of my husband, Malcolm.

Malcolm and I chose Andrew Lloyd Webber's 'Requiem' together to play at Ella's funeral. Is it too moving, too sad? Perhaps so. But life and love and happiness is deepened, yes, enriched by, not only the terrible ache and grief of loss, but also the great and privileged joy of having in the first place, indeed, the exquisite joy of having life and love. Andrew Lloyd Webber wrote 'Requiem' out of his experience both of hearing the painful stories of others and of his own personal grief at the death of his father in 1982. 'Requiem' was first performed on 25 February 1985.

We lost Malcolm on 12 November 2007, and a part of me was lost then as well. But at the end of the previous year we had had a wonderful adventure together: several months in England and Scotland, when we did lovely, dream-like things, like walking parts of Hadrian's Wall, where Malcolm revelled in browsing through some of the funny little places with old tools (very old – some from the Vikings, or so we were told). We drove slowly along the coast up to and past Edinburgh, getting out frequently and traipsing around the little fishing villages that are indented like studs below the surprisingly rugged cliffs. We meandered, as we had done on our honeymoon when driving through Queensland and up to Magnetic Island. That honeymoon trip was where Malcolm's obsession with 'old roads' first became apparent to me; it was to become part of every long driving holiday thereafter. Later, when we went on our seven years of caravanning holidays with the little kids, they would watch out as well and all shout together 'old road'. Malcolm loved breaking out and exploring the tantalising 'old road', and the family folklore concerning the 'road to Miriam Vale' dates back to our honeymoon. We were en route to Townsville when Malcolm saw it and we took it. We became very lost and very late, and we were never sure if we actually got to Miriam Vale or had passed it without noticing. But how much we enjoyed the looking!

So this long unhurried drive through the north of England and the south of Scotland was part of – a culmination of – a family tradition that reached way back to that long-ago honeymoon. We both enjoyed long drives and randomly stopping along the way. A few years before this UK trip we had driven through Ireland with no bookings, just stopping and seeking accommodation as our fancy took us. We were always successful.

As an aside, that Ireland drive along the Wild Atlantic Way took us from the sublime (Cashel House, a grandly furnished country home/

Requiem

By Andrew Lloyd Webber

Pie Jesu, pie Jesu, pie Jesu, pie Jesu,

Qui tollis peccata mundi

Dona eis requiem, dona eis requiem

Agnus Dei, Agnus Dei, Agnus Dei, Agnus Dei,

Qui tollis peccata mundi

Dona eis requiem, dona eis requiem,

Sempiternam

Sempiternam

Requiem

Merciful Jesus, merciful Jesus, merciful Jesus, merciful Jesus

Father, who takes away the sins of the world

Grant them rest, grant them rest.

Lamb of God, Lamb of God, Lamb of God, Lamb of God,

Father, who takes away the sins of the world

Grant them rest, grant them rest.

Everlasting

Everlasting

Rest.

https://www.youtube.com/watch?v=3loAcmBz044

https://www.youtube.com/watch?v=K-mLTAFrlEA

If you ever go across the sea to Ireland,

Then maybe at the closing of your day,

You can sit and watch the moon rise over Claddagh,

And see the sun go down on Galway Bay.

From the song 'Galway Bay'
composed by Dr Arthur Colahan

garden farm admired by Charles de Gaulle, where we stayed for two very expensive nights) to the ridiculous (an excessively neat bed and breakfast on the edge of Galway Bay – my choice of course, because of the view resonating with the song 'Galway Bay', one of Grandma's favourites). The bed and breakfast had the coldest bedroom I have ever slept in (and we've been into the Arctic Circle) and had freezing stiff sheets that felt like they were coated with ice.

Anyway, back to our lovely 2006 road trip. At one salty and sea-whiffy village just across the Scottish border on the way to Berwick-upon-Tweed, I remember a really tasty and vinegary fish and chips lunch. A bit further up towards Edinburgh, a rosy-cheeked Scottish lady gave us a slice of Dundee cake with a beautifully hot cup of tea. I am not a cake eater, but it seemed appropriate there (if not essential). It was getting late (both late in the day and late in the year), and the route had become prematurely grey and shadowy – creepy tendrils of white mist kept reaching out to our little car – and it was freezing cold. Thinking about poor little Mary, Queen of Scots (she apparently did not like the *glacé* cherries in fruit cakes, so they used almonds and Seville orange instead for her Dundee cake), I ate the blanched almonds off the top and Malcolm polished off the rest.

At another time during these months, we spent a wonderful day going across to the Holy Island of Lindisfarne, where at the priory (the monastery was founded around 634 AD) we tasted mead for the first time. This tiny tidal island became the centre for Christian evangelism in Northern England and is like a history of England in microcosm. We couldn't do the whole walk (times and tides were against us), but crossing the Pilgrims' Way at low tide was like crossing into another Lilliputian world with the history of centuries telescoped into one of those small glass domes that you shake to release the snowflakes (or in this case, the stories). Here Vikings pillaged, here saints prayed, here the Venerable Bede visited, and here Henry VIII used and abused the church to satisfy his own desires.

I learnt so much about Bede (672–735) at Lindisfarne. He was a medieval scholar, writer and historian, who in 1899 was made a Doctor of the Church. He is the patron saint of scholars and historians. His most famous work is the *Ecclesiastical History of the English People*, which tells the story of the conversion of the English to Christianity. Part of his most significant and far-reaching work was in the academic discipline of *computus*, the science of calculating calendar dates. He helped promulgate the practice of dating forward from the birth of Christ (*Anno Domini*, 'in the year of our Lord'), a practice which eventually influenced all medieval Europe. Bede was a polymath who had expertise not only in *computus* but also in astronomy, natural history and theology. I like the simplicity of one of his most well-known statements: 'He alone loves the Creator perfectly who manifests a pure love for his neighbour.'

When we weren't driving, we walked and walked and walked: across country, over stiles, through meadows and through small towns and villages, where we peered into little shops and into the warm lights of homes shivering/quivering across bare winter gardens, loving the tawny sparseness of the cold, quiet countryside. It wasn't 'a wood near Athens' and it wasn't spring (far from it), and nor was it on the banks of the Avon; but it *was* Shakespeare's England, and I found myself thinking of the fairy in *A Midsummer Night's Dream*, who wanders everywhere, 'over hill, over dale', seeking dewdrops and hanging dewdrop pearls on the wildflowers. What magical landscapes of ideas, thoughts, perceptions and sheer wonder – *mindscapes, thoughtscapes, dreamscapes* – have our poets and artists opened our eyes to see, opened our minds to take in and make our own!

We didn't come home until a few weeks before Christmas, and we were in the north of England in Newcastle-upon-Tyne in the run-up to the festive season. So, we were also

A wood near Athens. A Fairy speaks.

Over hill, over dale,
Thorough bush, thorough brier,
Over park, over pale,
Thorough flood, thorough fire,
I do wander everywhere,
Swifter than the moon's sphere;
And I serve the fairy queen,
To dew her orbs upon the green.
The cowslips tall her pensioners be:
In their gold coats spots you see;
Those be rubies, fairy favours,
In those freckles live their savours:
I must go seek some dew-drops here
And hang a pearl in every cowslip's ear.
Farewell, thou lob of spirits; I'll be gone:
Our queen and all our elves come here anon.

A Midsummer Night's Dream, Act 11 Scene 1 William Shakespeare

Cowslip is related to primrose and primula

able to go to that city's wonderful program of plays and seasonal music recitals. Then we went to London to see the decorations and the Christmas tree in Trafalgar Square.

I've been enjoying writing about these memories of those last months, but of course they are seeded in sadness, and in fact they seed sadness. Grief, like the artistry of poets, 'opens the mind'. As Lennon and McCartney wrote, both 'pools of sorrow' and 'waves of joy' can co-exist: can both possess and be all consuming and at the same time caress and soothe.

This part of my *passeggiata* is hard to walk, just as it felt hard at the time to keep going. Will you understand if I say that for me it was an other-worldly time, concerned with thoughts and feelings that are difficult to articulate or express in ordinary language? This is not to say that the language of grief is necessarily that of a grand ode or sad elegy, although there may be elements of both. Rather, it feels to me like a language filled, overpoweringly, with those sharp and strong emotions that prise open the mind, as the Lennon and McCartney song says, and that may be contradictory: gentle as well as fierce, lyrical as well as gruff and thankful as well as angry. Lyrical implies expressive, subjective, even aesthetic. There is a certain grandeur in grief; by that I mean a set-apartness that is both personal and communal, that opens up new and other-worldly, extra-temporal, even heavenly, perspectives. There is an awful alone-ness as well as an equally awful and unwanted communion with other mourners. Yes, there is that dreadful, ripping, agonising sense of loss, a yearning to recapture times past, but there is an equal passion, after giving in to loss, not to forget those times, not to lose them; an urgent desire to somehow commemorate, even consecrate, them. There is, at once, both a holy and

Pools of sorrow, waves of joy are drifting through my opened mind,
Possessing and caressing me.
The Beatles, 'Across the Universe'

I do not think I have ever seen anything more beautiful than the bluebell I have been looking at. I know the beauty of our Lord by it.

G. M. Hopkins Journal 18 May 1870

unholy concomitance of past and present, then and now, before and after.

'Break, break, break/ On thy cold gray stones, O sea', wrote a grieving Tennyson. I have watched the sea and observed and felt that inexorable breaking, that unstoppable coming in and going out of waves that seems to echo the relentless breaking and aching in our spirit. Tennyson expresses this, simply, in a profoundly universal cry:

> But O for the touch of a vanish'd hand,
> And the sound of a voice that is still!

This whole book, especially the later part, has been a lived exegesis of keeping on keeping on. The ache, leavened by faith and belief and God's grace, doesn't go away but becomes bearable. Thankfulness for what was. Celebrating that which we have had. Gratitude for family and friends, for the large beauties of the world and the tiny beauties of the everyday.

Christmas at Kerensa 2006. The new flugelhorn, an instrument he always loved, was my gift to Malcolm

Freesias – Malcolm's favourite flowers – in a wildflower patch at Kerensa

Like Hopkins, seeing the grandeur of all Creation, and indeed of a loving Creator, in small things, in a common flower, in a bluebell.

Our soul, like our mind, opens, enlarges, embraces, grows, enfolds, loves.

A beatitude of blessings.

From **'Joy and Sorrow'** by Kahlil Gibran

The deeper that sorrow carves into your being, the more joy you can contain. … When you are sorrowful look again in your heart, and you shall see that in truth you are weeping for that which has been your delight.

Kahlil Gibran (1883–1931) was a Lebanese-American writer, poet and artist. He is best known as the author of The Prophet and is generally considered to embrace Christian, Jewish and Muslim teaching.

I love my little angel. She is flawed but maintains her grace and serenity. She reminds me of the children's classic, The Velveteen Rabbit, by Margery Williams: 'Once you are Real, you can't be ugly, except to people who don't understand'

Malcolm playing in an orchestra with the world-famous musician, James Morrison – yes, that little boy who was so good in my plays for the local church. His parents live nearby and his mother taught dancing to our daughters

12. Keeping On

'Hope' is the thing with feathers –
That perches in the soul –
And sings the tune without the words –
And never stops – at all –
From 'Hope is the thing with feathers' by Emily Dickinson

Life goes on, and it must, for everyone's sake. There have been many sweet times since we lost Malcolm – as there should be. I have had some really nice adventures, and our family has shared all sorts of lovely milestones, as the grandchildren are starting to grow up into their own lives. That's good. Life is an amazing gift, and we are all entrusted to make the most of it, both for ourselves and for those around us.

Our continued family happiness is in fact a celebration and a tribute to Malcolm, just as it is to all those who have gone before us: Grandma Elsie and Grandpa Joe, Grandma and Grandpa Johnston, my father Roy and little mother Dorothy, and all the precious aunts and uncles. I wrote in one of the family emails that these 'dear departed' are part of the great 'cloud of witnesses' that I believe are always close by: in another dimension, perhaps, but still close.

I have also been fortunate enough to travel at various times with friends and family, as well as with some of our children. Visiting places with like-minded people adds another rich edge to the experience, and the many trips to places such as Oberammergau and Lake Como with dear colleagues (Barbara and Keith, Paul and Joyce) have been mind-enhancing, as have experiences with international colleagues with whom I have visited and whom we have welcomed at Kerensa (Kim and Peter Reynolds and Polly, Peter Hunt and family from England, Lynne Vallone from the United States, and Perry

> The *Oberammergau Passion Play* (Bavaria, since 1634) is performed every ten years by the villagers because, according to legend, they had made a vow to do so after being spared from a plague epidemic decimating the region.

and Billie Nodelman and Lissa Paul from Canada). I also had many wonderful trips with family all around England and Europe (Alistair and Stephen, Sarah, and Robert). Robert, as a youth, came with Malcolm and me to Thailand and Bali. Later, as mentioned, he became an invaluable research officer in the work we were doing in remote Indigenous communities in Australia. He studied for part of his postgraduate degree at Harvard, where I was able to visit him and have a tour of that exciting campus. On another trip when, as part of an education conference I was fortunate enough to meet Dr Jill Biden, later FLOTUS, Robert showed me around New York and Washington. In Boston we met and had a lovely meal at the home of my cousin Tanya, cousin Azim's daughter, who is a professor of pathology at Harvard Medical School and a senior scientist at Brigham and Women's Hospital.

With collegial friends at Lake Como (top l-r) Joyce, Barb, Keith, Paul, with RRJ standing; and with Alistair and Stephen in Croatia (bottom)

I noted earlier that I was asked to become a member of L. M. Montgomery Institute, which felt such an honour. Subsequently, I was able to attend a number of conferences (and at one was the keynote speaker) in the beautiful Canadian maritime province of Prince Edward Island, which Montgomery put on the literary world map. Sarah was able to accompany me to one of these, and we had great fun exploring PEI together,

With cousin Tanya at her home in Boston

which was very special. I'd earlier been able to visit her during her student year in Spain; she showed me around not only Salamanca, where she was studying at that famous old university, but Madrid, where she booked a hotel room facing the Reina Sofia, famous for Picasso's 'Guernica', which we visited the next day. I had had no previous idea of how big this painting is and how deeply it conveys emptiness and a bare, terrible futility. We then went together to London, where I had to leave her on my way to a speaking engagement in Zimbabwe. This parting was awful. We were at Gatwick (one of the few times I've been there) and the automatic doors of the little train taking her back to London closed so abruptly, I did not feel as if I had said goodbye. I wouldn't see her again for months, as I was then going straight back to Sydney. That flight to Harare was not an enjoyable one.

Rob in Washington in springtime

Family Trip to the Centre

One of the very special whole family times we have had was our trip together to Central Australia to visit Uluru. I had been to Uluru several times before, but it is a place of many moods and provokes not only a sense of wonder but a mystical and, yes, spiritual sense of contemplation. Early morning it is somehow so fresh, with the daintiest of pale green in the chiffonade of short grasses growing around the encircling tracks; at noon it ruggedly melds as one into the deep, heart-red, clasp of earth and rock; in late afternoon, the gleaming sun seems to probe nooks and crannies of age-old mysteries on its western face.

Family line up for plane to Alice Springs

There is, over the whole area, somehow an aura of timelessness, of being outside of time. I have written in various places about the power of perspective and how Aboriginal spatial perspective is an overhead one (rather than the vanishing point one we learnt about in school). Thus animal tracks can respectably lead off the top of the page. Ideas of temporal perspective are equally fascinating; time is not set in a linear organisation of past, present and future but in a circular pattern. This pattern of time circles has the individual in the centre and events placed closer or further away according to their relative importance.

Ideas about all this – time and space and identity and place – tumbled through my mind as the sun slowly went down over the fabled rock, and I found myself remembering snippets of a poem by Hyllus Maris: 'I am this land and this land is me.'

Writing, Writing, Writing … and an Ethics of Hope

Part of the work of a professor is writing and original research, and this I relished. I wrote and presented many papers in many places over the years; most were later published in journals or as chapters in various books.

Literacy: Reading, Writing and Children's Literature, written with colleagues Gordon Winch, Paul March, Lesley Ljungdahl and Marcelle Holliday, which was published by Oxford University Press, became an academic bestseller and ran to six editions over the years 2001 to 2020. In this and other writings I introduced the idea of an 'ethics of hope':

> Part of the idea of an ethics of hope relates to soul, and to a sense of the uniquely valuable quality in human life and human awareness. This is why education itself is such a hopeful enterprise: its thrust is forward-looking, ambitious and life changing.

I also wrote about an 'ethics of hope' in *Australian Literature for Young People* (2017):

> [We] need to muse on the way Indigenous cultures pass on wisdom to their young and make full use of the arts – literature (as story), drama, poetry, visual arts, music, dance. Story is told and danced and drawn and sung, to remember the past, map the present, and perhaps suggest a future. …
>
> And in a time of increasing concern about mental health and wellbeing, this might restore to centre the idea of 'soul' – that which is most deeply intimate, most deeply vulnerable. …
>
> An ethics of hope in children's books comprises that movement towards futures that offer possibilities. This ethics must inform national consciousness …
>
> It is surely the way forward for us and, most of all, for our young people – that they carry the poesis and imageries and imaginaries of hope into their own futures and into the future of the nation.

'The author and the publisher must be thanked for such a critical intervention'
Book Review: Rosemary Ross Johnston, *Australian Literature for Young People* — Rimli Bhattacharya, 2019 (sagepub.com)

I am a child of the Dreamtime People
Part of this land, like the gnarled gumtree
I am the river, softly singing
Chanting our songs on my way to the sea
My spirit is the dust-devils
Mirages, that dance on the plain
I'm the snow, the wind and the falling rain
I'm part of the rocks and the red desert earth
Red as the blood that flows in my veins
I am eagle, crow and snake that glides
Through the rainforest that clings to the mountainside
I awakened here when the earth was new
There was emu, wombat, kangaroo
No other man of a different hue
I am this land
And this land is me
I am Australia.

Aunty Hyllus Maris
(1933–1986)

Let Us Not Be Bitter

Away with bitterness, my own dark people
Come stand with me, look forward and not back,
For a new time has come for us.
Now we must change, my people. For so long
Time for us stood still, now we know
Life is change, life is progress,
Life is learning things, life is onward.
White men had to learn civilised ways,
Now it is our turn.
Away with bitterness and the bitter past;
Let us try to understand the white man's ways
And accept them as they accept us;
Let us judge white people by the best of their race.
The prejudiced ones are less than we,
We want them no more than they want us.
Let us not be bitter, that is an empty thing,
A maggot in the mind.
The past is gone like our childhood days of old,
The future comes like dawn after the dark,
Bringing fulfilment.

Oodgeroo Noonuccal (Kath Walker)
(1920–1993)

I Am

I am
the river,
gently flowing,
as I wind my way to the sea.
I am
the breeze,
softly blowing,
through the leaves of a
mighty tree.
I am
the snowcapped mountain,
the frost, the wind, the rains.
I am
a misty fountain,
the dry and dusty plains.
I am
the sparkle,
of the early morning dew.
I am
the dream,
of my mother's dreaming.
Who are you?

Mary Duroux (1934–2011)

Grandchildren at the base of Uluru. Out of respect for the traditional custodians, we did not climb the Rock

Patricia Wrightson (1921–2010), was one of the earliest writers to introduce young readers to Australian Indigenous ideas, beliefs, traditions and customs. She was a nurse and became an Assistant Editor of the School Magazine – how I loved that crisp promise of new stories when it landed on our desks! Her books brought glimpses of inspiring and colourful iconographies into the shabby and often very limited (and English dominated) primary and secondary school libraries of that time. For many young people, these introduced not only different ways of thinking about place and country, but the first realisation that there were different ways.

Poets and Poetry on Campus

We held many events in our own CREA room – not only seminars, but recitals, art shows, drama events, student acitivies, fora, lectures and evening functions.

One of these events featured poet Les Murray, who came to speak and read to our students.

Poet Les Murray in my university office at Kuring-gai. A colleague brought him to Sydney and I was fortunate enough to be able to invite him to speak to our students. Such a privilege!

Les Murray Seminar at Kuring-gai

The Meaning of Existence

Everything except language
knows the meaning of existence.
Trees, planets, rivers, time
know nothing else. They express it
moment by moment as the universe.
Even this fool of a body
lives it in part, and would
have full dignity within it
but for the ignorant freedom
of my talking mind.

This poem is an expression of Murray's idea of 'wholespeak' and 'Me-speak'. The best, and most harrowing, example of 'Me-speak' is 'The Cows on Killing Day'. I quote just a few lines here:

All me are standing on feed. The sky is shining.
All me have just been milked. Teats all tingling still
from that dry toothless sucking by the chilly mouths
that gasp loudly in in in, and never breathe out.
All me standing on feed, move the feed inside me.
…
And all me run away, over smells, toward the sky.

Les Murray (1938–2019)

'It was Murray's exceptional capacity to illuminate the edge of the clearing, the boundary of nature and culture, where the bush meets the establishment, the 'giddy line midway' which means that he will never be classed and done with.'

Dr John Vallance, NSW State Librarian, speaking at the State Memorial Service, 2019

Dynamic Rest

Six little terns
feet gripping sand
on a windy beach
six more just above
white with opened wings
busy exchange of feet
reaching down lifting off
terns rising up through terns
all quivering parallel
drift ahead and settle
bracing their eyes
against the brunt of wind

From 'Waiting for the Past' by Les Murray

… a field all foreground, and equally all background,
like a painting of equality. Of infinite detailed extent
like God's attention. Where nothing is diminished by perspective.

From 'Equanimity' by Les Murray

In the entrance of Lancaster House London, 'holding' an Olympic torch, 2012

So we have had birthdays and Christmases and multiple family events. I had more interesting years teaching and writing, with some lovely things happening along the way. One of these was that in 2012 I was invited as one of only several Australians to participate in the Cultural Olympiad, a Global Business Summit on Creative Content, Creative Services and Education, which was held concurrently with the London Olympic Games. I'm not sure if this happens with every Olympics, but this was a truly wonderful event. It was held in the Long Gallery at Lancaster House, right next door to Clarence House (then the town residence of Prince Charles and Camilla). The day functions were quite small and relatively intimate, in a long room with perhaps eight or nine tables seating eight people each. I was sitting next to Jony Ive, now Sir Jonathan. Unfortunately, I'd never heard of him and asked him politely what he did (he was then chief design officer of Apple Inc.). I think he said he worked with computers!

We met and were addressed by actors and producers. The cast of the latest James Bond film, minus the star (Daniel Craig), all spoke, and we were given a sneak preview of the film then in production, *Skyfall*. The Harry Potter stars were interviewed as were Julian Fellowes and many others, such as designer Stella McCartney (Paul's daughter), who was really interesting. It was an amazing experience. At one point on the second day we had an afternoon tea in the garden, and I looked up at the surprisingly close back windows of Clarence House. One small window was open. It looked like it could be a bathroom and I found myself staring at it; it was somehow delightfully ordinary. There was an evening function, from memory at the College of Arts, with special guest Kate, Duchess of Cambridge (now Princess of Wales). I didn't exactly meet her but was part of a small group with whom she spoke; she is surprisingly tall and I remember how shiny her hair was.

At Admiralty House, Kirribilli, Sydney

I was given tickets to a few events at the Olympics (the beach volleyball and the swimming, where I saw Michael Phelps win several of his multiple gold medals). I also lined up along the side wall of Buckingham Palace to watch the finals of the cycling. It was over in seconds!

CREA Board meeting at Admiralty House

They simply flashed by. Just as well, because that day I had walked from Notting Hill to Tower Bridge and back to the palace before waiting with the crowds. It was very warm and the roads were lined about ten deep. I ended up leaning against the tall brick wall of the palace grounds; I hadn't stopped to eat or drink and felt very faint. After the cyclists flew past, I gratefully found a place to sit down and have a cup of tea and a salad sandwich.

There have been many lovely times. My friendship with the former Governor-General Dame Quentin Bryce has been enriching, and she generously facilitated us being able to have several meetings at Admiralty House, which is so beautiful and looks out over the harbour to Sydney Opera House; it feels as if you are looking into the pulsing, beating, twinkling, pounding heart of the city.

Quentin Bryce also came down from Queensland to launch my book, *Australian Literature for Young People* (Oxford University Press). Afterwards, with some special friends and those of the family who were able to come, we all went out with her and dear Gregor Ramsey for an informal dinner just across the road from UTS. It was a memorable night.

Most precious of all, however, is the fact that I have been able to share in the lives of our children and grandchildren and watch the unfolding and growth of new generations. What a privilege!

Celebratory dinner with family

Family at book launch of 'Australian Literature for Young People' with Quentin Bryce

Around and about with family

12. Keeping On

In my end is my beginning ...

I retired in 2019. UTS gave me a lovely retirement function to which the whole family came – including my brother Chris, who came from Canberra with his wife and children – as well as many close friends and colleagues. The function was held immediately prior to the university graduation ceremony, at which I was presented with a Distinguished Service Award. I was also made an Emeritus Professor (Professor Emerita), which means I retain my professorship for life.

With Robert, Libby and Mary, at my UTS Farewell

The family all came to the graduation ceremony with me. After the graduation, we caught taxis downtown and all had dinner together at Sydney Tower, the revolving restaurant with its expansive city and harbour views. It was magical, seeing the glittering city below, vibrant and busy, aglow with colour and light.

To top it all off, out of the blue one afternoon a little

Receiving the UTS Distinguished Service Award

later, I received a call informing me that I was being considered for an award of Member of the Order of Australia (AM). I had heard nothing at all about this and am still not completely sure how it came about. It is a lovely honour and a very fulfilling way to finish my years at UTS. I was and am very grateful.

My UTS Farewell

My UTS Farewell

The investiture ceremony

5 September 2019 – Investiture as Member of the Order of Australia at Government House, Sydney. *Guests were limited; Emily couldn't come because of an important school function. I had her photo (and Malcolm's) with me and stood both on the table near me during the luncheon held at Parliament House prior to the investiture.*

12. Keeping On

Welcoming Thérèse Rein, Quentin Bryce, Chancellor, VC, Bruce, Leon, Amanda, Theo, Philip, Gregor

NBCS Board

With Excelsia Board: Neville, John, Phil

Lunch at Kerensa with international colleagues: Lynne Vallone, Lissa Paul, Kim Reynolds, Peter Hunt

Dec 2022 – One of the board farewells

13. A Blessed Congruence

As we drove home the stars came out thick: I leant back to look at them and my heart opening more than usual praised our Lord to and in whom all that beauty comes home.

Gerard Manley Hopkins, *Journal* 17 August 1874

At the top of the Jungfrau, in the Bernese Alps (Switzerland)

13.1 A cosmic symphony

Credo in Deum Patrem omnipotentem, Creatorem caeli et terrae
I believe in God, the Father Almighty, maker of heaven and earth

What a huge statement that is, especially in a world (earth) setting off to explore far-off planets (heavens)! And humans, both young and old, have done so, dreamed so, imaginatively, artistically for years.

*Twinkle, twinkle, little star,
How I wonder what you are*

'Starry Night'
Vincent van Gogh
*Starry, starry night
Paint your palette blue and grey
Look out on a summer's day
With eyes that know the darkness in my soul…*
From *'Vincent'* by Don McLean

This early nineteenth century lullaby, which is from a poem written by Jane Taylor (1783–1824), has several lesser-known verses and concludes with the couplet:

*Tho' I know not what you are,
Twinkle, twinkle, little star.*

242

Of course we know much more about the stars and the cosmos now than we did then, and we are learning more every year. We have even learnt to accept that what we are seeing in our today is a twinkle of light that happened perhaps thousands of years ago. In other words, when we look up at those 'little stars', we are seeing across time, through time, beyond time. The night sky is a glimpse into the faraway past. It is mind-boggling, even rather terrifying. How can this be? What does this mean for who we are? What is time? What am I? Where am I in all of this extravagant magnitude?

Nonetheless, despite the enormity of what they are saying, millions of small children throughout the past two hundred years, encouraged by their parents, have happily learnt and chanted and sung these simple words of seeing but not knowing: seeing something beautiful – 'like a diamond in the sky' – but not knowing what and how and why it is.

In our spiritual faith, I believe that we *know* but can't always *see*. Or perhaps we can see, or at least glimpse, what we think we know through the minds and artistry of others who give it expression, who help our hearts, as Hopkins says, to open 'more than usual'. Pico Iyer in his recent book *The Half Known Life* describes how the reclusive Emily Dickinson, writing her poems alone in her small bedroom at Amherst, 'travelled to the farthest reaches of doubt and conviction, seeing "how we both believe, and disbelieve a hundred times an hour"'.

> *My heart leaps up when I behold*
> *A rainbow in the sky:*
> *So was it when my life began;*
> *So is it now I am a man;*
> *So be it when I shall grow old,*
> *Or let me die!*
> *The Child is father of the Man;*
> *And I could wish my days to be*
> *Bound each to each by natural piety.*
>
> William Wordsworth (1770–1850)

There may always be questions and some element of doubt in a thinking person's belief, and words sometimes feel inadequate, even restrictive. But for me, the Latin is perfect; it seems to capture and express the grandeur and enormity of what we are saying: *Creatorem caeli et terrae*.

Every night, every day, we glimpse, if we look for it, a creation way bigger than our part in it, way beyond our small moment and the tiny space we seek to claim and fill with our own presences. It is difficult not to believe in a great power, a great mind, when you look up at the heavens and see the razzle-dazzle of stars that started their shining centuries ago! A big bang?

Perhaps. A big Creator? I believe, yes!

Perspective. An horizon glimpsed but forever beyond us. Yet, contrarily, perplexingly, we somehow know that our little dots of time and space, insignificant though they may appear in such a mighty scheme of things, are important, somehow special, somehow holy? sacred? as are Vincent's intense swirls of starlight and McLean's 'flaming flowers that brightly blaze'. The ache of trying to express that, trying to catch that elusive thought, that wisp of idea that enfolds a whole cache of creative plenitude, is the ache of the artist – the painter, the poet, the composer – who both glimpses and trespasses into the darkness (and light) of other souls and thus, as McLean says, magnifies the darkness (and light) in their own.

We like to think we live in neatly-controlled and humanly-ordered time and space; but of course we don't. We are shown this not only by our creative artists, as they seek to *portray* in word and image the complex profundity of life, but by our scientists, as they seek to *explain* a universe of complex profundity.

> *The world is charged with the grandeur of God.*
> *It will flame out, like shining from shook foil ...*
>
> From *'God's Grandeur'* by G. M. Hopkins

Yet there are amazing synergies and 'spillovers' of thought! And sometimes science turns to art to explain, as seen in this discussion of string theory by American theoretical physicist Professor Brian Greene in his book *The Elegant Universe*:

> [A]ccording to string theory, the observed properties of each elementary particle arise because its internal string undergoes a particular resonant vibrational pattern. This perspective differs sharply from that espoused by physicists before the discovery of string theory; in the earlier perspective the differences among the fundamental particles were explained by saying that, in effect, each particle species was 'cut from a different fabric.' Although each particle was viewed as elementary, the kind of 'stuff' each embodied was thought to be different. Electron 'stuff', for example, had negative electronic charge, while neutrino 'stuff' had no electric charge. String theory alters this picture radically by declaring that the 'stuff' of all matter and all forces is the same. Each elementary particle is composed of a single string – that is, each particle is a single string – and all strings are absolutely identical. Differences between the particles arise because their respective strings undergo different

resonant vibrational patterns. What appear to be different elementary particles are actually different 'notes' on a fundamental string. The universe – being composed of an enormous number of vibrating strings – is akin to a cosmic symphony.

A cosmic symphony. Hark, the herald angels sing!

Of course, scientific theory never stands still (any more than the artistic impulse to create does), and string theory is now questioned by some because it seems, after forty or more years, still impossible to test. But despite this, many physicists continue to consider string theory as the best hope for combining what we know about quantum physics and what we know about gravity into that scientific super-goal of creating a unified 'theory of everything'.

You dream. You sing. It is.

It is fascinating to consider these scientific descriptions of the physical universe alongside the Australian Aboriginal idea of the Dreaming: Ancestor beings made a noise, the noise became singing, and the singing created land, landforms and themselves as beings.

> You dream. You sing. It is.

This becomes even more interesting when Greene goes on to discuss what he calls 'the music of string theory'. It is also fascinating to consider both these views alongside the idea in Indian languages of 'Aum'. Blanche and Beattie write:

> According to Eastern belief, 'Aum' is the sound whose vibrations built the universe; it is at once all the voices, all the sounds of all beings in existence, past, present and future. Sound is at the centre of each person, and the greatness of the human soul is expressed through music and poetry.

Khushwant Singh, Indian author, lawyer, journalist and politician, points out that in Sikh theology, Aum is 'the symbol of God'.

These world views

Questions about space and time in early analytic philosophy:
Do space and time exist independently of the mind?
Do space and time exist independently of one another?
How can we explain the mystery of the flow of time? (unidirectional?)
Can times other than the present moment exist?
What is the nature of identity over time?

stress connectedness: Greene physically, the others more spiritually. But the images are runny and spill over into complex ontological spaces that invite even more questions. Professor Carl Sagan, that amazing American polymath (astronomer, planetary scientist, cosmologist, astrophysicist, astrobiologist and author), expresses this complexity deceptively simply but from a sort of challenging inside-out perspective:

> The cosmos is within us. We are made of star-stuff. We are a way for the universe to know itself.

Amazing, is it not? Awe-inspiring. All of us (string theory or whatever) as particles of energy and matter are connected to the universe, resonating with it as part of Greene's 'cosmic symphony', and the universe is part of us.

Sagan explained this further, and quite magically, in his 1980 television series *Cosmos: A Personal Voyage*:

> The nitrogen in our DNA, the calcium in our teeth, the iron in our blood, the carbon in our apple pies were made in the interiors of collapsing stars.

Astrophysicist Neil deGrasse Tyson, who presented a later series in 2020, *Cosmos: Possible Worlds*, said:

> It won't be wrong if I say that 'No one has ever explained space, in all its perplexing glory, as well as Sagan did'.

'In all its perplexing glory.' What a wonderful description! Yet in this grandness there is a sense of profound intimacy, of physical and spiritual connection, both to the cosmos (and especially to our world) and to each other: a sense of universal community. This is a *sharedness* but not a *sameness*. As Greene says, we each have our own 'fingerprint', are each 'tiny pieces of vibrating string':

> This overview shows how string theory offers a truly wonderful unifying framework. Every particle of matter and every transmitter of force consists of a string whose pattern of vibration is its 'fingerprint'.

So, we are not the same but we share our human-ness. We are also part of something bigger than ourselves, something deeply connected to others. Or rather, if we consider Sagan's words above, *it* is part of *us*: 'We are made of star-stuff'.

Professor Paul Davies, theoretical physicist, cosmologist, astrobiologist and winner of the Templeton Prize for 'harnessing the power of the sciences to explore the deepest questions of the universe and humankind's place and purpose within it', writes:

> Through conscious beings the universe has generated self-awareness. This can be no trivial detail, no minor by-product of mindless, purposeless forces. We are truly meant to be here.

For me, this expresses a mighty – and almighty – congruence of body, intellect and faith. The beginning (itself the most profound question of all) was not a mindless almost accidental big bang, although there may have been a big bang. We are not just talking about a concept of spatial matter – or even the spiritual – but a concept of time, the temporal, that scientists, including Einstein, agree is another dimension, a fourth dimension, which is sometimes called 'spacetime'. Time, perhaps itself in different dimensions, somehow exists and co-exists. Past and present overlap, as our Australian First Nations cultures – and others – celebrate.

Indeed, I find myself very attuned to the rich idea of the Dreaming, which the Australian anthropologist W. E. H. (Bill) Stanner sought to explain in English as 'everywhen'. Stanner spent many years working with Indigenous Australians, who traditionally don't describe time as a sequential linearity. In 1964 he was influential in setting up the Australian Institute of Aboriginal Studies (now the Australian Institute of Aboriginal and Torres Strait Islander Studies).

I have both felt and glimpsed intimations of this 'everywhen', which I summed up very simply a few years ago in a family email:

> We live in an amazing cosmos, huge and awe-inspiring, and I think what we call 'Heaven' is a virtual, time/space parallel, an **all-around-us**. Stephen Hawking talks about the universe having another kind of time which is at right angles to 'real' time. He also said that if we ever discover a theory of everything then 'we would truly know the mind of God.'

13.2 'This world is not conclusion'

A field all foreground, and equally all background,
like a painting of equality. Of infinite detailed extent
like God's attention. Where nothing is diminished by perspective.
Les Murray

Les Murray was a poet inspired by his faith, and I love this idea from his poem 'Equanimity': 'Of infinite detailed extent/ like God's attention.' And his following line reminds me of Aboriginal art with its emphasis on representing size regardless of position in relation to the viewer (or artist): 'Where nothing is diminished by perspective.' Nothing is made smaller or less important by being far away.

I want to reiterate the idea of *sharedness* but not *sameness*. There is a special, almost symbiotic, relationship, a congruence, between this immensity of creation and us, the created; between a universe tuned to such balance and integrity of fit and us, its inhabitants. Our little planet consists of countless different parts – huge continents and tiny islands, seas and rivers and lakes and billabongs, arid deserts and tropical rainforests and icy North and South Poles – that, somehow together, make up the whole. We, its peoples, may have (and do have) just as many differences, but we also have much in common that binds us together.

I think of Shakespeare's *Merchant of Venice* and Shylock's impassioned defence:

> [Are we not] Fed with the same food, hurt with the same weapons, subject to the same diseases, healed by the same means, warmed and cooled by the same winter and summer...?

And I think of Kennedy's later call:

> So, let us not be blind to our differences – but let us also direct attention to our common interests and to the means by which those differences can be resolved. And if we cannot end now our differences, at least we can help make the world safe for diversity. For, in the final analysis, our most basic common link is that we all inhabit this small planet. We all breathe the same air. We all cherish our children's future. And we are all mortal.

Yes, we are all – irrespective of different faiths and cultures – part of humanity, and we all obviously have a fundamental physical sameness. But here there is a caveat that may seem contrary to my previous comment about *sharedness* but not *sameness*. Please note, it is mainly a difference in emphasis. We share the physical state of being human, and in that we are basically the same. But as well as a body we have a mental life – a mind of ideas and thoughts and feelings, beliefs and expectations – that is uniquely ours. And these shape and colour not only how we see what we are, but *how we actually see what we see*.

Amid the intricacies of different time and space contexts and different experiences, perceptions of difference may confuse and oppose that sense of fundamental sameness. This becomes most problematic when difference is emphasised and becomes the main point of focus. Then the opposition can be incendiary.

And here is my point: thinking, perception, world view and subsequent behaviours are influenced and facilitated (or impeded) by our moment in time, our sociocultural circumstance, and our experience. Ways of believing and understanding the world and us in it, may thus have different labels and be branded differently, sometimes antagonistically. But even in those differences, there are often deep chords of likeness, of connection, of synchronicity. And, amid difference, we should surely concentrate on where we are similar and what we share.

I am a Christian, a lifelong believer in God the Father Almighty, maker of heaven and earth. I believe in a triune God, a Trinity: God the Creator, the Father; Jesus Christ His Son, our Saviour, who shared our earthly humanity but rose beyond it in a living promise to us; and God the Holy Spirit, the Comforter, the Helper, 'the Spirit of truth, who proceeds from the Father'. The Holy Spirit brings many and diverse *gifts* to us, which may include wisdom, understanding, counsel, fortitude, knowledge, piety, teaching and leadership. The *fruits* of the Spirit, that is, what it produces and how it manifests in us, are love, joy, peace, patience, kindness, goodness, faithfulness, gentleness and self-control.

For me, Jesus offers a unique intimacy of divine relationship that is powerful, challenging and enlarging. It is at once other-worldly but profoundly of this world. While it points to another realm, where there is 'life everlasting', it relates deeply, inherently (and Jesus emphasised this), to the here-and-now, to us in this world as well. Luke records that Jesus said: 'Behold, the kingdom of God is within you.'

I also believe, as I've intimated above, that we as humans may be limited by our language and culture and earthly time and earthly place, and that – and here I get into deep waters – there have been and are other God-inspired leaders. I have personally met so many dear people across the world who are badged with a different religion or a different belief system but with whom I share an affinity of values, a deeply spiritual affinity, an affinity of soul. They are doing good and loving and caring for others; indeed, they are living out, sometimes without naming or perhaps even knowing, and sometimes in the most challenging of places, the precepts of Jesus.

I have long been drawn to the work of some of the medieval Persian poets and philosophers. Rumi (Jalāl al-Dīn Muḥammad Rūmī) was a thirteenth century poet, scholar, theologian and Sufi mystic. Sufism emphasises spiritual closeness to God, transcending sects and labels and focusing on the importance of the inner life. One of Rumi's well-known writings 'Do not feel lonely, the entire universe is inside you' resonates for me with Carl Sagan's scientifically-inspired words quoted earlier: 'The cosmos is within us. We are made of star-stuff.' Another Persian poet I admire is Ḥāfeẓ – Ḥāfeẓ-e Shīrāzī (1325–1390) – also a Sufi mystic. His work expresses the ecstasy of the Divine and of Divine inspiration: 'I am a hole in a flute that the Christ's breath moves through. Listen to this music.' Ḥāfeẓ also writes: 'I am in love with every church and mosque and temple and any kind of shrine, because I know it is there that people say the different names of the One God.'

I can understand these thoughts, have felt similar emotions. Without any diminishing of my Christian faith (Dare I say as part of it? It's what I believe.), I think the way forward in an often sadly divided world is to focus on what we have in common, what we can share. Three of the world's great religions – Christianity, Judaism and Islam – share as their patriarch Abram-Abraham, the 'father of many nations'. These are called the Abrahamic religions and Abraham is extensively referred to in the Hebrew and Christian Bibles and in the Qur'an.

I also believe that all three religions share a basic idea or principle – that of *lovingkindness*. Such a beautiful word; such a beautiful concept! Psalm 36 extrapolates lovingkindness as mercy and love and goodness and grace and faithfulness. For Christians lovingkindness is both humanly and divinely expressed in Jesus. In the Jewish faith the idea is usually translated as *chesed,* meaning mercy and goodness: 'I am the Lord which exercises *chesed* (lovingkindness)' (Jeremiah 9:24). Islam also encourages kindness and compassion. What is described as the most authentic record of the teachings of Mohammad says: 'You do not do evil to those who do evil to you, but you deal with them with forgiveness and kindness.' Islam, it says, encourages kindness and compassion towards everyone, no matter one's religion, status or colour. What a difference it would make in our world if we all tried to truly abide by this beautiful ideal of lovingkindness!

There is another core teaching that many religious leaders have openly supported and which is, almost universally, accepted as a foundation of education and citizenship. It is of living well in a world of others. This is at the very heart of the teachings of Jesus and, in various expressions, is part of many faith traditions. Indeed, its principles are readily adopted across an increasingly secular world:

> Do unto others as you would have them do unto you. (Matthew 7:12)

Consider the following:

1. Preparing for a visit to the United States in 2008, Pope Benedict XVI said:

   > Do to others as you would have them do to you, and avoid doing what you would not want them to do. This 'golden rule' is given in the Bible, but is valid for all people, including non-believers. It is the law written on the human heart; on this we can all agree, so that when we come to address other matters we can do so in a positive and constructive manner.

2. In his book *Islam and the Secular State* (2008), Abdullah An-Na'im, a Sudanese born Islamic scholar who is the Charles Howard Candler Professor of Law at Emory University School of Law in the United States, writes:

   > My right to be myself requires me to accept and respect the right of others to be themselves too, on their own terms. The golden rule is the ultimate cross-cultural foundation of the universality of human rights.

3. From about 700, Shintoism in Japan taught:

   > Be charitable to all beings, love is God's representative. Don't forget that the world is one great family. The heart of the person before you is a mirror; see there your own form.

4. And around 1060, Zhang Zai, a Confucian philosopher, wrote:

   If one loves others just as one is disposed to love oneself, one realises benevolence completely. This is illustrated by the words 'If something is done to you and you don't want it, then for your part don't do it to others'.

5. On a wall inside the United Nations hangs a large carpet that contains lines from *Gulistan* (گلستان), generally transliterated as 'The Rose Garden', written by Sa'di (1210–1291), another one of the great medieval Persian poets. For many years the *Gulistan* was widely known and studied and Persian was the language of literature from Bengal to Constantinople.

   Human beings are members of a whole,
   In creation of one essence and soul.
   If one member is afflicted with pain,
   Other members uneasy will remain.
   If you have no sympathy for human pain,
   The name of human you cannot retain.

6. In a 2015 address to the United States Congress, Pope Francis said:

   Let us remember the Golden Rule: 'Do unto others as you would have them do unto you' (Matthew 7:12). This Rule points us in a clear direction. Let us treat others with the same passion and compassion with which we want to be treated. Let us seek for others the same possibilities which we seek for ourselves. Let us help others to grow, as we would like to be helped ourselves.

Harry J. Gensler, Professor of Philosophy at Loyola University in Chicago, has compiled an interesting and occasionally humorous (he begins with Fred Flintstone!) chronology of 'the golden rule' through the centuries in his book, *Ethics and the Golden Rule: Do unto others* (2013).

In 1747, in Sermon 30, John Wesley, the founder of Methodism, said the golden rule 'commends itself, as soon as heard, to every man's conscience and understanding; no man can knowingly offend against it without carrying his condemnation in his own breast.' And in 1943, in his classic *Mere Christianity*, C. S. Lewis writes: 'The golden rule sums up what everyone had always known to be right.'

Our universe is a miraculous creation and life is also miraculous. I find it hard to believe that this world, even as beautiful as it is, is the end story or indeed the whole story. For me, intimations of another world – of a parallel dimension, of a 'what comes after' and, yes, of a 'Heaven', somehow *a within us* and an *all around us* beyond our human perceptions of time and space – abound. As Emily Dickinson says, those in the pulpit may thump out strong assurances, but we in the pews may waver and question and doubt and grab onto little 'twig[s] of evidence'; we may even slip and be ashamed, but something deeper than ourselves, that elusive yet captivating 'something more' that we glimpse and feel, inspires and persuades us to laugh and rally. Our faith, the poet writes, both beckons and baffles: Jesus bore the cross because of it. This tantalising and persistent idea of something beyond knowing, beyond any wisdom on our part, beguiles and captivates our spirits just as sound and music do; it spikes our minds and intrigues our intellect.

Those glimpses and intimations of a something beyond, 'nibble at our souls'; I believe they also season and sweeten and, yes, sanctify our hearts.

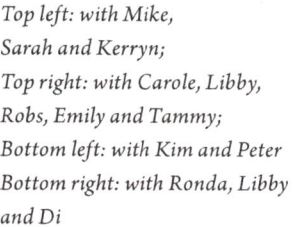

Top left: with Mike, Sarah and Kerryn;
Top right: with Carole, Libby, Robs, Emily and Tammy;
Bottom left: with Kim and Peter
Bottom right: with Ronda, Libby and Di

This World is not Conclusion

This World is not Conclusion.
A Species stands beyond -
Invisible, as Music -
But positive, as Sound -
It beckons, and it baffles -
Philosophy, dont know -
And through a Riddle, at the last -
Sagacity, must go -
To guess it, puzzles scholars -
To gain it, Men have borne
Contempt of Generations
And Crucifixion, shown -
Faith slips - and laughs, and rallies -
Blushes, if any see -
Plucks at a twig of Evidence -
And asks a Vane, the way -
Much Gesture, from the Pulpit -
Strong Hallelujahs roll -
Narcotics cannot still the Tooth
That nibbles at the soul -

Emily Dickinson

The LORD will guide you always; He will satisfy your needs in a sun-scorched land and will strengthen your frame. You will be like a well-watered garden, like a spring whose waters never fail. (Isaiah 58:11)

An armful of grand babies: Malcolm Luke, Evelyn, Caleb, Toby, Samuel, Isabella (Anna coming)

From emails to the family during Lockdown

Dear all,

Well, what a day!! Such well-deserved results for Evie and Izzy – both incredible, both into the university courses of their choice, both such excellent choices for them. We are all rejoicing with them, and for them!

And we should not only congratulate the girls, but their mums as well – both have worked so very hard to make sure their little girls have had every possible opportunity. And we know that their dads are incredibly pleased and proud of them also. As indeed we all are!! Well done everyone for the part you have played in the lives of these two little sweethearts …

Isabella Rose and Evelyn Ada, HSC graduates

Because today is all about Isabella (dance) and Evie (violin), I want to share this famous poem by Irish poet William Butler Yeats. Yeats here is celebrating, as we do, the intimate connections between music and music maker (Evie), and between dance and the dancer (Isabella). Is a tree, he asks, the leaves or the flowers or the trunk (bole)? Of course it is all of them, one beautiful whole:

> O chestnut tree, great-rooted blossomer,
> Are you the leaf, the blossom or the bole?
> O body swayed to music, O brightening glance,
> How can we know the dancer from the dance?

All of you have got all this, and much more, through Dad and the other mums and dads– what a heritage!!

Much love.

Christmas 2020 (in lockdown), in reply to article reminding us that, whilst family events were postponed, Christmas was not cancelled

Hi Em - I loved this when you read it to me on the phone and I loved reading it now! Thanks for sending.

Yes, it's so perceptive and also challenging. We of course are terribly disappointed not to be at Boat Harbour with you as planned on Christmas Day and not to be able to be all together over our extended days of Christmas. And we all feel for you – I know all the planning that goes into our usual big family Christmas. Thank you!

But how blessed we have been – and are – to share in such a wonderful extended family. And this article highlights the depth and richness and strength of that extended family! It is Christians everywhere who celebrate the mystery and wonder of the incandescent hope that Jesus has brought into the world. It is a gentle yet strong and vibrant peace within, isn't it? A surety which as we learn more and more to live it out and express it, spreads and grows.

So thank you for sharing! I'm so sad not to be with you and yours, and Robs, and Mal and Helen and gang. But in the deepest, most eternal way, we are!!!

Much love forever!

Christmas Day 2020 (in lockdown)

Dear family,

Sending you all prayers and thoughts for a happy and blessed and fun Christmas Day!

We are all in little bubbles but we are part of a strong and vibrant whole, and I am seeing all your faces so clearly. It's like bubble wrap – a large sheet of connected bubbles, each little bubble making the whole stronger and bigger and more effective.

Thank you, children and grandchildren and extended family – you are each one very precious.

Have a great day!

Much love always,

Mum/Grandma/Bana/Rosemary

We eventually were able to get together for a Christmas meeting, not in a home (numbers were still limited and there were too many of us) but in a pretty park on the edge of beautiful Pittwater.

Benediction

Benediction: Special words at the end of an event, a prayer asking for divine blessing

So, here is the place where we end this *passeggiata* – this leisurely stroll through the ups and downs of a mindscape, lifescape, dreamscape, remembering bits here and there, as we do, in tangles of past and present. The longer the stroll, the more there is to try to unravel, the more the present is superimposed on the past – or is it past superimposed on present?

It is sometimes said, mainly by my siblings, whom I love dearly – after all, they are the living links, the anchors, to the earliest, the 'pastest' of my past – that I remember only the good, that I see through rose-coloured spectacles. Perhaps so. However, I believe this is not so much a washing *out* as a washing *in* – a drenching in time ongoing, in experience, in enlarged perspectives both glimpsed and lived. There may well be a gloss, but it is a gloss not only of distance but surely, hopefully, of the 'getting of wisdom'.

For this memoir has recorded, with honesty, the deepest of me. Yes, I do believe in the power and comfort and life-changing capacities of hope. I do believe that life is a precious gift. I do believe in the transforming power of love.

I am inspired and grown by those around me, not only family and friends but also that great cloud of witnesses and thinkers and scholars who have gone before us all and whose legacies have both shaded and illuminated our paths. Life is a richly intertextual experience. It is an innate democracy of lived and living thoughts, words, images and sounds, that have been created and transmitted by others and that reach us in what may be very different ecologies of space and time. In turn, we see what we see and hear what we hear and translate these in our own way, sometimes admiringly, sometimes argumentatively, sometimes with a close focus, sometimes expansively; they become new and different shapes and forms and applications and indeed new thoughts and ideas.

The A. E. Stallings poem 'Peacocks' is a comment on memory and how some things, like the flamboyant colours of the peacocks, are overwhelming in their richness.

> *When he absconds, he leaves behind*
> *A duller shade, a haunt of blue,*
> *A dazzled blindspot in the mind.*

There is a 'dazzled blindspot'. You can't remember the colours as quite as bright as you are sure they were and as you want to; the mind is overcome by such extravagance.

Memory, no matter how sad, no matter how beautiful, is always tinged, shot through, with loss, with *what was not* but should or could have been or with *what was* but now *is not*.

Board Meeting at the beautiful Dromkeen Picture Book Art Museum in the Victorian Macedon Ranges (think 'Picnic at Hanging Rock'). Peacocks roamed freely around the lovely old homestead. I was privileged to serve on the Board for years. Here we are: Ken Jolly, statue of stockman, RRJ, Leon Paroissien, Gregor Ramsey, John Oldmeadow

Research in neuroscience reveals interesting findings about memory and recall. In *Growing Young Minds: Reading, Thinking and Aspiration* I noted the findings of Eric R. Kandel, who, with Arvid Carlsson and Paul Greengard, shared the 2000 Nobel Prize in Physiology or Medicine for their work on memory. Kandel is Professor of Biochemistry and Biophysics at the College of Physicians and Surgeons at Columbia University, and his work shows how thoughts and imaginings can change the structure and function of the brain. As I wrote:

> In a paper on the molecular biology of memory Kandel describes a gene (the 'CREB' gene) which can be switched on with thoughts. In my very simple terms, and thinking about memory as a vast and complex network of branches, they say that we switch the gene on when we need space to 'house' a new thought; this switching on creates a protein synthesis which, at a synapse – the minute gap at the junction of two nerve cells (neurons) – develops and grows a new little twig or branch to accommodate and place this new thought.

This *passeggiata* has been all about memory. It has been an emotional, sad-happy, calm-edgy, lingering-hastening stroll, sometimes challenging yet most times exhilarating. Sometimes I've forgotten what I want to remember and remembered what I want to forget.

I would like to conclude this long meandering walk with a brief description of a recent day – just an 'ordinary' everyday – and relate it to some thoughts written years ago in my PhD thesis. I have been exploring and elaborating on these thoughts (if only to myself) ever since, inspired first by a medieval scholar, second by a late nineteenth century poet and third by a twentieth century Irish novelist.

As I wrote in the thesis, I was fascinated (and still am) by ideas of time (temporality):

> *Memory, all alone in the moonlight*
> *I can dream of the old days*
> *Life was beautiful then.*
>
> From 'Memory' by Andrew Lloyd Webber and Trevor Nunn, inspired by the poem 'Prelude 1' by T. S. Eliot (below).
>
> *The winter evening settles down*
> *With smell of steaks in passageways.*
> *Six o'clock.*
> *The burnt-out ends of smoky days.*
> *And now a gusty shower wraps*
> *The grimy scraps*
> *Of withered leaves about your feet*
> *And newspapers from vacant lots;*
> *The showers beat*
> *On broken blinds and chimney-pots,*
> *And at the corner of the street*
> *A lonely cab-horse steams and stamps.*
> *And then the lighting of the lamps.*

> The concepts of 'everydayness' and 'this-ness' (haecceitas) are thematic extrapolations of each other, although one concentrates on the elements of ordinariness and one on the elements of what can perhaps be called, in a specialised sense, the extraordinary ... The quality of being 'extraordinary' in this sense is a quality of the inherent difference, distinction and individuation which exists within things; it is the innate essence of something ... It is not 'supra-ordinary', outside of the ordinary, but inside it, deeply, exceptionally ordinary as someone who is happy says they are 'extra happy', or as something which has the quality of being dry, deeply, is 'extra dry' ...
>
> The very nature of temporality makes everydayness of value ... This is a perception of time at its most continuous but also at its most transient. But it is ... precisely because of the nature of temporality that the apprehension and appreciation of 'this-ness' becomes so significant a part of human experience. (pp. 219–220)

I noted at the very beginning of this *passeggiata* the lovely idea of what poet Gerard Manley Hopkins called 'inscape': the unique characteristics and impact of a particular thing, a particular scene, at a particular moment in time. Then, in Chapter 5, this was related to the concept of philosophical thought that the medieval scholar, Johannes Duns Scotus (c. 1267–1308), professor of theology at Oxford University and known as the 'Subtle Doctor', conceived of as *haecceitas*, 'this-ness' – the unique and particular of this one among many similar.

Now I want to add into this heady mix Irish writer James Joyce and his concept of 'epiphany' and the 'epiphanal moment'; these are built on the philosophical idea of *quidditas*, 'whatness' and inspired his own concept of 'radiance'. Joyce wrote in his posthumously published autobiographical novel *Stephen Hero*:

> *Claritas is quidditas* … This is the moment which I call epiphany … The soul of the commonest object … seems to us radiant. The object achieves its epiphany.

So, Duns Scotus, Hopkins and Joyce have all inspired and indeed inflamed my thinking – my everyday thinking as well as my thinking about the everyday. This relates to what Proust describes as 'a precious essence'. They have all made me perceive and relish the value of a particular moment, a particular time, a particular event or something I treasure more and more. I love how in her song 'Apple Tree', Sarah Sydney encourages us all to 'seize the day' (*carpe diem*) and writes the perceptive line 'Don't shelter in the corner of the known'.

Sarah Sydney is our Sarah's professional name. She was a semi-finalist in the Nashville International Songwriting Competition, for her first song 'Apple Tree'. Her most recent release is 'Come to Me'

If I may, I want briefly to precede the following with a short comment about the word 'happiness'. Etymologically 'happiness' derives from the Old Norse '*happ*' meaning 'luck' or 'chance', and you can see this meaning in the related words 'mayhap', 'perhaps', 'happen', 'happenstance' and 'haphazard'. The Irish philosopher Francis Hutcheson encouraged a new, more political interpretation of *happiness*

with his 1725 treatise 'An Inquiry into the Original of our Ideas of Beauty and Virtue', where he wrote: 'That Action is best which accomplishes *the greatest Happiness for the greatest Numbers.*'

This conflated the idea of 'happiness' with the idea of civic responsibility (helping others) and, even more importantly to my mind, with something that the individual can play a part in, can do and can achieve.

This is such an important point – I believe, a life point. Happiness is a state of mind, even (perhaps!) a discipline, something we can work at, both for the good of others and for the good of ourselves.

So, come with me ...

I am thinking now of an evening, not so long ago, still in lockdown but with some restrictions at last lifted, and my younger son has been able to visit us for the first time in months. He has come over to stay for almost a week – such a gift – and has spent hours, with Sarah, doing repair jobs around our much-loved but fifty-year-old house, replacing the high light bulbs, fixing this and that, organising a new mower (the wheel kept falling off the old one), and both of them spending two full days in the garden, mowing and tidying up. The loveliest thing was, they were both enjoying it!

As evening draws in, Annabel and the kids come up from next door, bringing her brazier. It has been a heavenly spring day – clear skies, warm, prescience of summer. The jacaranda shading us, barely, leafless, but with twigs of bud – is a promise of incipient violet and lilac. Birds are everywhere; especially I hear at this moment the magpies and kookaburras, signing off for the day, but there is still a persistent clamour of sociable rainbow lorikeets, probably attracted by all the activity. Robs lights the brazier ('Be careful!' I can't help saying, 'Are there any fire restrictions at the moment?') and we all sit around, they on the grass, me just a couple of feet higher on the end of the verandah. Night creeps across the valley – silkily, gently, and suddenly the small fire is accentuated – moving light against the dark, flickering warmth and conviviality, defined and definite, a focus for the inner quietness of our dreamings. It is the epicentre of our vision, for this moment of our very communal beingness.

We have a simple tea – salad and sausages on bread rolls for the meat eaters, tomato and hummus and tangy red capsicum for me. Delicious. Annabel has brought up some marshmallows to share with everyone and they are all toasting them enthusiastically on bits of twig. I am brought one – it tastes like this moment, sweet, transient, melty and warm and lovely. I want to hang on to it, but it's already evaporating.

Against a backdrop of chatter and laughter, the night establishes itself more solidly; the turpentines are now just dark shadows against a richer, deeper blackness. The moon is not yet visible over the hill but there is one star, oh! so bright; it's Venus, the Evening Star in the north-western sky. The scent of newly mown lawn is mixed with fire and smoke and laughter, the shapes of those sitting around the fire are suddenly for me joined by the shadows of my children not able to be here, my older daughter Emily and son Mal and their families – as well of course by that ever-present great cloud of other loved ones. Time and space for an instant are fused – past on present, *then* on *now*. Perhaps dimensions collide, infinitesimally. There is an incredible traction of memory in my heart.

I bow my head for a moment, in gratitude and profound thanksgiving.

Yes, I, like Hopkins, have felt and heard and smelt and touched the *inscape* of that ordinary everyday twilight and evening, like Joyce have felt that *epiphany* and *radiance*, like Duns Scotus have celebrated the exquisite beauties of *'this-ness'* – this moment of time, this particular thing this place.

So, I hope you understand. And I wish all of this – and more – for all of you, every one of you, down through the generations.

The words of this *passeggiata* and the images shared, hopefully give just a glimpse of what I have seen and been and hoped and dreamed along the way.

Thank you for walking with me and lighting up my path!

Kerensa, Newport, NSW

Jacaranda Afterglow

Mists and drifts of beauty-been, a sticky lake,
Would I could leave such beauty-seen
    In my wake.
Lilac trails, brocades of past, a smokey haze,
A cast of love, a plenitude,
    Brims o'er my days.

Professor Emerita Rosemary R. Johnston AM

'This is my lovely day …' (a line from a very old song that Malcolm loved)

With Robs last summer at Soldiers Point

Thank You

What a lovely walk we have had together, stopping here and there at various times: sometimes alongside each other, sometimes on different tracks that merge along the way. Thank you, each one, for your company, for your bright and sparky spirits, and for the fun and fellowship we have shared. Thank you for all you have been and done in my life. I feel very blessed and am so very grateful.

Brothers and sisters-in-law – Royston and Sandra, Christian and Ming, Danny and Adina

Dancing with Mal

Birthday party on Pittwater 17 Feb 2024 (back row l-r) Janine, Helen, Mal, Annette, Ronnie, Paul, Eric, Betty, Ron, Cliff, Sue, Bruce, Andrew (middle row l-r) Noreen, Di, Joyce, Rosemary, Keith, Barb, Lesley, Marion, Jodi, Annabel, Viv, Libby, Carole, Sarah, Rob (front row l-r) Alistair, Emily, Isabella, Stephen, Luke, Anna, Evelyn, Caleb

(back row l-r) Ronnie, Libby, Eric, Cliff, Ron (front row l-r) Carole, Marion, RRJ, Di, Betty

(back row l-r) Paul, Joyce, Cliff (front row l-r) Keith, RRJ, Barb, Lesley

(back row l-r) Andrew, Jodi, Robert, Helen, Mal, Janine, Emily, Annabel (front row l-r) Noreen, RRJ, Sarah

Remembering Ronda and Judy

(back row l-r) Anna, Evelyn, Caleb, Luke (middle row l-r) Emily, Rob, Mal, Isabella (front row l-r) Helen, Annabel, RRJ, Sarah (Absent: Samuel, Toby)